Ben West

Buying a property
ABROAD

CADOGANguides

Contents

About the author

Ben West has written on property, health, travel and numerous other subjects for many newspapers and magazines including the *Guardian*, the *Independent*, the *Daily Telegraph*, *The Times*, the *Daily Mail*, the *Evening Standard*, *Vogue* and *Readers' Digest*. He was chief property correspondent of the *Daily Express* and the *Sunday Express* from 1999 to 2001, and currently writes a weekly property column for the *Daily Express*. His books, *London for Free* (1996), *Fun for a Fiver in London* (2002) and *Fun for a Fiver in Amsterdam* (2002), were published by Pan Books. He has also written *Buying a Home: The Virgin Guide* (2003) and *Cameroon: the Bradt Travel Guide* (2004). He has written a short film, *Gertrude*, featuring Prunella Scales, which was filmed in 2004.

Acknowledgements

Navigator Guides would like to thank the author Ben West for his expertise and hard work, plus Antonia Cunningham and Susannah Wight for their editing, Sarah Gardner for cover design and Isobel McLean for indexing; also Linda McQueen for her invaluable efforts in bringing this book to print.

Titles available in the *Buying a Property* series

Buying a Property: France
Buying a Property: Spain
Buying a Property: Italy
Buying a Property: Portugal
Buying a Property: Ireland
Buying a Property: Greece
Buying a Property: Turkey
Buying a Property: Abroad
Buying a Property: Retiring Abroad

Forthcoming
Buying a Property: Cyprus
Buying a Property: Emerging European Countries

Related titles

Working and Living: France
Working and Living: Spain
Working and Living: Italy
Working and Living: Portugal

Forthcoming
Working and Living: Australia
Working and Living: New Zealand
Working and Living: Canada
Working and Living: USA
Starting a Business: France
Starting Business: Spain

Conceived and produced for Cadogan Guides by
Navigator Guides Ltd, The Old Post Office, Swanton
Novers, Melton Constable, Norfolk NR24 2AJ, UK
www.navigatorguides.com
info@navigatorguides.com

Cadogan Guides
Network House
1 Ariel Way
London W12 7SL, UK
info@cadoganguides.co.uk
www.cadoganguides.com

The Globe Pequot Press
246 Goose Lane, PO Box 480, Guilford,
Connecticut 06437–0480, USA

Copyright © Ben West 2004

Cover design: Sarah Gardner
Cover photographs: John Miller
Editor: Antonia Cunningham
Proofreader: Susannah Wight
Indexing: Isobel McLean

Printed in Italy by Legoprint

A catalogue record for this book is available from
the British Library
ISBN 1-86011-124-6

Introduction

01

Just 10 years ago it was still quite unusual for someone in Britain to have a home abroad, and even then that property would most likely have been in Spain or France. Today, the market for homes abroad has changed beyond recognition and people are setting up home in the most remarkable places, including ex-war zones only vacated by the soldiers in very recent years, and an increasing list of countries few people could find easily on a map.

A whole raft of factors have collided to make this huge sea-change happen: a financial environment ideal for investing in a foreign home, with low lending rates and a high proportion of UK homeowners with more equity in their homes and an unprecedented ease of access, with low air fares and new air routes to unsual places enabling homeowners abroad to visit their properties quickly, easily and cheaply. The huge growth in foreign travel has encouraged a real spirit of adventure and led many holidaymakers to look beyond our nearest neighbours on the continent; having visited on vacation, they are then more likely to consider more unusual or exotic countries to invest in – especially when they see the low price tags of properties in many of these places.

Not only is there a new breed of buyer wanting a holiday home or somewhere to retire to, but also an increasing band of buyers intent on totally transforming their lifestyles, desiring to relocate full time to experience a new life abroad.

The main headache for many buyers of properties abroad now is, therefore, the huge spectrum of choice. The intention of this book is to present, in an accessible way, the pros and cons of buying a property in a wide range of countries, to help the buyer decide exactly where they will find their dream home abroad. The book provides a wealth of contacts to help make that search for a dream home become reality. The buyer is directed step by step through the practicalities, from the legal and fiscal implications and logistical considerations to the numerous things to look out for before you commit to buy. There are also tips on selling and letting your property as well as sources of further information.

Whether you are primarily guided by price, climate, a love of winter sports, vibrant cities or the countryside, hopefully this book will steer you through the maze that is property-buying abroad, and help you to avoid the pitfalls along the way.

First Steps and Reasons for Buying

Long gone are the days when owning a second home abroad was a distant dream for most people, enjoyed by a smattering of film stars and tycoons, and precious few others. Nowadays you often don't need a lottery win or inheritance to buy a villa on a sun-kissed beach or farmhouse deep in the unspoilt countryside to escape the grey skies of Britain.

In 1994 only 250,000 Britons owned properties abroad. Ten years later the number, according to a survey by *Saga* magazine, has reached 1.38 million. It is reckoned by one recent survey that one in ten Britons will own a home abroad by 2008.

It is no surprise that recent research by the Royal Bank of Scotland found that buying a home abroad was now the main wish-list achievement for British people.

Why are so many people now buying abroad?

There are many factors causing a mass migration of Brits to other shores, either to buy a holiday home, an investment property or a retirement home or perhaps to emabrk upon a completely new life abroad.

These factors include increased general affluence, plunging international travel costs, and a sustained period of low rates of borrowing and of soaring property values in many areas of Britain, which has allowed many homeowners to release equity in their homes at a time when property prices remain low in other areas of the globe.

Widespread disappointment with disastrous pension and endowment plans have increasingly encouraged older members of the population to search for other ways to create wealth for their senior years. Couple this with widespread disillusionment with the UK's education, crime and health records and a challenging, often damp and cold climate, and the huge surge in numbers of people buying abroad becomes easier and easier to understand.

A wider choice

Britons are the largest group of overseas buyers in Europe and have confidently moved on from choosing largely to locate only in familiar destinations like Spain, France, Portugal, Florida and Cyprus. Now a bewildering and adventurous list of countries has emerged as perfectly sensible options to consider, including exotic territories as varied as Croatia, Dubai and Morocco. Agents, developers, lawyers and other professionals and organisations have swiftly sprung up geared to making the task of searching and buying a home relatively enjoyable, secure and easy.

It is no surprise that more and more buyers are looking further afield than the familiar few countries so popular in the past, considering that much of the coast from Portugal all the way through Spain to France, the Greek Cypriot coast and swathes of Florida are made up of concrete, often high-rise, developments. This guide explores and compares both the most popular choices of location and a huge number of more uncommon options that you may not have thought of.

Some people are even buying properties in several countries, casually flitting between them on the mushrooming choice of bargain air routes, able to support the lifestyle by plugging into the ever-expanding network of global communication links that allow business to be carried on from almost anywhere in the world.

More affordable housing abroad

With the price of an average home in Britain standing at £160,565 according to HBOS plc (The Halifax Building Society) in August 2004, clearly many buyers are having to look further afield to buy. Properties in countries like rural Italy and Greece start at little more than £5,000, although at that price they may be little more than a glorified pile of rubble, and little town houses and remote cottages ready to move into but in need of renovation are still available for under £15,000. In some parts of London £50,000 may buy you little more than a cupboard or parking space these days, but cross the Channel and you can take your pick from a fabulous range of beautiful villas, rustic farmhouses and beachside apartments. Just focus on unfashionable rural areas and keep well away from the more glamorous and recognised resorts. Cap d'Antibes is unlikely to be a possibility, but Carcassonne may be; Chiantishire's Arezzo, no, but Marche's Ascoli Piceno, yes.

What you get for your money differs surprisingly from country to country. Prices tend to differ least in big cities: In May 2003 *The Economist* compared the price of a two-bedroom flat in a smart central area in various capital cities around the world and found the costs for these to be $975,000 in London, $925,000 in New York, $500,000 in both Paris and Sydney and $180,000 in Brussels. The biggest bargains emerge the more rural you go.

For what you get property-wise, France, for example, remains generally substantially cheaper than neighbouring Spain, which in turn is substantially cheaper than southern Portugal on the whole. Similarly, Belgium and the Netherlands are not only usually notably more costly than neighbouring France, but very few agents are geared to the UK market and language difficulties can greatly hinder your search in such places. Whereas you can do much research at home on the internet for France or Spain, for other countries your research will have to be in person and therefore costly and time consuming.

You have to be prepared to investigate carefully to find the bargains, especially since homeowners in many countries have woken up to the profit potential of turning neglected properties into holiday homes. And even smaller properties available at this price range often need a considerable amount of work, which can be tricky to price, organise and oversee if your main home is in Britain.

Better, cheaper transport options

For many buyers, owning a home abroad is also proving irresistible because transport is now so much easier, quicker and cheaper. Vastly improved transport links include the Eurotunnel's 35-minute Channel crossing, fierce competition from ferry companies, bargain-basement fares offered by the 'no-frills' airlines (and now standard airlines also), as well as better motorways and an expanding high-speed train network. All these developments are making house-hunting and owning abroad quick, cheap and easy and allowing buyers to look further and further for their dream holiday home abroad.

Even so, 2004 saw the beginnings of a threat to the era of low-cost air fares. In April and May alone, easyJet announced falling profits, Ryanair axed several routes, and Birmingham airline Duo went out of business. It is a stark warning not to buy a property simply because a low-cost airline has launched a service there. The low-cost airlines keep ahead of the market by reacting quickly to chanmges in travel fashion – today Riga, tomorrow Reykjavik – and some destinations are winter routes only.

The golden era of cheap borrowing

A long period of enticingly low mortgage rates have made house hunting abroad even more attractive, and a number of UK lenders now have branches on the Continent to cope with the increased demand and generally offer cheaper mortgages there as interest rates are likely to be lower than in the UK.

High UK property prices have allowed many homeowners, awash with equity gained from their UK properties, to extend their UK mortgage to fund a property abroad and some are taking on big projects that would have been almost unheard of a decade ago, such as owning and running a vineyard or buying a big house abroad to live in, plus a couple of cottages nearby to rent out for income.

Choices, choices...

The huge choice of countries now suitable as a possible location for a holiday home, investment opportunity or place to live in full time throws up many tempting possibilities, but also many questions. Should you buy brand new and hopefully maintenance-free, or buy an old rambling farmhouse in need of extensive renovation? Is it better to buy inland or on the coast, and can you cover the mortgage payments through holiday lets?

It is vital to research the options thoroughly before you commit yourself. As well as selecting the ideal region, lifestyle and culture, you need to know how to buy the property legally and safely using the best form of finance and lessening as far as possible any adverse effects of exchange rate fluctuations. When you come to buy, you need to be legally represented by an experienced, independent lawyer. The maze of conveyancing laws around the world open up considerable potential pitfalls for the ignorant and unwary. You need to have the necessary safeguards in place to prevent you from buying a property with no title, one with inadequate or no planning permission, one that has also been sold to someone else or may be subject to debts, or even one that does not even exist.

Hopefully this book will help guide you through the foreign property maze, avoiding the pitfalls and exploiting the benefits, as painlessly and pleasurably as possible.

Things to consider before buying a property abroad

Before buying a property abroad, and maybe making a decision that you later regret, make sure that you carry out enough research to ensure you are buying exactly the property you want in the place that you want it to be. So many people buy in a rush, taking none of the precautions they would in their home country, intoxicated by the pleasures of a short holiday but without investigating the possible alternatives, pitfalls and disadvantages.

What do you want from the property?

Ask yourself what you want from the property. Is it to be a holiday or retirement home, a place where you can relocate full time or possibly a home that can also bring in income, such as offering a bed-and-breakfast arrangement or being available for renting out part of the year? Will you want the home principally for long summer holidays, or for both summer and winter visits? Choose somewhere too far away and weekend breaks are out. If letting, you will have to do a fair amount of homework to be assured you will get enough custom to make the enterprise worth the effort. Is it vital that the property can be easily maintained?

If you wish to indulge in a sport, such as golf, skiing or sailing, that will narrow choices down considerably. If you plan to retire abroad, many countries impose strict restrictions that will narrow your choice. If you have pets, and don't wish to put them in kennels continually, that is another major factor that will influence your choice of location.

Do not assume that, just because your UK property has appreciated well in recent years, the same will happen abroad and you will make quick profit. In many countries properties increase annually in value by under 5 per cent, if at all, which means that the costs of buying will probably not be covered for at least three years. And capital gains taxes (*see* p.220), should you come to sell, can greatly reduce any profits that you do make.

As with buying art or antiques, buy principally for the pleasure a foreign home can bring, rather than for financial gain. Generally the people who make significant financial gains are developers, housebuilders and those running successful holiday rentals businesses.

The responsibility of a home abroad

Most people buy a property abroad to improve their quality of life and some owners will also benefit considerably financially from it. Yet it is a sizeable responsibility. If you need to let the property, there is the ongoing pressure to find tenants, and when you are absent from the property there is always the worry of the ongoing maintenance or that a neighbour will telephone because of a calamity like flooding or burglary. You may have to consider enlisting a paid minder to oversee the property regularly while you are absent.

Before committing yourself to purchasing, ensure that you are satisfied that you can actually afford it. The mortgage may seem affordable now, but the economy and your personal circumstances may be different a few years down the line. Also, although a property abroad may seem very cheap by UK standards, the final amount can swiftly rise once the purchasing costs are added, which can be far higher than in Britain, not to mention the ongoing running costs, from local taxes to possibly a gardener and someone to clear the swimming pool when neccessary.

The climate is very important: many of the things that people tend to enjoy in a holiday home are dependent on the weather, like golf, sailing, walking, swimming and sunbathing. Even regions known for their hot climates can be bitterly cold, windy and rainy for several months of the year. It is a good idea to spend time in the country throughout the year before deciding to buy.

Your knowledge of the local language is also important. If you plan to spend your days with other Brits in a gated development within an overwhelmingly English resort or village, an ability to speak the local language is not so vital, but if you plan lengthy renovations of your property requiring much interaction with builders, architects and suppliers, or if you plan to start a business, good knowledge of the local language may be almost essential.

Also ask yourself whether your partner likes the idea of a property abroad as much as you. If the husband is attracted to a property because of the nearby golf course, in which the wife has no interest, or one partner wants the bright lights and a lively social life while the other wants the solitude of a remote village, it is obviously a good idea to come to some compromise before buying. Some buyers try a new life abroad to try and improve or save a troubled union, but instead of taking focus away from the negative, emigrating can put so much stress on a relationship that the marriage is irredeemably damaged, possibly only to fall apart, rather than be salvaged.

Also, the property and location may be idyllic, but will there be enough there to stimulate and distract you? Many people relocate or retire to a beautiful spot only to find after the initial excitement that they are bored out of their minds and that life lacks purpose when they are simply lounging by the pool week after week.

If you plan to live abroad full time, what kind of property would have everything that you require? The commitment of a second home means that you are far less likely to make trips to pastures new, as you will feel obliged to visit your home abroad as much as possible to realise value for money. Do you love the area sufficiently that visiting will always be a pleasure, or could it easily become a burden, or would you start to resent the fact that owning a property abroad is preventing you from visiting other lands?

Visas and permits

Before even considering buying in a specific country, ensure that you will be able to use the property as you wish. You can do this by checking with the embassy or consulate of the country concerned. In some countries the rules change regularly and so it is important to get up-to-date details. In the US, for example, non-residents can buy a property, but cannot stay for more than six months per year unless they have an appropriate visa or permit. And the other way round, Americans may not be allowed to retire in some EU countries. EU nationals can both live and work in other EU countries, but cannot retire unless they can show they reach the minimum income level required.

For embassy addresses, see under each country in **Chapter 03**.

Fees

Another important thing to consider is the associated costs of buying a home abroad. In many foreign countries the fees involved with buying are proportionally far higher than in Britain. They may include a valuation and/or surveyor's fee, estate agent's fee, notary's fee, title search fee, mortgage tax, value added tax, insurance, transfer tax, property registration fee, conveyancing fee and utility connection fees.

Before committing to buy, make sure you have details of all fees payable in writing. Most of these fees are paid by the buyer, but in some cases some fees, such as for the estate agent, are paid for by the vendor or fees are shared by both parties.

Health

Many Britons buy homes abroad to escape the cold, grey weather of Britain. Hot weather and sun are well known to make people feel healthier and happier, and sunlight and a dry climate also help eradicate conditions such as arthritis, eczema, psoriasis and asthma.

Health care facilities and health risks

Health care facilities vary greatly from country to country, and this should be fully investigated prior to deciding on a country to buy in. In some areas it may be vital that you take out private health insurance, and in others decent health facilities may be free but a long distance away.

Potential health problems may also be very different from those in your home country, ranging from an added risk of sunburn to serious tropical diseases like malaria. Provision for the disabled may be considerably lacking compared with what is seen in the UK. Some countries, especially in the tropics, have strict entry requirements where certain inoculations are mandatory. For example, a jab for yellow fever is necessary to enter certain African countries.

In many countries, various medical precautions are advised but are not mandatory. However, ignoring them could be fatal (in the case of malaria, for example) and it is, therefore, advisable to research the medical risks of the country you are going to. Even countries not thought of as being a particularly high risk may pose significant medical dangers not seen in the home country.

Travel clinics

If you are considering investing in a property in a country that is less developed than your home country, or has inferior medical facilities or significant health risks, visit a travel clinic to assess the possible health risk of the country you are considering. A list of travel clinic websites worldwide is available on the International Society of Travel Medicine's website, **www.istm.org**; and **www.traveldoctor.co.uk** contains a list of UK travel clinics.

UK

- **British Airways Travel Clinic and Immunisation Service**, 213 Piccadilly, London W1J 9HQ, **t** 0845 600 2236; **www.britishairways.com/travelclinics**.

- **Hospital for Tropical Diseases Travel Clinic**, Mortimer Market Centre, 2nd Floor, Caper St, London WC1E 6AU, **t** (020) 7388 9600; **www.thehtd.org**.

- **MASTA (Medical Advisory Service for Travellers Abroad)**, London School of Hygiene and Tropical Medicine, Keppel St, London WC1 7HT, **t** 09068 224100; **www.masta.org**. Details of clinics around the UK.
- **www.fitfortravel.scot.nhs.uk**: the **NHS travel website** provides country-by-country advice on immunisation and malaria, plus details of recent develop- ments, and a list of relevant health organisations.
- **www.doh.gov.uk/traveladvice/index.htm** and **www.nhsdirect.nhs.uk**: also have medical travel advice.
- **Travel Health Online, www.tripprep.com**. Journey preparation info.

Irish Republic

- **Tropical Medical Bureau**, Grafton Street Medical Centre, Grafton Buildings, 34 Grafton St, Dublin 2, **t** 01 671 9200; **www.tmb.ie**.

USA

- **Centers for Disease Control and Prevention**, 1600 Clifton Rd, Atlanta, GA 30333, **t** 800 311 3435; **www.cdc.gov/travel**.
- **International Association for Medical Assistance to Travelers (IAMAT)**, 417 Center St, Lewiston, NY 14092, **t** (716) 754 4883; **www.iamat.org**.

Canada

- **International Association for Medical Assistance to Travelers**, Suite 1, 1287 St Clair Ave W., Toronto, Ontario M6E 1B8, **t** (416) 652 0137; **www.iamat.org**.
- **Travel Doctors Group**, Sulphur Springs Rd, Ancaster, Ontario, **t** 905 648 1112; **www.tmvc.com.au**.
- **www.travelhealth.gc.ca**: details of travel clinics in Canada.

Insurance

Various insurances are particularly important when you have a property abroad, such as household (both buildings and contents), motor, holiday and travel and/or health insurance. Note that in the event of needing to make a claim, you may be required to report the incident to the police, often within 24 hours. *See* **Chapters 05** and **06** for further details on insurance.

Health insurance

Most European residents are covered for health treatment in other European countries, and numerous countries provide emergency treatment for visitors under reciprocal agreements. In the EU, to obtain cover from a reciprocal health agreement you usually need to complete form E111, which is obtainable from your local post office, social security office or the Department of Social Security,

Overseas Department, Newcastle-upon-Tyne NE98 1YX, UK, before leaving home. This covers you for up to 90 days each trip.

Despite such arrangements, health insurance should also be arranged, not only because the national health service or compulsory health scheme in other countries is often inadequate, but also as a foreigner you may not qualify. And you can still be saddled with a large bill even when there is a reciprocal health agreement. Many countries do not have reciprocal agreements, including the USA, Canada, Switzerland and Japan.

While travel health insurance should be taken out for short visits abroad, often a private health insurance plan should be in place if you are living abroad full time. Private health insurance may also allow you to be treated by an English-speaking doctor in a country where this would otherwise most likely not be possible. Both the cost and extent of cover can vary greatly and therefore care should be taken in selecting a policy. **BUPA International** (**t** (01273) 208181; **www.bupa-intl.com**) offers international private health cover.

Pets

Check the latest regulations for taking pets abroad, not just for your destination, but for any countries you may pass through if travelling overland. Shipping companies and airlines may have restrictions and impose specific requirements.

Some countries require a period of quarantine and you may need to organise health and vaccination certificates and other documentation.

Pet passport schemes are now operated by a number of countries and have allowed many animal-lovers to consider buying a home abroad who previously would have been unhappy with putting their pets into kennels. Pets on such schemes are typically required to be microchipped, or sometimes tattooed, for identification, and to be administered anti-rabies inoculations and various blood tests. Some dog breeds are not permitted pet passports. More information on the subject is available at **www.petsabroad-uk.com** and from the Department of the Environment, Food and Rural Affairs (**t** 0845 933 5577).

Bear in mind that there may be additional potential dangers and diseases for a pet abroad. Health insurance for pets should be considered, especially as veterinary care can be very expensive, as should third-party insurance if there is a possibility of your pet biting or injuring or causing an accident.

Language

If the language spoken in your chosen country is not your own and you plan to spend considerable time there, then obviously the more you can understand and speak the local language the easier and more rewarding the whole experience will be. Although many foreign buyers get by in English-speaking enclaves, such as on the Spanish or southern Portuguese coast, obviously you are going to have considerable problems if you are not at all acquainted with the local language in an area where only the native tongue is likely to be spoken, such as the wilds of rural Lithuania. Also, if you plan to restore a property or run a local business, some command of the local language is going to be more necessary than if you are buying a holiday home for infrequent visits in a tourist area.

Language skills are more important in some countries than others. Generally, the Spanish are more relaxed if you do not speak the language, while in France it is expected that you should do so, and your not doing so can cause resentment, especially if your shopping trips normally consist of pointing feverishly, waving your arms and shouting in English without even a *bonjour*.

Not only will you find it easier to integrate into the local community if you speak the local language, but the cost of living will reduce as you will be able to do more, more quickly, without possibly involving outside paid help, and the endless routine things like deciphering bills, reading instruction manuals or taking a parcel to the post office will become quick and easy. Living full time in a country where you do not understand anything from the road signs to the local newspaper is at best infuriating, at worst isolating and depressing.

There's even less excuse not to learn the language, considering the wide range of language course options available now, whether on CD, computer or video, or by attending an evening course.

Don't underestimate the time and effort required to learn a language, especially as many languages, such as French, are more structured than English and, therefore, require sustained study.

Whichever way you learn, becoming fluent can take time, but is invariably well worth the effort in the end and you will benefit immeasurably by doing so.

Living abroad

A survey by the UK's YouGov in 2002 found that 55 per cent of participants had seriously considered settling in another country, often because of discontent with the state of Britain. A 2004 survey found that 52 per cent of Britons want to leave their homeland, with 20 per cent wanting to relocate to Australia, 16 per cent to Spain and 11 per cent to the USA. Data from the Office for National Statistics shows that in 2001 some 159,000 Britons emigrated or moved to work overseas for at least a year.

Can you hack it?

It can be a very enticing idea, when you're crammed in like a sardine on the early morning commuter train, struggling with everything from the mortgage payments to the rain and bitter cold of a British winter, to picture upping sticks to some foreign field in a gorgeous sun-drenched villa or farmhouse.

Yet some people find that the grass isn't necessarily greener on the other side and, within months, return to the UK because they find the rural bliss interminably boring, they miss their friends and family and such British pleasures as the local pub; and they feel isolated by the language and cultural differences of their new country of residence.

Those who tend not to stick it out speak little or none of the language, have unrealistic goals and struggle to integrate, while those who manage to survive tend to arrive with a realistic view of the limitations and how they intend to spend their days in their new country.

Financial implications

The practical and financial implications of such a move should be addressed many months in advance. For example, note that savings and investments obtained in the UK may not qualify for the same tax breaks in the country you are planning to emigrate to.

The differing tax regimes, property regulations and pension rules all need to be investigated thoroughly. The Inland Revenue website, **www.inlandrevenue. gov.uk**, has links to sites that explain tax rules in different countries.

An independent financial adviser and/or an accountant may be able to advise on how to protect savings and transfer them abroad tax-efficiently. Dual taxation arrangements are in place between Britain and some other countries, so that tax is only paid once rather than twice when investments are assessed.

Savings may benefit from being left in a UK deposit account, which will require an **Inland Revenue IR85** form, available from banks and building societies. This form allows for tax-free interest payments for the non-resident. Savings can also be put into offshore bonds to benefit from tax-free growth, and pension funds can remain in the UK until retirement overseas.

Those planning to emigrate should also check whether life and critical illness insurance cover, income protection plans and similar insurance will still be valid for those living abroad.

The emigration application itself may be costly, and may involve an application fee to the immigration authorities, proof of assets, medical fees, legal fees and other such costs.

Friends and family

If you want to stay in touch with friends, family and business colleagues, the availability, efficiency and cost of communication, whether telephone, mobile phone, mail or email, should be a major consideration. While this may not be such a problem in a country like France or America, it may be a real issue in a less developed country. International mobile phone tariffs can vary greatly.

Fortunately, technological advances and widespread competition in recent years have generally brought down prices and improved quality of service greatly for all forms of communication.

Many people who move abroad underestimate how much they will miss family and friends when they go abroad. People you leave in the UK may not visit as much as they initially planned as the complications of life plus time and money pressures take their toll. And when they do stay, it can sometimes seem as if you are running a hotel, where instead of being paid hotel rates you receive a box of chocolates and a bottle of wine.

Older buyers often find that they underestimate what a wrench their leaving the country can be, even for their young adult children who, instead of welcoming independence, can feel rather abandoned.

Working abroad

Before anything else, it is imperative to know whether you are permitted to work in your country of choice, whether by birthright, marriage, as a national of a country that is a member of a larger community such as the European Union, or maybe through being able to invest in a business there.

Even if you fit the criteria for a work permit, is there enough demand for the qualifications, experience and skills you have to offer? France, for example, has high and inflexible entry requirements for most professions and, currently, with a 10 per cent unemployment rate, does not have a skills shortage.

Another thing to consider seriously is whether your grasp of the language is strong enough for successful employment. Are the sorts of salaries on offer adequate for your needs? There may be plenty of work in the ugly, heavily industrialised part of the country, but opportunities are likely to be far fewer in the beautiful rural region you may picture yourself being in.

Working for yourself

Because in many countries both homes and businesses cost less than in Britain, working for yourself can be a relatively painless way of leaving the daily commuter grind, especially with the advances in communications, which allow many workers to keep in touch worldwide through the telephone and Internet. In particular, buildings big enough to become guest houses or small hotels are affordable in many countries, where they would be out of the reach of aspiring hoteliers in Britain.

But if you like the idea of running your own business abroad, are you prepared for the in-depth research you need to do to have a good chance at succeeding? Could you handle the invariably baffling bureaucracy you will come across should you start your own business? Could you cope with the long hours with small profits often associated with running a business like a restaurant or bar?

Running a bed and breakfast

Many Britons are renovating larger buildings in order to run bed-and-breakfast properties abroad, especially in France, but are finding to their cost that instead of a steady flow of paying guests financing the easy life, there are too many times where customers do not materialise, and when they do they demand almost 24-hour service.

The problem is compounded by too many people doing the same thing in the same area – as commonly happens in popular areas of France and Spain – so that sheer competition diminishes any chance of reasonable profits. You can find yourself working a 60-hour week, greeting, washing, ironing, cooking, doing the paperwork and redecorating, just to make a profit.

Many people going into the B&B business underestimate the cost, and over-estimate how long the season will last and how much can be charged.

It is imperative, therefore, to research the area and competition thoroughly before committing to buy. A swimming pool can make a huge difference to the amount you can charge guests and increases the possibility of bookings. Tennis courts help too. A property that is easily accessible by road, rail or air will have more chance of filling up, as will one near good tourist sites.

Many people who relocate to start a new business bite off more than they chew. It is a good idea to be absolutely clear of your capabilities and try to imagine everything that could possibly go wrong before deciding on a business plan. Owning a vineyard or olive grove may sound idyllic, but do you have any background in agriculture? A little village restaurant may look like bliss, but do you have any experience of the catering trade?

You would need to employ an experienced English-speaking lawyer as well as an accountant (for example one from an international firm such as Price Waterhouse or Ernst and Young) to guide you through the laws and regulations.

Often the best way to finance buying or starting up a business abroad is to remortgage your UK home, as British banks are frequently not keen to lend against commercial property abroad.

The website **www.businessesforsale.com** features small business opportunities abroad.

Education overseas

Fortunately most countries have at least an adequate choice of educational options for the children of people relocating abroad, and in some countries, notably in most of Europe, there is a good choice of private English-speaking schools and colleges as well as of local state ones.

Education abroad offers children an early introduction to the international scene and can broaden horizons greatly. Young children educated in a foreign country can also often benefit from becoming bilingual quite effortlessly.

For further information, the **European Council of International Schools** (21 Lavant Street, Petersfield, Hants GU32 3EL, UK, **t** (01730) 268244; **www.ecis. org**) publishes an international schools directory, while the website **www. ibiblio.org/cisco/schools/international** lists international schools. Overseas schools for English-speaking children are included in some of the larger country sections in **Chapter 03**.

Retirement abroad

Retirement abroad may hold many attractions: possibly a more favourable, health-improving climate, a more relaxing way of life, a higher standard and lower cost of living, anything from lower taxation and utilities costs to the price of everyday groceries and meals out.

In 2004, of the 11.3 million people who receive the state pension in the UK, about 930,000 live abroad. Many of these have found that they can sell their UK home for a sizeable sum and buy a comparatively cheap home abroad and invest the rest to provide income, enjoying the lower cost of living many countries popular for retirement enjoy.

Yet retiring abroad also has its disadvantages. You are separated from family and friends, and may have language problems and difficulties settling into what may be an alien culture and way of life.

Health care facilities may be lacking compared with the standard you are used to, and there may be new dangers of disease or infection.

Lounging in the sun can seem very attractive initially, but after a few weeks the attraction may wane and health benefits the climate may bring could be cancelled out if you take too little exercise and too much sun, alcohol and food. You may have financial difficulties caused by exchange rate fluctuations, higher taxes or cost of living.

Some countries offer significantly inferior state support for the elderly, and your state pension can be lost by moving to some countries. Many senior citizens planning to relocate abroad do not realise that even in popular retirement destinations, like Canada, New Zealand, Australia and South Africa, state pension increases are not annually index-linked by the government in the UK. This means that often pensioners living abroad receive a state pension that is a fraction of the current one offered at home.

Be aware that there can be a big gap between the dream of retirement abroad and reality, and that the beautiful landscapes and better climate may not be enough to sustain you, and that missing friends, family and the British way of life may cause you to want to move back to the UK. Not all retirees end up with a big beachside villa, nice boat and comfortable income. There are many in sunnier climes that find themselves living hand-to-mouth and working hard well into retirement.

It is good to plan for the eventuality of living abroad's not being all it is cracked up to be. There are many British retirees abroad who want to move back, but do not have the finance in place to be able to sell up and do so.

Potential expats should thoroughly investigate their region of choice before committing themselves. The first thing to clarify is whether the country of choice will permit you to retire there, and whether there are any conditions you have to meet. For example, you will probably have to satisfy the authorities that you have sufficient income, and/or may be required to show that you own the freehold on a property in the country. Once you have got over those hurdles, can you actually afford to retire there?

Do you know the country well enough to be sure you want to live there? It may be a good idea to rent first to see how you like it. Although you know the summer is delightful, the winter there may be miserable, the local municipality a ghost town and most facilities and services closed until the summer season. On the other hand, spring and autumn may be delightful, while summer becomes unbearable with the stifling heat and huge influx of tourists.

The tax implications of retiring abroad should be thoroughly investigated, too. Many retirees have a considerable sum available through the sale of their UK home, their savings, pensions and possibly other assets, and this needs to be put into a tax-efficient package so that the tax man doesn't get too high a proportion of it.

Find out what the position of retired people is in your country of choice. Are there any tax breaks? Would it be advantageous to leave some of your assets in an offshore account? Is health care free? Is there much of a choice of state and private residential nursing homes, home nursing services or private sheltered homes, should the need arise? Sheltered housing developments often have significant service charges and these may increase annually.

More information on state pensions for those living abroad is available from the **Pension Service International Pension Centre (t** (0191) 218 7777).

Country Profiles

This chapter makes a detailed comparison of many of the countries that have proved popular for purchasing property. For shorter summaries of a further 14 countries that you may wish to consider, *see* **Appendix: Further Countries**, pp.253–64.

Andorra

Why buy here?

Pros: More people could probably find the Lost City of Atlantis than place the tiny landlocked country of Andorra on a map. But, along with France, Germany, Spain, Italy, Switzerland and Austria, Andorra is one of the key countries to focus on if you enjoy skiing. Sandwiched in the eastern Pyrenees between Toulouse in France to the north and Barcelona in Spain to the south, this mountainous country has seven excellent winter ski resorts, with drops of 3,000 feet and runs of a couple of miles or more. Andorra's popularity is further boosted by its being a tax haven: there are no income, capital gains, inheritance, sales or value-added taxes.

In spring and summer, when the snow and ice has melted, the resorts are transformed into beautiful mountain holiday destinations with hot summers, unrivalled air quality, wonderful walking country and unspoilt villages. Horseback-riding, mountain-biking, fishing, hiking and hunting are popular, and there is an 18-hole golf course just across the border in Spain. There are beautiful streams, lakes, waterfalls, forests and meadows.

Cons: Andorra's small size and exclusivity make it significantly more expensive and more difficult to buy in compared with neighbouring France and Spain. It suffers from very bad traffic, aggravated by seasonal and holiday visitors, as well as air pollution in the valleys caused by the country's incinerators and by lorries travelling to and from Spain and France.

Access: Andorra enjoys the excellent transport options available in neighbouring southwest France and northern Spain.

Property

Types: Housing is not cheap and many properties are on plots hewn from the side of a mountain. Apartments in the ski resorts are most popular with foreign buyers, and town houses and chalets are also quite widely available.

Where to buy: The most popular area for foreigners is the parish of La Massana (population 6,000) in the northeast of the country. Good locations include the outskirts of the town and the nearby villages of Anyos, Sispony, L'Aldosa, Pal, Erts,

Xixerella and Arinsal. The smaller parish of Ordino, adjacent to La Massana, is also popular, but few properties are available and prices are high.

Property prices: Andorra's size, tax-haven status and strict controls on building ensure that property prices are among the highest in Europe. Apartments in one of the ski resorts would typically set you back more than £100,000, and commonly £200,000. Chalets are typically £700,000 plus.

In the La Massana area, the minimum asking price for a detached house would be about £150,000, and some hover around the £1 million mark. Low-rise apartment buildings are common, especially in Arinsal. Small apartments here are available for under £60,000.

Legal restrictions: Foreigners may own only one property, and it and the land it sits on may not exceed 1,000 square metres.

Finance

Currency and exchange rate: Euro (€); £1 = €1.50

Local mortgages: Andorran banks offer loans in euros, but better terms may be available in the UK. Local banks typically offer mortgages up to 25 years for 60 to 70 per cent of the purchase price.

The buying process: When both parties agree on the purchase price, typically a non-refundable deposit of 10 per cent is paid to the vendor and official permission to buy is sought from the government. The purchase contract is signed in front of a notary, who duly issues the deeds to the property.

Costs of buying: On top of the 1 per cent (maximum) fee for the notary, a property transfer fee of up to 2 per cent of the purchase price is payable. Although a small fee is payable for applying for government approval of the sale, no stamp duty or land registry fees are charged.

Is property a good investment? Andorra's political stability, steady property market and enduring demand for both summer and winter holiday rentals (on which there are no restrictions) make property generally a good investment.

Selling: With Andorra being a tax haven, no capital gains tax is payable.

Inheritance tax: With Andorra being a tax haven, there is no inheritance tax.

Living in Andorra

Around a quarter of the 70,000 population of this 486 sq km principality are native Andorrans, with the remainder principally coming from France and Spain. The official language is Catalan, with French and Spanish also spoken.

The granting of a residence permit, a *residencia*, is subject to strict financial conditions concerning income and requires a financial deposit to be paid. Foreigners wishing to be full-time residents (technically, resident for more than

90 consecutive days in any one year) fall into two categories: retirees and those wanting to work or start a business. Unless you're an EU national, a working residence permit is almost impossible to obtain. Work permits are also difficult to obtain.

Foreigners are permitted to own a property and spend more than 90 days in the country without a residence permit provided they can prove that it is their second rather than their main home.

Residents enjoy both a low cost and a high standard of living, boosted by there being virtually no taxes. A nominal annual property tax is payable, however.

The crime rate is low and medical facilities are good, although private health insurance should be taken out.

Further information

- **Andorra: t** (00 376)
- **Andorra Delegation**, 63 Westover Road, London SW18 2RF, UK, **t** (020) 8874 4806.

Estate agents

- **Servissim** (Andorra), **t** 737 800; **www.servissim.ad**.
- **www.propertyandorra.com**. A useful resource.

Australia

Why buy here?

Pros: Currently around 10,000 Britons a year leave to live in Australia, and in 2001 around a thousand Brits applied to buy property compared with around 700 the year before. That is unsurprising, considering Australia's high standard of living, fabulous climate with its blazing summer during the depths of our winter, and huge geographical diversity. Prices have been especially attractive to British buyers in recent years, with sterling performing well against the weak Australian dollar.

Cons: Obviously the long distance makes weekend visits rather unattractive. It is a long way from family and friends.

Access: Mile for mile, air fares to Australia are comparatively cheap. There are numerous carriers offering a wide choice of special offers including tempting stopovers to break the long journey.

Property

Types: A very wide range, as can be expected of a prosperous first world country. Many buyers purchase a plot of land and have a home built on it.

Where to buy: Sydney is eternally popular with foreign buyers. The inner-city Sydney suburb of Paddington, 20 minutes from the centre, has charming convict-built period terraced homes. Modern loft-style apartments are located at Woolloomoolloo. Glebe, Randwick and Birchwood boast grand old mansions, and Potts Point contains splendid Art Deco apartments. The neighbourhood of Toorak in Melbourne has some of the country's most expensive real estate. Far cheaper is Melbourne's answer to London's Docklands, Port Melbourne.

Property prices: Prices are significantly lower than in the UK. In most city suburbs, two-bedroom apartments and houses are available from under £40,000. Sydney property, generally the most expensive in the country, costs at least four times as much, although central one-bed apartments are still available for under £150,000. Three-bedroom suburban bungalows start at £60,000 or so. Terraced homes in Paddington, Sydney, are available for under £300,000. Melbourne is also expensive – Toorak in Melbourne has many properties topping the £1 million mark – but it is still cheaper than London.

Many newspapers carry property auction statistics, allowing potential buyers to track the property market in their chosen locality.

Legal restrictions: Apart from holiday homes situated in officially designated 'integrated tourism resorts', foreign investors generally are required to register with and seek prior approval from the Foreign Investment Review Board.

- Foreign nationals with a permanent visa are permitted to purchase residential property, otherwise they may only buy property off plan.
- Foreigners living in Australia are required to sell the property if they leave.
- Usually there is a restriction on spending more than four weeks per year at a timeshare property.
- Although most property and land is freehold, in Canberra (the Australian Capital Territory) land is sold on a 99-year lease.
- Foreigners purchasing for investment reasons may buy only new property, a restriction designed to ensure that the local population is not priced out of the market.

Finance

Currency and exchange rate: Australian dollar (A$); £1 = A$2.60

Local mortgages: British banks do not offer mortgages for Australian property, but a mortgage from a local lender should be straightforward to arrange. There is a large choice available, up to 100 per cent and for up to 30 years.

The buying process: This is very different from the process in the UK. Most property is sold by auction. The property is typically open to the public for viewing during the three weekends preceeding the sale. The auction is usually held in the property itself, unlike in the UK where a succession of properties is sold at a neutral venue. The auction system can be nerve-racking as the buyer can so easily lose out and the seller may not raise the price wanted. At least it is straightforward and quick, and eliminates gazumping, although there have been problems with dummy bidders driving prices up. State governments intend to stop this by introducing a purchaser registration system.

If you are planning permanent residence it is advisable not to start looking at properties until you are in possession of a visa.

Costs of buying: These average around 5 per cent of the purchase price and include legal fees, stamp duty, which varies from region to region, and a small land transfer registration fee.

Is property a good investment? Australia's property market is comparatively stable. Waterside property, especially, is likely to appreciate well because such homes are generally in short supply.

Selling: Capital gains tax is not applicable on a taxpayer's main residence and is 33 per cent on gains on properties by non-residents.

Inheritance tax: None is payable.

Living in Australia

The climate is tropical in the north and temperate in the south; summer is from December to February and winter from June to August.

Australia is politically very stable and the crime rate is relatively low.

The cost of living is rather lower than that of northern Europe, although some items are considerably more or less costly when compared with the UK. For example, a good restaurant meal would only be around £5–10, yet cars cost as much as double the amount as in the UK.

Medical facilities are very good, although there are no reciprocal agreements with the UK. Residents contribute 1.5 per cent of taxable income to the national health scheme, which covers most medical costs. Non-residents and the retired require private medical insurance.

Property taxes can vary greatly from region to region. Income tax is payable by those remaining in the country for more than six months per year and ranges from 17 per cent on incomes of £2,300 to a maximum of 47 per cent on incomes above £23,000.

There are various ways to emigrate to Australia. You can marry or live with an existing Australian citizen; you would be required to prove that your relationship is genuine and has lasted for a minimum of a year, demonstrating this through such things as a joint bank account and other examples of shared or joint commitments. You can also apply as a skilled professional, with success decided using a points system linked to age (45 is the cut-off age), qualifications, experience and skills offered. Applications can take over a year, and jobs most in demand include teachers, nurses, accountants, engineers, chefs and workers in the building trades. Typically education, jobs and personal records are examined, and numerous references and documentation are required. Health and police checks can cost around £1,000. The application can be undertaken by a specialised emigration agent on the applicants' behalf, who typically will charge from £500 to £2,000.

Residency can also be obtained through investing a sizeable amount of money into the country. Also, retirement visas are granted, on condition that you do not work in Australia.

Further information

- **Australia: t** (00 61)
- **Australian High Commission**, Australia House, Strand, London WC2B 4LA, UK, **t** (020) 7836 7123; **www.australia.org.uk.**
- **Australian Tourist Commission**, Gemini House, 10–18 Putney Hill, London SW15 6AA, UK, **t** (020) 8780 2227; **www.australia.com.**
- **Australian Embassy,** 1601 Massachusetts Avenue, NW, Washington, DC 20036, USA, **t** (202) 797 3000; **www.ausemb.org.**
- **Foreign Investor Review Board,** Treasury Department, Parkes Place, Parkes, ACT 2600, Australia, **t** 26263 3795; **www.firb.gov.au.** For information on property purchase by non-residents.
- **Australians Abroad, www.australiansabroad.com.** Relocation info.
- **Southern Cross Group, www.southern-cross-group.org.** General expatriate advice.
- **www.fed.gov.au:** Government website with details about immigration.
- **Global Visas** (UK), **t** (020) 7009 3800; **www.globalvisas.com.** A specialist emigration agency that can help with emigration.

Estate agents
All are located in Australia.
- **First National, t** 29240 6165; **www.firstnational.com.au.**
- **Laing and Simmons, t** 29223 4888; **www.laingsimmons.com.au.**
- **LJ Hooker, t** 29283 5511; **www.ljhooker.com.au.**
- **McGrath, t** 29568 0811; **www.mcgrath.com.au.**

- **Raine and Horne, t** 29258 5400; **www.raineandhorne.com.**
- **Ray White, t** 29262 3700; **www.raywhite.com.au.**
- **www.realestate.com.au:** A good search tool.

International schools

- **Redlands Church of England School**, 272 Military Road, Cremorne, Sydney, NSW 2090, Australia, **t** 29909 3133; **www.redlands.nsw.edu.au.** Co-educational grammar school for 5–18 years.

- **Queenwood School for Girls**, 47 Mandolone Road, Mosman, Sydney, Australia, **t** 29960 6751; **www.mosman.org.au/members/queenwood/htm.** 5–18 years.

Books

Nick Vandome, *Getting a Job in Australia* (HowTo Books, £10.99).

Austria

Why buy here?

Pros: Austria is not an obvious choice for foreign buyers, yet it has much to offer. It is in the heart of Europe, gorgeous cities such as Prague, Venice and Budapest are very easy to reach, and it is rich in culture – past distinguished citizens include Mozart and Strauss.

Although it is landlocked, more than half of the country is situated within the eastern Alps, offering stunning mountains and beautiful valleys. Much is forested. The winter sports season is generally from December to early April, although the higher ski resorts are active as late as May. Other distractions include skating, sailing, tobogganing, horse-riding, cycling, scuba-diving, hang-gliding, thermal baths, cable cars, mountain railways and horse-drawn sleigh rides.

Cons: As it is landlocked and has a milder climate than the Mediterranean countries, Austria isn't for beach-lovers or sun-worshippers; and if you are not strong on languages the national language, German, may be a problem.

Access: Various airlines, including Austrian Airlines, British Airways and Air Berlin, fly to Vienna, while Ryanair, BMIbaby and Flybe have daily flights to Salzburg. In addition, there are many flight options in neighbouring countries, and motorway access through Germany is straightforward and efficient.

Property

Types: A wide mix from studio apartments to large detached chalets.

Where to buy: The ski resorts are the most popular for foreign buyers, and are excellent summer destinations for outdoor pursuits such as hiking. It is best to avoid the resorts frequented by the package tours as, although they are lovely for a holiday, they are geared to mass tourism. The resorts further afield represent true Austria and are far better for repeated visits or residency.

The swankiest areas, such as Kitzbühel in Tirol, should only be considered if you have a budget of over £600,000, but prices are lower around such towns as Zillertal, Soll, Scheffau, Kufstein and Worgl. The attractive city of Salzburg is a popular urban destination, and elegant Vienna is gaining in popularity.

Property prices: Compared with France and Spain, where property prices have risen substantially in recent years, property has fallen relatively in price over the past few years, stabilising in 2004. The capital, Vienna, unsurprisingly has the highest prices, with asking prices in excess of £80,000 for a one-bedroom apartment. A large detached chalet would start in the region of £600,000. On the outskirts of the city, three-bedroom houses are available for around £150,000. A studio flat in the 'Sound of Music' region, around Sonnenalm, Bad Mitterndorf, would be available for under £50,000.

Legal restrictions: Each province (*Bundesland*) imposes restrictions on ownership (whether by an Austrian or foreigner) of property and in some regions, such as the Tirol, it is almost banned completely for holiday use (*Zweitwohnsitz*). Buyers are required to have their purchases approved by the appropriate *Grundverkehrsbehörde* – part of the local authority.

Finance

Currency and exchange rate: Euro (€); £1 = €1.50

Local mortgages: Local banks offer mortgages to foreign buyers, and rates are generally cheaper. They can usually be arranged within a few days. Typically local lenders require a 40 per cent deposit over 10 or 15 years.

The buying process: Conveyancing for both buyer and seller is normally administered by the same lawyer. A deposit, usually of 10 per cent, is usually but not always payable and then a purchase agreement is drawn up and signed by both parties. As this is in German, a translation may be required.

Neither purchaser nor vendor can back out, which prevents gazumping, and means the finance must be in place before you can make an offer. The lawyer then draws up the sale contract on behalf of both parties.

Registering the title typically takes between three and six months. The lawyer acting for the sale then pays all the necessary taxes and fees and the balance owing to the vendor.

Costs of buying: Conveyancing fees average around 3 per cent of the purchase price, while there is an additional property transfer tax of 3.5 per cent and stamp duty, land registry and title registration costs of around 2 per cent. Estate agents' fees are controlled by law and typically cost both buyer and seller 3 per cent. VAT at 20 per cent is payable on fees.

Is property a good investment? The property market is stable, and prices are unlikely to be reduced because of the scarcity of properties available. Property in the ski resorts is attractive to renters all year round and there are no restrictions on holiday letting.

Selling: Capital gains tax is set at 50 per cent on the profit of a sale, and main residences are not liable for the tax after 10 years of ownership.

Inheritance tax: There is an inheritance tax ranging from 15 to 50 per cent.

Living in Austria

Austria is an all-year-round location and the cost of living is relatively low, with bottles of wine around £2 and food much cheaper than in the UK.

It has a mild, pleasant climate, although this can vary greatly around the country, depending on altitude and geographical situation. Austria is a very clean country, from the hotels, restaurants, trains and roads to the fresh, clean water of the rivers and lakes.

Almost the entire population of eight million speak German, although English is common in the resorts and cities. The country is politically stable, has a low crime rate, excellent public transport, and a very good standard of medical care.

Income tax ranges from 15 to 50 per cent, and there is an annual property tax of 0.8 per cent on the assessed value of a property. EU nationals as well as non-EU ones are required to register for a residence permit, although this is essentially a formality.

Work permits are difficult to obtain by non-EU nationals. Foreigners running a business require a *konzession*, a permission to trade, from the authorities. Sometimes these can be handed down from the previous owner. The better the business plan you can present, the greater the chance for success.

Further information

- **Austria: t** (00 43)

- **Austrian Tourist Office**, PO Box 2363, London W1A 2QB, UK, **t** (020) 7629 0461; **www.austria.info.**

- **Austrian Embassy**, 18 Belgrave Mews West, London SW1X 8HU, UK, **t** (020) 7235 3731.

- **Austrian Embassy,** 3524 International Court, NW, Washington, DC 20008, USA, **t** (202) 895 6700; **www.austria-emb.org.**

Estate agents

- **Euroburo** (Austria), **t** 6137 20099; **www.euroburolimited.co.uk.**
- **www.homesbyweb.co.uk**: Features Austrian properties.

Bulgaria

Why buy here?

Pros: This largely rural country is approximately the size of England yet has a population of only around eight million. Its lack of development and rural tranquillity provide a glimpse of Europe that has long since disappeared elsewhere. In many ways, Bulgaria has the mass-market appeal that Spain had many years ago. It is relatively near to the UK, has a great climate (clear blue skies and temperatures of 30–35°C in the summer) and fabulous coast, a low cost of living and extremely low property prices. It has a wealth of historic towns, unspoilt villages, castles, churches and monasteries, and unchanged rural traditions.

There is increasing interest from foreign buyers in investing in the areas popular for skiing and other winter sports as well.

Bulgaria is set to join the EU by 2007 and this would undoubtedly do much to secure the property market and increase property values. Until then, the European Union has been investing millions of pounds in upgrading the country's roads, airports and other infrastructure.

Cons: Most buyers are focusing on the coast but, as this is not a long stretch, it is likely to become increasingly like Spain with overdevelopment and high prices. Also, the Slavonic language in this country takes a considerable effort to get to grips with.

In recent years the country has suffered from numerous economic problems, including the devaluation of its currency and a struggling economy. Although many Bulgarians welcome foreign buyers, whom they see as regenerating neglected rural areas, others resent them. While £10,000 houses are very cheap by UK standards, they are not to Bulgarians, who on average earn around £1,000 per year. Although Bulgaria has very much left its communist past behind, some grim buildings, including towering grey hotels in popular resort areas, still remain. There are problems with crime and corruption; however, the present government is relatively stable.

Until the low-cost airlines launch rumoured routes to Bulgaria, getting there is expensive.

Restrictions on foreigners buying property with land, which includes anything with a garden, remain (*see* opposite). Setting up a company, which can be arranged by agents, solves this, but is an added complication.

Access: Direct international flights are available to the capital, Sofia, all year round while direct charter flights to the Black Sea at airports at Varna and Burgas are available during the spring and summer months. A number of budget airlines are planning routes in response to the increasing tourism in this country.

Property

Types: These vary from apartments and villas in new-build developments to larger, older, run-down rural properties.

Where to buy: Although on the eastern part of the Balkan peninsula, Bulgaria feels Mediterranean. Bulgaria's Black Sea riviera is especially popular, at Sunny Beach, Golden Sands and Bourgas, and the resort city of Varna. But there are some stretches scarred by unsympathetic development.

Inland, there are beautiful Dordogne or Tuscany-like hilltop towns such as medieval Veliko Turnovo. Shabla and Durankulak are tranquil rural communities north of Varna.

Bulgaria has several magnificent mountain ranges – the Rila, Balkan, Sredna Gora and Prini. The ski areas in the Rhodope Mountains in the south of the country are increasingly popular, and in summer these mountainous areas are ideal for trekking and climbing, and discovering the many traditional villages, monasteries, national parks and rich wildlife.

There are attractive properties along the Danube, on Bulgaria's northern border with Romania, and the Danube towns have much to offer, not least historical Ruse, with its splendid architecture.

Culture vultures will appreciate the numerous museums and galleries of vibrant Sofia, Plovdiv and Veliko Turnovo.

Property prices: Although Bulgarian property is among the cheapest in Europe, like most Eastern European destinations it is beginning to see an upsurge in foreign investment in some areas, and in 2003 prices rose by around 20 per cent, with signs of rises of around 25 per cent in 2004. Bargains still exist, but the last year or two have seen phenomenal interest from bargain-hunters, and really cheap property is becoming more rare.

A new apartment on the coast would average £35,000, although Black Sea villas are still available for half that cost or £50,000 new. Three- or four-bedroom rural houses in need of renovation are still widely available for under £20,000, sometimes even under £5,000.

Legal restrictions: You need to set up a local private limited company to buy property with land (for example a garden), and this can usually be arranged by the estate agent or property consultant. The process costs around £600 but this fee is likely to be abolished as EU membership draws near.

The company is subject to tax in Bulgaria but also corporation tax has to be paid in the UK on any company profits, i.e. when you sell or from rental income. Currently UK corporation tax is 23.75 per cent on profits of between £10,001 and £50,000. However, tax paid on the property overseas can usually be offset against your British tax bill.

Finance

Currency and exchange rate: Lev; £1 = 2.95 Lev

Local mortgages: The local lending market is undeveloped and using a UK lender is preferable.

The buying process: After reserving a property with an agent, the first thing to do is to determine whether the sale is with land. If it is, a company needs to be incorporated to hold the land. If not, no company is required. There are also strict zoning restrictions that need to be adhered to.

When a sale is agreed, a notary draws up a purchase contract in the form of a notary deed which is similar to 'Sold subject to contract' in the UK. The notary will require various documents certifying such things as the ability of the buyer to pay for the property, the ownership rights of the vendor, and the vendor's declaration that all fiscal obligations to the state have been paid. Details concerning the status of buyer and seller and proof that the property is unencumbered are also required.

The buyer's lawyer should make the necessary checks on the property. These include examination of the title documents, licences and permissions, any debts on title and terms of the contract. When everything is seen to be in order, the vendor and purchaser sign the contract of purchase in front of a notary. The notary then registers the notary deed in the local court's land registry.

Costs of buying: Both purchaser and vendor pay commission to the estate agent, with charges typically ranging from 3 to 6 per cent. Stamp duty is a further 2 per cent of the price. Agents typically charge several per cent extra for admisistration expenses such as legal and translation costs and the cost of setting up a company to buy the property.

The buyer is usually responsible for paying the notary tax for the deeds and land tax of 2 per cent.

Is property a good investment? Upcoming EU membership, house prices the cost of a good kitchen back home and a healthy rise in tourism make Bulgaria a good bet for the future. However, the risks are considerable, as in other emerging eastern European states, with legal, financial, property market and physical infrastructure not as solidly in place as in many other countries in Europe.

Selling: Non-resident investors pay 15 per cent tax on rentals and capital gains.

Inheritance tax: This varies depending on individual circumstance.

Living in Bulgaria

The cost of living is very low, with a typical three-course meal with wine costing just £3 or so, a beer 50p, and a coffee 15p.

Non-resident investors pay 15 per cent tax on rental income.

UK passport holders do not require a visa in order to visit Bulgaria for a period of up to 30 days. Long-term visas are obtainable from the Bulgarian Embassy in London. Visa control has been considerably relaxed between the UK and Bulgaria.

Further information

- **Bulgaria: t** (00 359)
- **Bulgarian Embassy,** 186–8 Queen's Gate, London SW7 5HL, **t** (020) 7584 9400; **www.bulgarianembassy.org.uk.**
- **www.sofiaecho.com, www.bulgariaski.com** and **www.travel-bulgaria. com:** information about Bulgaria.

Estate agents

- **Avatar International** (UK), **t** 08707 282827; **www.avatar-international.com.**
- **Balkan Ski Chalets** (Bulgaria), **t** 889 633086; **www.balkanskichalet.com.**
- **Barrasford and Bird** (UK), **t** (01566) 782642; **www.barrasfordandbird.co.uk.**
- **Bulgarian Dreams** (UK), **t** 0800 684 8502; **www.bulgariandreams.com.**
- **Stara Planina** (Bulgaria), **t** 887 203364; **www.staraplanina.com.** As well as being a source for properties, for a fee of around 10 per cent of the cost of the property Stara Planina can organise all the necessary legal work, accounting, translating and logistics.

Canada

Why buy here?

Pros: Although Canada has a reputation for extreme cold weather, in many regions the climate is terrific. The north has Arctic conditions with temperatures below freezing for much of the year, but Ottawa, for example, has a severe winter for four months but also has excellent long, hot summers. Vancouver has warm summers and mild winters.

Foreign property-buyers attracted to Canada are largely lovers of 'the great outdoors'. Canada, a country the size of Europe, is sparsely populated and has vast areas of natural beauty, a good infrastructure and a comparatively wealthy society – and the attendant lack of social problems.

The very varied topography includes forests, mountains, polar desert and many lakes, including four of the world's largest. Its mountains provide excellent skiing conditions.

Cons: The flight time to Canada does not encourage short visits.

Access: There are plenty of daily flights from the UK to Canada. British Airways, for example, has a daily flight to Vancouver from £350 return. Cut-price carrier Zoom has begun flights for under £300 return from Stansted, Gatwick and Glasgow to Vancouver.

Property

Types: A great variety, from apartments to large detached buildings, both old and new.

Where to buy: Properties in cities such as Toronto, Ottawa, Montreal and Vancouver are popular with foreign buyers, as are lakeside, forest and ski-resort properties. British buyers are increasingly being lured by new developments in the Rockies and other areas. Calgary is the country's sunniest spot, with an annual average of more than 320 days of sun.

Property prices: These vary greatly in such a large country and are generally substantially lower than in the UK. In 2003 the average cost of a home in Canada was C$207,699 (£83,000) according to the Canada Real Estate Association.

A small city flat costs from £40,000 and a detached three- or four-bedroom city home is typically in excess of £80,000. Building plots and simple accommodation in remote areas cost a small fraction of that.

A large three-bedroom flat in the centre of Vancouver costs about £60,000, while out of town luxury six-bedroom homes are available for under £200,000.

Legal restrictions: There are generally no restrictions concerning foreign owner-ship, although there are some exceptions, such as Banff, where only those who live or work in Banff may buy.

Finance

Currency and exchange rate: Canadian dollar (C$); £1 = C$2.50

Local mortgages: Mortgages up to 75 per cent (but normally 65 per cent or so for foreign buyers) of the property value and of a maximum duration of 30 years are available, but strict lending criteria are applied, with proof of income and expenditure required. Interest rates are historically low and often there is the option of long-term fixed rates.

The buying process: This is speedy and efficient when compared with the UK. Each province has its own conveyancing laws and the process is in English except in the province of Quebec, where it is conducted in French.

Once your offer to buy is accepted you cannot be gazumped (beaten by a higher offer from another buyer). The searches can be completed within a week, whereas in the UK this can take several weeks.

Sellers usually provide a property condition disclosure statement providing basic information about the property. Purchasers usually impose conditions when making an offer, for example that the property has an acceptable survey report. The buyer, along with their solicitor, often visits the municipal hall before buying to ensure such things as the lot size, maximum building size and occu-pancy permit are in order.

If you pay cash, the whole deal can be completed within a couple of weeks. It is a good idea to use a buyer's broker who acts on your behalf.

Costs of buying: This typically represents about 3 per cent of the purchase price made up of land transfer tax (0.5 to 2 per cent), conveyancing costs (1 per cent), survey costs, title registration and a compliance certificate. In some provinces, newly built homes attract a 15 per cent harmonised sales tax. Realtors (estate agents) typically charge 6 per cent on the first £45,000 of the purchase price and 3 per cent thereafter.

Is property a good investment? The property market is generally stable and there are no restrictions on holiday letting. New tax residents can use an immi-grant trust to shelter non-Canadian source income and capital gains for a maximum of five years. After five years, this can be transferred from the trust without attracting tax.

Selling: Capital gains tax is payable on the purchase or sale of assets other than the main residence.

Inheritance tax: None.

Living in Canada

Canada is particularly multiracial, with three-quarters of the population of British or French origin and the remainder consisting of German, Dutch, Hong Kong, Ukrainian and other nationalities. English and French are the official languages. Politically very stable, the country enjoys a very high standard of living coupled with a cost of living lower than that of much of western Europe. Several times in recent years the United Nations has voted Canada as having the best standard of living in the world. Currently around 4,000 to 5,000 Britons move from the UK to Canada annually.

Both federal and provincial income taxes are payable by residents, as well as annual property taxes, all of which vary greatly from region to region. It is important to pay your council tax on time: in Montreal, for example, those failing to pay have their name and address published in the newspaper, and their home is seized and auctioned off to the highest bidder.

The crime rate is low, and medical facilities are very good and free to those covered by the national health scheme. Those not covered should have private health insurance in place.

Work permits are easiest to obtain by those with close family ties, or able to bring investment or to start a business; refugees and those with skills are in great demand. Work permits or close family ties are generally required for those wanting a residence permit. Skills as a linguist, age, level of education and ability to adapt to a new country are all taken into account.

An application to emigrate currently involves charges similar to these: application fee to Canadian government (£245); right of permanent residence fee (£435); birth certificate reissue (£25); medical fees (£150); language exams (£165); legal fees (£500).

Further information

- **Canada: t** (00 1)
- **Canadian High Commission**, 1 Grosvenor Street, London W1X 0AB, UK; t (020) 7258 6600; **www.canada.org.uk**.
- **Canadian High Commission**, 501 Pennyslyvania Avenue NW, Washington DC 20001, USA, t (202) 682 1740; **www.cdnemb-washsc.org**.
- **Canadian Real Estate Association**, 334 Slater Street, Suite 1600, Canada Building, Ottawa, ON K1R 743, Canada, t (613) 237 7111.

Estate agents

- **Chesterton International, t** (020) 7201 2070; **www.chesterton.co.uk**.
- **Premier Resorts, t** (020) 8940 9406; **www.premierresorts.co.uk**.

The Caribbean

Why buy here?

Pros: The Caribbean consists of thousands of islands divided into two main chains, the Greater and the Lesser Antilles. It extends nearly 4,000km/2,500 miles from the Bahamas, off the coast of Florida, to Trinidad, off the coast of Venezuela. The islands are characterised by white, sandy beaches, clear blue seas, rainforests and mountains.

Britons are increasingly waking up to the benefits of buying a dream holiday home in the Caribbean rather than the sunnier climes of Europe. Plunging air fares and sunshine 365 days a year, which peaks during the depth of the UK winter, in what is often thought of the world's premier tropical paradise – with, therefore, excellent rental potential – are all behind the property boom. The official language on many of the islands is English. The political stability on many islands is good.

Cons: Strong sea breezes and the tropical weather can result in high maintenance and gardening bills. Some islands have been badly hit by hurricanes.

The most popular islands are increasingly becoming the victims of their own success. Barbados, for example, is becoming increasingly crowded, while traffic jams are becoming more and more of a regular occurrence on the pricey Cayman Islands.

Access: Access is getting easier with an increase in new flights to the islands. There are plenty of direct flights from the UK to the Caribbean, with daily ones to all Caribbean countries popular with the British. The cost ranges from around just £260 to £500, and flights take around seven to ten hours from the UK. Return fights are cheapest in the winter, the most popular time to visit. Many visitors fly via Miami (under two hours flight time), New York or Toronto.

Property

Types: These vary from ocean-front villas and apartments to town houses and rural farms. There is a wide range of luxury homes on many islands. Newer detached homes usually have a swimming pool, and developments often have a management and letting service, tennis courts, swimming pools and other sports facilities, as well as restaurants and shops.

Where to buy: Developments are now widely being constructed on many of the islands. The most popular islands with the British are the ones people can get to easily, like Trinidad and Tobago (population 1.3 million), Antigua and Barbuda (pop. 80,000), Barbados (pop. 260,000), St Lucia (pop. 150,000) and the Bahamas (pop. 290,000). But these are also the most expensive places to buy.

Barbados, for example, with a population of 250,000, is by many considered number one in sophistication, rental prospects, management and investment potential, but this image is reflected in its prices.

The **Turks and Caicos Islands** (population 10,000), however, remain very much a tropical paradise. Consisting of a small archipelago of eight major islands and 40 small cays southeast of Florida, they boast plenty of deserted beaches and unspoilt areas. A 90-minute flight from Florida, they enjoy the lowest crime rate by far in the Caribbean and are a wonderful destination for sailing and diving among the coral reefs. They've become a popular haunt for celebrities: Cindy Crawford, Richard Gere, Bruce Willis, Donatella Versace, Paul McCartney, John Galliano, Brad Pitt and Demi Moore have all visited in recent years.

Antigua has 365 beaches and is especially popular with the yachting fraternity. **St Barthélemy** in the French West Indies is seldom considered by British buyers despite being the Caribbean's answer to St-Tropez.

An upsurge in holidaying Brits has also led to increased interest in the **Dominican Republic**, a 49,000-square-kilometre island with a population of 75,000, making up the eastern two-thirds of Hispaniola (the remainder being Haiti) and one of the prettier of the Greater Antilles. Not only does the island possess, at 3,175 metres, the highest peak in the Caribbean, but also fertile valleys, desert and palm-tree-fringed beaches. Resorts started appearing from the 1970s and one of the newest – and largest in the Caribbean – is the luxurious Cap Cana, which features eight kilometres of beach. When completed, it will feature around 5,000 homes including beach-side and golf-side apartments, three golf courses and a marina large enough to take 500 boats.

Other islands that are particularly popular with foreign property buyers include **Jamaica** (pop. 2.5 million), **Puerto Rico** (pop. 4 million) and **Guadeloupe** (pop. 350,000).

Property prices: The Caribbean is largely not for the budget property-buyer: whether you want an old colonial-style home with verandas or a new villa, you are likely to be paying in excess of £500,000, and many homes cost several million pounds.

Prices are relatively high on the islands as a whole, especially near the beach. Apartments tend to start at around £200,000 and detached homes cost £280,000 plus. Properties at the livelier, more well-known islands usually cost the most, with properties at the quieter less well-known ones costing less.

Two-bed villas in the Turks and Caicos Islands typically start at around £200,000 and one-bed apartments start from £150,000 in the Grace Bay beach area, resort capital Providenciales' best beach and home to the majority of hotels and apartments.

On Barbados the most popular properties with overseas buyers cost between £400,000 and £550,000 for detached houses in secure developments, although colonial-style mansions are still available on the island for under £150,000.

A luxurious four-bed, four-bath villa in one of the most select neighbourhoods boasting an ocean frontage would set you back at least £700,000. If your budget doesn't stretch quite that far, cheaper houses on the islands start at around £90,000 in the Blue Hills residential area, one of Providenciales' original settlements.

Property is clearly not cheap when compared with, say, France or Greece, but the islands offer fabulous rental income and investment opportunities. And there are properties at cheaper developments being built all the time on many of the more popular islands. Plus it has been noticed that recently prices have reduced significantly – generally they are as much as 35 per cent lower in 2004 than in 2001.

Legal restrictions: Some islands restrict or forbid the export of local currency and some require foreign currency to be declared on entry and exit.

In Barbados, foreign buyers are required to import all funds for the property purchase and register the funds with the Central Bank of Barbados. Almost always this is simply a formality, but permission to purchase must be obtained from the Bank.

There are numerous other restrictions: for example, on Antigua foreigners need an alien landholder's licence to buy a property. This costs 5 per cent of the property's value and can take six months to obtain.

Finance

Currency and exchange rate: There are numerous currencies, but US dollars ($) are widely accepted and the official currency on some islands.

Local mortgages: Local mortgages typically run for 15 to 20 years and are available for up to 80 per cent of the property, but usually for 50 or 60 per cent.

The buying process: This varies from island to island as each island retains autonomy and has its own conveyancing system. Although usually things run smoothly, it is important to employ the services of an experienced local solicitor. The conveyancing process in the Caribbean can be slow.

Buying new property involves paying in stages: 10 per cent deposit, 10 per cent when the foundations are laid and so on.

The Turks and Caicos are a British dependent territory and therefore have an accountable legal and political system. There are no restrictions on foreigners buying property and no income or capital gains taxes to pay. The only taxes are stamp duty on your property at 9.75 per cent, and a $15 (around £10) departure tax at the airport and on importing certain goods.

In the British Virgin Islands (population 15,000), however, purchasers from overseas are required to obtain a non-belonger's land-holding licence from the government of the islands, supported by documents indicating their solvency and non-criminal record. A deposit of 10 per cent is usually paid; both purchaser and vendor sign a sale agreement drawn up by the vendor's solicitor and final payments are made when the land holding licence is obtained.

Costs of buying: Conveyancing fees are generally around 3 per cent of the purchase price. In addition, many Caribbean countries levy transfer tax at between 5 and 10 per cent and/or stamp duty from 1 to 9.75 per cent. Estate agents' fees typically vary between 5 and 6 per cent.

In the British Virgin Islands, conveyancing fees average 2 to 3 per cent of the purchase price of the property, and stamp duty is 8 per cent.

In Barbados, conveyancing fees average 2 per cent but property transfer tax of 10 per cent was removed in 2002.

Is property a good investment? If you're looking to become an absentee owner planning to earn good income from rentals, the Caribbean is a good investment. Rental returns of 10 per cent or more on your investment are aften achievable because many of the islands are eternally popular due to the fabulous climate and strong tourism.

The important thing is to look beyond the house to the management. Make sure that the property is going to be in safe hands.

Numerous islands, notably the Bahamas (pop. 290,000), the Turks, the Caicos and the Cayman Islands (pop. 40,000), are an attractive investment and rental proposition because they are international tax havens with no income, property, capital gains or inheritance taxes.

The smaller islands retain a more exclusive cachet, but bear in mind that they are more likely to suffer from political instability.

Selling: Most islands have no capital gains tax.

Inheritance tax: Most Caribbean countries operate no system of inheritance tax.

Living in the Caribbean

The Caribbean offers a large cultural mix including British, American, French, Dutch, Spanish and Afro-Caribbean cultures, along with many sports, art festivals, fishing, golf and many other leisure activities. Most islands have a sizeable population of British and American retirees and expatriates working in tourism and finance.

The climate is widely thought of as almost perfect. There is a rainy season, although it is seldom cold, and strong sun invariably follows any downpour. The hurricane season is officially from June to the end of October but in reality damage-causing storms rarely occur outside mid-August to late October.

The crime rate is generally low, although it has increased on some islands in recent years, and the more populated ones like Jamaica, Trinidad and St Lucia have crime problems. The medical set-up is generally good, although lacking in facilities on less developed islands. Private health insurance is required.

The cost of living, generally, is comparable to that in western Europe, but higher than the USA, and many items are expensive as they have had to be imported. Income tax is usually either low or non-existent, but property taxes are common, usually 1 or 2 per cent of the assessed value of the home.

Residency rules vary from island to island. Permits are generally granted to those able to prove that they have adequate funds and who own a property valued at above a specified amount or who have invested to a certain level. Citizens of the UK and Ireland can stay in the Dominican Republic, for example, for a maximum of 90 days with a tourist permit (obtainable for $10 from a Dominican Consulate when purchasing a ticket, or on arrival at one of the country's ports or international airports). In the British Virgin Islands visitors can stay for a maximum of six months at a time.

Work permits are generally only available to those who are starting a business and creating employment or who can demonstrate that their position cannot be filled by an existing Caribbean resident.

Further information

- **The Caribbean: t** (00 1 + island code)
- **USA: t** (00 1)
- **High Commission for Antigua and Barbuda**, Antigua House, 15 Thayer St, London W1M 5LD, UK, **t** (020) 7486 7073; **www.antigua-barbuda.com**.
- **Trinidad and Tobago High Commission**, 42 Belgrave Square, London SW1X 8NT, UK, **t** (020) 7245 9351.
- **High Commission for the Commonwealth of the Bahamas**, 10 Chesterfield Street, London W1X 8AH, UK, **t** (020) 7408 4488.
- **Trinidad and Tobago Embassy**, 1708 Massachusetts Avenue, NW, Wahington, DC 20036, USA, **t** (202) 467 6490.
- **Embassy of Jamaica**, 1520 New Hampshire Avenue NW, Washington, DC 20036, USA, **t** (202) 452 0660; **www.emjam-usa.org**.
- **Dominican Republic Department of Immigration, t** (809) 685 2535.

Estate agents

General

- **Caribbean Property Services** (UK), **t** (020) 7622 6515; **www.caribbeanpropertyservices.co.uk**.
- **Prestigious Properties** (Caribbean), **t** 649 946 4379; **www.prestigiousproperties.com**.

• **Sotheby's International Realty** (Caribbean), t 561 659 3555; **www.sothebysrealty.com.**

Barbados

• **Eugenie Smith International** (UK), t (01268) 685273; **www.esi.barbados.com.**

• **Hamptons International,** t (020) 7824 8822; **www.hamptons-int.com.**

• **Knight Frank** (UK), t (020) 7629 8171; **www.knightfrank.com.**

• **Big Mac Real Estate** (Barbados), t 246 423 5830; **www.barbados.org/ realest/bigmac.**

Antigua

• **Tradewind Realty** (Antigua), t 268 460 1082; **www.tradewindrealty.com.**

• **Waterside Properties** (Antigua), t 238 023 0066; **www.watersideproperties-worldwide.com.**

Tobago

• **Hamptons International** (UK), t (020) 7824 8822; **www.hamptons-int.com.**

• **Real Estate Tobago** (Tobago), t 868 639 5263; **www.realestatetobago.com.**

Bahamas

• **Grand Bahama Realty** (Bahamas), t 242 373 9999; **www.grandbahamarealty.com.**

• **Shoreline Grand Bahama** (Bahamas), t 242 373 3174; **www.shorelinebahamas.com.**

Turks and Caicos

• **Trade Winds Realty** (Turks and Caicos), t 649 941 3389; **www.twrealty.com.**

• **Turks and Caicos Realty** (Turks and Caicos), t 649 946 4474; **www.tcrealty.com.**

Schools for English-speaking pupils

• **Lucaya International School**, PO Box F 44066, Freeport, Bahamas, t 242 373 4004; **www.lucaya-is.org**. Co-educational, 3–18 years.

• **The Ashcroft School**, PO Box 278, Leeward, Providenciales, Turks and Caicos Islands, t 649 946 5523. Co-educational, 2–13 years.

Croatia

Why buy here?

Pros: Often dubbed 'the new Tuscany', the Adriatic coastal country of Croatia, with a population of 4.4 million people, is often compared to St-Tropez. As well as having breathtaking though seldom sandy beaches, it is a magnet for yacht-owners and has better sailing than Turkey. A very diverse country, it boasts beautiful unspoilt scenery and Venetian-style towns and villages, 1,000 islands that rival those of Greece, and a cuisine that is on a par with Italy's.

A popular tourist destination in the 1980s, Croatia became independent in 1991 after the collapse of Yugoslavia but was immediately engulfed in the Balkan Wars, which ended in 1996. It has recovered well, as it wasn't physically greatly affected by the conflict, and is set to become the 28th member of the European Union, possibly in 2007. Its tourist industry has recovered and 170,000 Britons are expected to holiday here in 2004 alone. Robert de Niro, Clint Eastwood and Sharon Stone have apparently gone further: they are all rumoured to have bought private islands in Croatia.

Cons: Prices are high compared with other Eastern European countries. If you are buying on some of the islands, like Korcula, poor transport connections can mean that it takes more than a day to travel from London. And there can be a long wait for ferries when the tourist season is in full swing in August.

There have been cases of title-deed disputes and corruption in Croatia. For example, buyers are required to form a company to buy the land their property stands on. Having such a company requires purchasers to employ a receptionist who will answer the telephone on their behalf, but the employee also has rights of access to the owner's bank account, which could cause serious problems if the receptionist is dishonest.

There is always a concern about a resurgence of political instability, although Croatia's move towards EU membership should dissipate this.

The language barrier can also be frustrating and means that contact with local builders, should your home need renovating, can be fraught with difficulty. Fortunately, younger Croatians are increasingly speaking English as well as German and Italian.

Will Croatia be able to absorb all the foreign interest and keep its reputation as one of Europe's most unspoilt tourist destinations?

Access: The buoyant tourism ensures that there is plenty of choice. Czech Airlines, Aer Lingus and Croatia Airlines fly from several British airports, while British Airways has a scheduled service from London to Dubrovnik three times a week and an increasing number of charter flights are being launched. Other airports served with direct flights from the UK include Pula, Rijeka, Split and Zagreb. You can also get a budget flight to Trieste in northern Italy, which has frequent buses to Zagreb and the north Croatian coast; or to Ancona, Pescara or Bari on the Italian Adriatic coast, which are a short ferry journey from Split, Dubrovnik, and many coastal islands. See **www.visitcroatia.co.uk** for extremely thorough details.

Property

Types: These commonly vary from beachside and city apartments to large, luxurious detached villas and rambling rural piles.

Where to buy: Most foreign buyers head for the long, unspoilt coastline. Much of the buying occurs on the sleepy, unspoilt, uncrowded Dalmatian coast, with its bustling town of Split and numerous tourist resorts, old walled towns, small villages and pine forests. Beach-lovers should focus their sights on the more pleasant resorts such as low-key Tucepi, Brela, Mlini or Cavtat.

The Istrian coastline is also worth considering. The largest peninsula in the Adriatic, Istria has strong ties with Italy and boasts a cosmopolitan atmosphere distinct from the rest of Croatia as well as pine forests, olive groves, vineyards and old stone houses. Resorts and areas worth checking out here include quiet, good-value Pula, the capital of the region, which is famous for its Roman amphitheatre and other remains, as well as Porec and the fishing port of Rovinj, whose old town is contained within an oval peninsula surrounded by forested hills.

The Croatian coast also boasts a huge variety of islands that are just a short boat ride away. Of the 1,000 or so islands, only 67 are inhabited. The island of Brac, the largest of the Dalmatian islands and a short ferry ride from Split, is popular. Another, Hvar, is noted for its vineyards and lavender fields and is good for views, beaches and exclusivity, as is Korcula.

Lovers of winter sports should consider the Slovenian Alps. Sea kayaking, rock-climbing, white-water rafting, night canoeing, mountain-biking, canyoning, hydrospeeding and boating are all possible in this region. Many foreign buyers wanting to purchase in culture- and history-rich Dubrovnik head for the picturesque yet rather cramped Old Town, which perplexes locals because it is where the poorer local inhabitants live, and where property is largely run down.

Split is another popular city foreign buyers focus on, while stately Zagreb is reminiscent of such cities as Budapest and Vienna. It has a pretty medieval section as well as an elegant 19th-century zone, and some excellent museums and galleries.

Property prices: Prices rose by around 40 per cent in 2003 and spectacular rises are set to continue. Apartments in new developments on popular islands like Korcula and Brac, in the harbour of Milna, for example, currently range from between £50,000 and £80,000. Houses average £80,000–£180,000, while apartments in Dubrovnik sell from £80,000. If you're looking for an island, £1m-plus should fit the bill, although one was recently for sale for under £300,000, and recent sales include a 17th-century castle eight miles from Dubrovnik for around £375,000.

Legal restrictions: You need permission from the Ministry of Foreign Affairs to buy here, which can take three to 12 months. To speed things up, you can avoid the need to obtain permission by setting up a local company to buy property here – this can usually be arranged by the estate agent or property consultant. The company is subject to tax in Croatia and corporation tax also has to be paid in the UK on any company profits, i.e. when you sell or from rental income. Currently UK corporation tax is 23.75 per cent on profits of between £10,001 and £50,000. However, tax paid on the property overseas can usually be offset against your British tax bill.

Finance

Currency and exchange rate: Kuna; £1 = 11 Kuna

Local mortgages: The local lending market is in its infancy and simpler, better deals are available in the UK.

The buying process: The estate agency sector is still evolving and it is well worth looking in shops and bars, where details of properties for sale may be on display.

It is important to engage a bilingual lawyer experienced in Croatian conveyancing to safeguard you against possible pitfalls.

There are two options for private investors: either to buy as a foreign national, which requires permission from the Foreign Ministry and typically takes around six months but can take 12; or to form a company in Croatia to buy the property on the buyer's behalf.

The buyer should check the legality of the sale, as estate agents in the country are unregulated. Establishing ownership can be complex, especially with older properties, as they may have been inherited by an extended family, all of whom are required to agree to the sale.

The buyer's lawyer draws up a contract that contains relevant details of the sale including price, buyer, seller, completion date and description of the property. The buyer's lawyer should include conditional clauses protecting the buyer should there be an unforeseen problem such as with title or obtaining a loan.

Buyers pay a deposit, typically of 10 to 20 per cent of the purchase price. If the purchase is not completed within the specified time, buyers lose their deposit, while vendors are required to pay back twice the amount of the deposit should they subsequently sell to another party.

The buying process can drag on and involves a government-appointed notary who oversees the signing of the sale contracts. The local tax office must be informed of the sale within 30 days of completion; 5 per cent tax is payable after that and income tax of 35 per cent is payable on any profit made if the property is sold within three years.

Costs of buying: Estate agents generally charge around 3 per cent to both buyer and seller, while stamp duty is 5 per cent of the purchase price. Conveyancing costs average 2 to 3 per cent.

Is property a good investment? Capital has been appreciating well in recent years. Prices rose about 20 to 30 per cent between 2002 to 2003 but the market is still young, so there is plenty of opportunity for further price rises. Dubrovnik is a good place for rental return as it has rental opportunities in both high and low season.

Selling: There is no capital gains tax payable on properties owned for more than three years.

Inheritance tax: Inheritance and gifts are exempt from taxation.

Living in Croatia

Croatia is one of the wealthiest parts of former Yugoslavia, with an average income in 2004 of £4,790/$8,800. The crime rate is very low and people are generally unthreatening and friendly.

As well as speeding up a house purchase, forming a company as described makes it easier to open a bank account, own a car and so on.

Travelling around can be patchy. An extensive ferry network links 40 islands as well as 60 coastal resorts. A new motorway is currently being built from Zagreb to Dubrovnik.

Further information

- **Croatia: t** (00 385)
- **Croatia Tourist Office**, 2 The Lancasters, 162–164 Fulham Palace Road, London W6 9ER, UK, **t** (020) 8563 7979; **www.croatia.hr**.
- **Croatia Embassy**, 21 Conway Street, London W1P 5HL, UK, **t** 0870 005 6709/(020) 7387 1790; **www.croatiaembassyhomepage.com**.
- **www.visit-croatia.co.uk** : lots of information on many aspects of Croatia.

Estate agents

- **Avatar International** (UK), **t** 08707 282827; **www.avatar-international.com**.
- **Broker Nektretnine** (Croatia), **t** 2154 7004; **www.broker.hr**.
- **www.croatia-estate.com** (Croatia), **t** 2154 7004.
- **Croatian Sun, t** 2031 2228/2131 5602/2031 2228; **www.croatiansun.com**. An agency specialising in dealing with British clients.

- **Homes in Croatia** (UK), **t** (020) 7502 1371; **www.homesincroatia.com.**
- **Passage Real Estate** (Croatia), **t** 5281 1403; **www.passage.hr.**

Czech Republic

Why buy here?

Pros: The Czech Republic, with a population of 10 million, is bordered by Germany, Poland, Austria and Slovakia and boasts forests, castles, spas, lakes and rivers. It is the most visited of the Eastern European countries and boasts one the most beautiful of Europe's capital cities, Prague, which is extremely popular with British tourists. European Union membership from May 2004 is already boosting the property market no end.

Cons: There are restrictions on foreign ownership. The years of Communism have blurred ownership in many cases and disputes are sometimes a problem.

Access: Prague is around two hours' flying time from the UK and there are several carriers, including low-cost ones.

Property

Types: Anything from newly renovated or new-build city apartments to rural villas and village houses.

Where to buy: Prague is a gorgeous city and is an architectural delight with buildings dating from the 11th century as well as Art Nouveau, Art Deco, Cubism, Bauhaus and 18th-century Hapsburg grandeur. It has remained cheap, compared with other European capitals, although prices are now steadily rising. UK buy-to-let investors have recently been flooding into Prague because returns have been appreciably higher than in Britain.

Property prices: Prices in Prague rose by about 35 per cent from 2000 to 2004 although it is still possible to buy apartments for under £40,000. Foreign buyers favour Prague's districts 1, 2 and 6.

The most expensive property is close to the historic Old Town (Staré Mesto) in district 1. District 1 also includes the Jewish Quarter (Josephov) and Mala Strana, below the castle. A two-bedroom apartment in a traditional block would currently be around £200,000 and there is very little in the centre under £125,000, although studios are still available for half that.

District 2 has a cheaper but very pleasant residential neighbourhood, Vinohrady, while district 6 has the capital's most expensive property, with town houses and villas of £650,000 and more.

Legal restrictions: You need to set up a local company to buy property here, and this can usually be arranged by the estate agent or property consultant. The company is subject to tax in the Czech Republic but corporation tax also has to be paid in the UK on any company profits, i.e. when you sell, or receive rental income. Currently UK corporation tax is 23.75 per cent on profits of between £10,001 and £50,000. However, tax paid on the property overseas can usually be offset against your British tax bill.

Finance

Currency and exchange rate: Koruny; £1 = 48.21 Koruny

Local mortgages: Typically, local banks will lend up to a maximum of 70 per cent of market value.

The buying process: The legal system is similar to that of Britain and ownership is much more clear-cut than in some Eastern European countries, such as Croatia. Even so, there have been property disputes and, therefore, it is important to engage an experienced lawyer to ascertain title. Prague has a central registry of ownership known as the Kadastra to help do this. Many overseas buyers purchase in restored apartment blocks because these are generally not liable for ownership disputes. You also have to buy a limited company for about £1,000–1,500 to enable you to buy. The property registration process before a property can be lived in takes about six months. Documents are likely to be in Czech and will require translation.

After the buyer and seller have negotiated the sale conditions, typically the purchaser lodges the purchase price in a notarial or escrow account to which the seller will have access when the purchaser has been registered as the new owner.

Costs of buying: Estate agency fees vary: some charge the buyer, others charge the seller or both parties. The seller is liable for a property transfer tax of 5 per cent, which the buyer becomes liable for in the event that the seller does not pay up.

Is property a good investment? In Prague prices have doubled in the last five years and demand continues to outstrip supply. Yet the property boom may soon be past its prime. For those considering letting out their property, Czech tenants are protected by rent controls, although there are no such restrictions on foreign tenants.

Selling: Capital gains tax is payable according to a progressive personal income tax rate.

Inheritance tax: The rate is progressive and dependent on the relationship between donor and recipient.

Living in the Czech Republic

The cost of living is low, with a meal for two at a good restaurant in the capital costing less than £12. The climate is continental, with cool summers and cold, humid winters.

If the property has been acquired through a company then the company is subject to Czech corporation tax on net taxable income. The rate is currently 31 per cent.

Further information

- **Czech Republic: t** (00 420)
- **Embassy of the Czech Republic**, 26 Kensington Palace Gardens, London W8 4QY, **t** (020) 7243 1115; **www.czech.org.uk.**
- **Czech Republic Tourist Office**, 320 Regent Street, London W1B 3BG, UK; **t** (020) 7631 0427; **www.czechtourism.com.**

Estate agents

- **Continental Realty** (Czech Republic), **t** 222 517 105; **www.continental.cz.**
- **EHS** (Czech Republic), **t** 257 328 281; **www.ehs.cz.**
- **Hanex** (Czech Republic), **t** 224 217 648; **www.hanez.cz.**
- **Lexxus** (Czech Republic), **t** 224 812 611; **www.lexxus.cz.**
- **Letterstone** (UK), **t** (020) 7348 6061.

Dubai (United Arab Emirates)

Why buy here?

Pros: The Gulf State of Dubai, one of the seven emirates that consitute the United Arab Emirates in the Middle East, has emerged rapidly as a foreign property hotspot, undoubtedly helped by its tax-free status, very low crime rate and year-round sunshine. Some stunning new resorts are emerging, with apartment blocks, villas, hotels, golf courses, shops and water parks all appearing out of both the desert and the sea. It is aiming to be a sort of cross between Hong Kong, Miami and Barbados, or the new Caribbean.

Cons: Sun-lovers will probably concede that the sun can get too hot: 47°C and 100 per cent humidity in mid-summer means an unbearably hot June, July and August. Also, with its being very much an artificial resort, there is precious little in the form of traditional culture.

There are complex ownership laws and some things are very different, for example the criminal justice system, which is based on Sharia law.

Dubai may be comparatively stable, but it is about 200 miles from Iran, 400 miles from Iraq and, as part of the United Arab Emirates, is next to Saudi Arabia. It is, therefore, in a very politically unstable region. It is politically and financially controlled by one family, the Maktoum family, which is fine at present in some respects if you disregard the lack of democracy and freedom of speech, but things could change considerably in such circumstances.

Access: Flights from London, with British Airways and Emirates, take around seven hours and cost in the region of £400.

Property

Types: Many of the properties now becoming available are apartments and villas that are bought off-plan (i.e. before they have been built – *see* p.196). Typically the developments will have swimming pools, children's clubs, gyms, room service and other features that you would normally expect at a luxury hotel rather than a holiday home.

Where to buy: In the next five years or so, the city state of Dubai is set to be the second fastest-growing metropolis in the world after Shanghai. By 2008, there will be an amazing 200 new skyscrapers and 250,000 new homes. Already a number of the England football team, including David Beckham and Michael Owen, and comedian Jim Davidson, have put their names down for properties.

Many British buyers have been focusing on the extraordinary Palm Jumeirah complex, expected to be completed in 2005. This vast array of man-made palm-shaped islands reclaimed from the sea will house 2,000 apartments starting at around £165,000 and luxury villas costing up to several million pounds. It will feature 120km of sandy beaches.

An even bigger offshore development, Jebel Ali, is also currently being constructed, as well as Burji Dubai, which is set to become the world's tallest building.

Property prices: Properties start at around £50,000 for a sea-facing one-bedroom apartment, and three-bedroom villas start at £80,000. But more common are two-bedroom apartments from £140,000 or so and three-bed houses from £200,000 with five-bed houses nudging £500,000.

These prices are relatively cheap compared with similar properties in the Caribbean or Portugal.

Legal restrictions: The United Arab Emirates, of which Dubai is a part, have complex property ownership laws. Usually foreigners are forbidden from buying freehold property, although exceptions are being made in Dubai. These properties can be rented out, but the owner may be liable for tax in the UK.

Finance

Currency and exchange rate: UAE dirham; £1 = 6.76 dirhams. The dirham is pegged to the US dollar at 3.67.

Local mortgages: Muslims cannot pay or receive interest under Islamic law, but major banks, such as HSBC, have local branches offering mortgages, typically on a 10- to 30-year basis with interest rates linked to the UK. Another local lender is Amlak Finance.

The buying process: Recent changes in property laws have meant that Dubai is the only place in the Persian Gulf where property can be bought freehold. Property contracts are based on British conveyancing laws.

Is property a good investment? At present this looks the case, but, with little investment history to go on and the instability of the region and a virtual dictatorship running the country, in the long term investment potential may be very different. With so many properties being created it is impossible to predict future rental yields or resale values. There are no restrictions on letting or resale.

Selling: There is no capital gains tax.

Inheritance tax: There is no inheritance tax.

Living in Dubai

This state on the Persian Gulf may be in the Middle East, yet security is good, crime is low, the cost of living in many respects is low, the economy is booming and there are few restrictions on day-to-day living. There are no taxes at all, including no income tax. Although the local language is Arabic, English is widely spoken. The criminal system is based on Sharia law and therefore crimes and punishments are often very different from what westerners are used to.

Alcohol is permitted, and western dress is acceptable, although topless sunbathing is discouraged and homosexuality is not tolerated.

New property-owners and their immediate family are given permanent residence visas providing that the owner visits Dubai at least once every six months. Visas are renewable every three years at a cost of around £1,000.

Further information

- **Dubai (United Arab Emirates): t** (00 971)

Estate agents and developers

- **FPD Savills** (UK), **t** (020) 7022 0055; **www.fpdsavillspropertyoverseas.co.uk**.

- **Homes Dubai** (UK), **t** 08700 992400; **www.homesdubai.com**.
- **Damac** (Dubai), **t** 4 390 8804; **www.damacproperties.com**.
- **Emaar** (Dubai), **t** 4 316 4608; **www.emaar.com**.
- **Nakheel** (Dubai), **t** 4390 8804; **www.thepalm.ae**.
- **Oryx Real Estate** (Dubai), **t** 4 351 5770; **www.oryxrealestate.com**.

Estonia

Why buy here?

Pros: This lovely, if at times chilly, little Baltic State joined the EU in May 2004, and is one of the least costly and least spoilt countries in Europe. It boasts large tracts of beautiful unspoilt countryside, lakes and beaches, and property prices that are exceptionally cheap owing to low levels of owner-occupation and years of a problematic, sluggish economy as well as a troubled history. Yet EU membership from 2004 will change this former Soviet state rapidly, with large-scale EU investment improving the infrastructure, and mortgage finance becoming increasingly available to locals causing prices to shoot up. Early investors will undoubtedly be able to rent or sell at a good profit.

Cons: As with the other Baltic states, Lithuania and Latvia, investment here is more of a risk than in more familiar eastern European countries like Poland, Hungary and Croatia.

From October to March the country is generally very cold and dark.

Access: There are daily flights to Tallinn from the UK.

Property

Types: Despite Estonia's small size, there is a wide variety of property types, from city apartment blocks to tall merchant's houses, several thousand manor houses built in the pre-Soviet era, wooden homes in the forests and chalets by the sea.

Where to buy: Estonia's fairytale capital, Tallinn, will see the biggest boom. As an ex-Soviet metropolis, rather than being a grey and grim city of concrete tower blocks and ugly factories, it is a medieval gem, home to more than a third of the country's 1.5 million inhabitants. The very best restaurants charge £15 at most; superb opera and ballet costs around £6 a ticket; woodland boasting wolves, bears and elks, and unspoilt beaches, are a ten-minute drive away on the Gulf of Finland. The old town has cobbled streets, medieval and neoclassical merchant houses and well-preserved churches. Helsinki in Finland is a boat trip away and St Petersburg a few hours away by car.

Property prices: Although prices have boomed in the capital, Tallinn, you can still pick up a studio flat from £12,000 to £18,000, a two-bedroom apartment for under £30,000, and a four-bed home for under £50,000. Conversely, a very good apartment in the old city can go for more than £1 million. Prices drop in the elegant, leafy suburbs, such as Kadriorg. In rural areas, run-down mansions can still be picked up for a song.

Legal restrictions: None.

Finance

Currency and exchange rate: Krooni (EEK); £1 = 23.85 EEK

Local mortgages: The local lending market is still in its infancy, and for simplicity, flexibility and the best rates a UK lender would be preferable.

The buying process: Buying in Estonia can have its difficulties and therefore it is important to engage an independent lawyer to protect your interests and ensure that you are obtaining true title. This is made more secure by there being an efficient land registry.

Costs of buying: Costs, such as conveyancing, notary fees and a survey, typically add around 15 per cent to the asking price.

Is property a good investment? Currently Estonia is a good place to invest, with many undiscovered pockets and property prices rising rapidly. It is seen as a leading example of a country that has made a successful transition from Communism to capitalism.

There is no corporation tax and therefore, instead of being taxed on profits from investment, you can reinvest. But it is a complicated place, with many opportunities for being swamped by baffling bureaucracy or ripped off, so care must be taken at every stage.

Selling: In most cases capital gains are added to an individual's regular income.

Inheritance tax: There is no tax on inheritance or gifts.

Living in Estonia

In 1991 Estonia quickly opted for a free market economy after independence from the Soviet Union and left annual inflation that had exceeded 1,000 per cent to now enjoy one of the fastest growing and most stable economies in Eastern Europe.

Estonia enjoys a relatively high standard of living combined with a low cost of living. The climate can be harsh, however, with mild, warm summers followed by freezing winters.

Further information

- **Estonia: t** (00 372)
- **Estonian Embassy,** 16 Hyde Park Gate, London SW7 5DG, UK, **t** (020) 7589 3428; **www.estonia.gov.uk.**
- **www.visitestonia.com**: information on the country.

Estate agents

- **Bristol and Stone** (UK), **www.bristolandstone.com.**
- **East European Property Secrets** (UK), **t** (01270) 627514; **www.easteuropeanpropertysecrets.co.uk.**
- **Ober Haus** (Estonia), **t** 665 9700; **www.ober-haus.ee.**
- **Raid and Co** (Estonia), **t** 627 2080; **www.raid.ee.**
- **Rime Real Estate** (Estonia), **t** 683 7777; **www.rime.ee.**

France

Why buy here?

Pros: While the low property prices, enchanting way of life and easy access from the UK tempt second-homers to France, frustrations with a stressful, noisy, expensive life in Britain is what seems to cause many people to choose to live full time in France. In France, not only are the property prices far lower than in the UK, but the climate is often considerably more clement, the cuisine far better and cheaper, trains are efficient and roads relatively empty, while health and education are of a very high standard.

The UK bank Abbey estimates that more than half a million Britons own homes in France now, and one estate agent recently estimated that around 65 per cent of rural properties in Normandy are now bought by the British.

Although the popularity of Peter Mayle's *A Year in Provence* may have helped to price many buyers out of the south of France, there are plenty of other areas to consider. In some rural areas, £50,000 still goes quite a long way.

Cons: We've all heard of people who supposedly bought a vast château for the price of a new Citroën. It's true, French property prices remain far lower than those in Britain and genuine bargains exist, but buying in France is very different and there can be many potential pitfalls to overcome.

Before you sign up for that beautiful barn ripe for conversion for the price you paid for the conveyancing on your British home, ask lots of questions. If you see something that's very cheap, ask why. First ask where it is. Check out the beach, airports and train stations. Many people see France in the summer and assume the climate will be the same all year round. There's a small area where the weather is better but prices are correspondingly high. The north may be convenient for the ferry ports, but you could have six months of mud. The south has lots of sun but could be at least a 12-hour trip. It seems romantic to live in a huge, rambling pile in the middle of nowhere, but wouldn't a modest, manageable home near a village be more practical?

Although much of France enjoys long, hot summers, the winter can be wet and freezing in many regions. Even Provence, despite harsh 95°F summers, can have winter nights well below freezing. The Mistral, a strong wind affecting the coast from Marseille to St-Tropez, should not be underestimated. It reaches Force 10 at least once a year, peaking from November to April. There are also regular strong winds on the plains between Narbonne and Carcassonne in Languedoc.

One fatal mistake, also, is to underestimate the cost of restoration. Often it can be cheaper to buy a property that has already been restored.

The British invasion of recent years, where whole French villages are now dominated by British owners who have opted for a French second home because a cottage in the UK would be too expensive, has caused resentment and tensions in some areas. In early 2004, for example, English residents in Chamonix, in the French Alps and where 10 per cent of the 10,000 population are British, suffered slashed tyres and 'English go home' daubed on their cars or property.

At the same time, Bourbriac in Brittany, with a population of about 2,700 and where one in three properties sold is British, has been subject to a rash of anti-British grafitti on roadsides and on the front wall of the village estate agent and local notary. Slogans included 'Brits out' and *Anglais intégrés, oui. Colons, non'*, which translates as 'Integrated English, yes, colonisers, no.' Locals at Bourbriac resent the British pushing up property prices so far that locals cannot compete, especially as house prices have risen by 50 per cent or so in three years. Some French nationals resent British homebuyers who make no effort to integrate, are unable to speak the language and create an enclosed all-Brit community. To make things worse, many Brits already in the country also resent the hordes of newcomers from the UK. The best thing you can do to get the most out of France is to learn the language and try to integrate as much as possible.

Access: Ferry ports have long been the traditional gateway to France, but bargain flights to a wide range of French airports have allowed buyers of holiday homes to infiltrate eastwards and southwards, where the climate is so much hotter.

No country has been affected more by the air travel revolution than France, which is littered with little airports opening up whole new areas for Britons to buy in. The emergence of budget airlines has, without question, improved accessibility in parts of France that were inaccessible before, especially if you live north of Birmingham. Increasingly, the cheap airlines have meant that being nearer an airport has become more important than being near a ferry port. People are flying and buying an old car to keep in France – houses often come with a barn for garaging and there is usually a friendly local to look after it.

As an example, flights to La Rochelle are ideal for Vendée and the Charentes; Dinard is good for Brittany and Lower Normandy; and Carcassonne for Languedoc-Roussillon and the Pyrenees. These airports are small and therefore entry formalities are quick.

Cheap flights providing access from the UK within the day have therefore transformed the French property market. In two hours you can be in Biarritz, Toulouse, Carcassonne, La Rochelle or Poitiers. That accessibility means the British are showing an interest in areas that, until now, haven't been popular, like the Basque country, east of Biarritz. There one has access to Spain, and wonderful surfing beaches. There's all the charm of Biarritz with its casino, restaurants and great night life, and just south is the fishing village of St-Jean de Luz, and skiing in the Pyrenees.

Stansted offers the best choice of flights. From here Ryanair flies to Biarritz, Carcassonne, Dinard, St-Etienne, Nîmes, Montpellier and Perpignan. Ryanair's daily bargain flights from Stansted to Carcassonne and Perpignan have provided access to the until now often overlooked Tarn, east of Toulouse: particularly around Albi and Gaillac the countryside is very beautiful and full of vineyards and attractive stone farmhouses.

Currently, Nice is the French airport best served by the bargain carriers for buyers outside the southeast.

For really easy access not dependent on the airlines, of course, you can't beat a pad near Calais, with the 35-minute Eurotunnel service and ferries serving the Dover–Calais route, or in Lille, where the Eurostar stops – but you'll pay for it in the lack of hours of sunshine.

Property

Types: The whole range, from smart city apartments to townhouses to cosy village homes to manor houses to châteaux to working farms and isolated houses with outbuildings.

Where to buy: Many Brits considering buying a property in France first focus on the most familiar areas like Normandy, Brittany, the Dordogne and Provence. According to Abbey in 2003, the Côte d'Azur remains the most popular area with Britons. Yet France is a large country with 95 *départements* (or provinces) organised into 22 regions. Each has a charm of its own, and many are overlooked by UK buyers. Hotspots in 2004 include areas north and east of the Dordogne, such as Limousin and the Auvergne, while Carcassonne and Bergerac have been boosted by low-cost airline routes. The Vendée on the west coast is being discovered as a region with an all-year mild climate, while Poitou-Charentes offers cheaper, more rural properties than the Dordogne and the Côte d'Azur.

It can be tempting to go for the bargains, which nowadays are usually in remote regions in the centre of the country. Yet these can be difficult to get to, isolated (think rural Scotland) and away from distractions such as lively towns and restaurants that often make a stay in France so pleasurable.

Prices begin to rise rapidly in fashionable coastal towns like Le Touquet, or the prettier ones like Deauville in Normandy and Dinard in Brittany.

The Loire Valley near Angers has good access, with cheap airlines operating in the region, high speed trains and good roads. People shy away from the Loire thinking it's just châteaux and vineyards but there's a good choice of cheap properties.

The north is generally cheapest but the three things people always want are good access, climate and value for money, and central France is best for these. Foreigners often underestimate the great variations in climate in France, which is the only European country to experience three distinct climates: Mediterranean, maritime and continental. Varied geographical factors create many further microclimates.

Limousin is a very good value area, and Charente is worth investigating, too, although there is not such a choice of properties. Normandy and Brittany have similar prices to Limousin but have a climate that is quite similar to England, with mild winters and warm summers, while in central France you are unlikely to get a bad summer. The western Atlantic coast is reckoned to have the most favourable summer climate. South of the Loire is considered by many to be the point where the northern European climate begins to disappear, to be replaced by the warmer southern one.

Here is a more detailed run-down of the various pros and cons of just a few of the areas of France popular with buyers, and the types of property available.

Brittany (the *départements* of Finistère, Côtes d'Armor, Morbihan and Ille et Vilaine) has long been a favourite destination for buyers of holiday homes as well as those moving to France permanently. Travel to the area has become easier, with the introduction of low-cost flights, the Channel Tunnel, ferry services to St-Malo and road improvements from the Pas de Calais through Normandy to Brittany.

Brittany is the wettest region in France and can be windy, although the Gulf Stream warms things up slightly. You don't get the guaranteed hot summers of the south of France, but in the north of Brittany the climate is generally a bit better than that of the south of England and it improves gradually as you move southwards.

Brittany is reminiscent of Cornwall, with undulating countryside and sandy beaches and a dramatic granite coast always under an hour away. It offers quiet country life and a bit more going on at the attractive coastal towns and ports like Dinan, Dinard and St-Malo. Fishing, horse-riding, sailing, boating, tennis, cycling and walking are all popular, and there is a good selection of golf courses in the region.

Stone and granite cottages built using local materials abound, and the more recently built properties in Brittany are usually built in keeping with the older styles. *Manoirs*, mill houses, *maisons de maître* and châteaux are also often available. Many Brittany properties have less land than those in **Normandy**, probably because farming has never been as important here.

The southeastern **Poitou-Charentes** department of Charente, whose capital is Angoulême, is becoming increasingly popular as more buyers appreciate how transport improvements have made the area easier to access, and how prices compare very favourably with those elsewhere, especially next door in the Dordogne. The Charente is an area of rolling landscapes – vineyards, wooded river valleys, sunflower fields and scattered forests. The river Charente meanders through the region and is navigable from the town of Angoulême through to the coast.

The region has a microclimate that makes it one of the warmest areas in France, and it compares quite well with the Provence area. Buyers find that they can usually eat lunch outside from February through to the end of October. The local people are welcoming, and make you feel part of the community. The French have holiday homes here and retire here too, and that's a good sign.

Access to the area is supported by an excellent road system – Limoges and Bordeaux airports are less than two hours away by car, and the Eurostar train from London to Lille and then a fast TGV train to Angoulême takes just seven hours in total.

Charentais buildings are typically made from a lovely local, light, sandy stone with orange-tiled roofs and many have courtyards and grand entrance gates. Interior features abound, including old stone sinks, stoves and fireplaces and charming little round windows.

The Charente-Maritime department, with its stretch of the Atlantic south of Nantes and north of Bordeaux, enjoys the second-sunniest climate in France after the Côte d'Azur. Despite this, it is little known to Britons compared with its expensive neighbours Brittany to the north and the Dordogne to the south, and is relatively untouched both by building or high property prices. Indeed, unrestored inland properties (of which there is a good choice) still start at under £40,000 and you'd be hard-pressed to pay over £500,000 for the very best houses in top condition. This area has a network of pretty waterways, and off the coast of the elegant 17th-century port of La Rochelle there are some pleasant holiday islands with good, sandy beaches – Ile d'Aix, reached by ferry, and the Ile d'Oléron and Ile de Ré, reached by toll bridge. Properties on the islands are substantially more expensive than on the mainland – a small village house on the Ile de Ré would be about £375,000 upwards.

The resort of Châtelaillon-Plage, just to the south of La Rochelle, is very family-friendly, with a good sandy beach.

Access is good: Ryanair operates a 75-minute direct flight to La Rochelle, while a journey by Eurostar and TGV from London takes about nine hours, with a two-hour stop in Paris. You can also arrive by sea with Brittany Ferries to St-Malo, a three-hour drive away.

The **Rhône-Alpes** region consists of the *départements* of Ain, Haute-Savoie, Savoie, Isère, Drôme, Ardèche, Loire and Rhône. Many French Alpine communities have imposed restrictions on property development, which has caused prices to rise steadily and by as much as 50 per cent from 2002 to 2004 in popular resorts like Mégève, Courchevel, Méribel, Val d'Isère and Chamonix. Foreign buyers flock here, attracted to the skiing in the winter and hot summers in the mountains where mountain-biking, lake-swimming and hiking are popular. Prices start at £50,000 or so for a studio apartment to over £2 million for a spacious chalet in the best locations.

It is a good idea to view a property when the snow has melted, as this can show up such things as an ugly roof. The lower resorts, like Mégève and Courchevel 1850, are more ideal for all seasons and mixed-ability skiiers, while the higher ones like Val d'Isère are better for experienced skiiers.

The Chamonix Valley, which lies at the foot of Europe's highest mountain, Mont Blanc, is a mecca for skiers and mountaineers from small children upwards as the range of activities include skiing on the easiest green pistes, descending the north face of the 3,847m-high Aiguille du Midi, and ambling on the local golf course. Hang-gliding and paragliding, ice driving, rafting, canooing, ice skating, ice hockey, mountain biking, horse riding and hiking are all popular here. There are plenty of restaurants, bars, casinos and nightclubs to while away the evenings.

Fortunately, there are many surprisingly inexpensive properties available in and around some of the smartest skiing areas, and in spring and summer, when the snow and ice has melted, many resorts are transformed into beautiful mountainous holiday destinations with hot summers, fresh air, wonderful walking country and unspoilt villages. Ice rinks are turned into tennis courts, outdoor swimming pools are opened up and you can enjoy a vastly different break at your ski resort home.

Bear in mind that if you choose a detached home in a ski resort, heavy snowfall may greatly impede access, winters can be hard and long, and you may require someone to visit your property regularly to clear the snow and check the central heating. Uncleared snow can result, once the temperature has risen and it re-freezes, in a glacier forming around the property, causing access problems.

As gorgeous, romantic cities go, **Paris** is hard to beat. And with access from the UK better than ever, with Eurostar trains whisking you there from London's Waterloo International station every hour or so, and a good choice of bargain

The power of numbers

Paris is divided into 20 districts, or *arrondissements*, radiating from the centre in a spiral, and referred to by number: 'the 6th' for instance, as you might say 'West One' in London.

Forget the 1st and 2nd; they are not for mere mortals. The 3rd to the 6th are both central and desirable and include areas like the Latin Quarter, still an academic centre that gets its name from the medieval student ban on speaking any other language but Latin there, and the newly trendy and desirable Marais district. The 7th (the Eiffel Tower) is very posh and very expensive. The 8th (the Elysée Palace, the Champs-Elysées) is even more so, and potential residents would rub shoulders with the president, among others. The 9th does have some residential properties but is mostly home to the head offices of big companies. The 10th to the 14th (with the Bois de Boulogne) tend to be less glamorous and consequently less expensive. The 15th is a mixture both of reasonable and expensive and of old and new, and is residential. The 16th (the Arc de Triomphe) is grand, exclusive, expensive and conservative. The 17th (also running from the Arc de Triomphe) is posh, too, but more trendy and lively, with some democratic pockets. The 18th, which includes Montmartre and Pigalle, is the reverse – a few fashionable pockets in an otherwise mixed and rumbustious area that includes the largely immigrant Bàrbes. The 19th (Gare du Nord) is a quieter continuation of the 18th. The 20th (around Père Lachaise cemetery) is quieter, bigger and cheaper still. Take your pick: Paris's urban transport network of métro, RER and bus is cheap, fast, reliable, and so nowhere is really very far away.

airlines, now is definitely the time to buy – especially as prices have been rising steadily, a far cry from the slump of the early 1990s.

The Parisian property market is very different from that of the rest of the country and although there are great buys around, with apartments costing considerably less than their London equivalents, many are increasingly realising dizzying asking prices. In a fashionable district like St-Germain a two-bedroom apartment is likely to set you back over £400,000, and even more near the Champs Elysées. Move away from the centre of the city, however, and prices can plunge (*see* box). Studio apartments in outer *arrondissements* are available for under £50,000. British buyers looking for a holiday home in Paris would find the 9th and 10th *arrondissements* ideal because they are good value as well as being close to the Gare du Nord railway station for the Eurostar to London. A two-bedroom apartment there is about £100,000, and 30 per cent less for a one-bed.

Forget Provence or Paris if you want a bargain, and consider the **Loire**. The Mayenne, the northernmost *département* of the Loire, is a tranquil farming region well worth investigating but which has all but been forgotten by British buyers, who instead flock to neighbouring Brittany and Normandy.

Let the train take the strain

The UK rail system may be in a perpetual sorry state, but the French network remains first class. Coupled with an unprecedented range of bargain air and ferry routes, it has never been easier for owners to visit their French properties.

Rapid expansion of super-fast TGV routes throughout France has meant that journey times are increasingly being shortened. One recent improvement has been the launch of the London Waterloo to Avignon service in the south of France, which takes just six hours and 20 minutes. The improved line from Valence to Marseille has cut journey times from Paris to three hours.

Because some areas of France are far better served by express services than others, some routes, despite serving areas that are considerably southern or eastern, are surprisingly quick. Slower lines relatively near to home can equally take a remarkably long time. For example, it takes the same time to reach Charlesville-Mezieres, northeast of Paris, and Grenoble, in the far southeast, from London – around seven hours.

Improving rail routes awaken people's interest in an area. This tends to start with the no frills airlines and then visitors realise that by the time you've got to the airport, waited to fly and all the rest of it, going by train is often just as fast. Also, the airlines go from airports like Stansted or Luton which isn't necessarily convenient. Once you are in France the trains are quick, punctual and clean. Fast trains go to some of the most pleasant areas of France popular with British buyers, such as Charente (via Angoulême station), Aquitaine (via Bordeaux), and the Vendée (via Nantes or La Rochelle).

When you are considering buying a property it is important to study timetables carefully, as travelling at different times of day can considerably affect journey times. For example, the afternoon train from Bordeaux to London currently takes more than an hour longer than the early morning service. A

The typical stone houses are very attractive and the Devon-like countryside of rolling hills and lanes particularly peaceful. Village cottages start at just £15,000 or so, and you could get a group of farm buildings to renovate with ample land for double that. The drive from Caen or St-Malo (with Brittany Ferries, from Portsmouth) is a manageable 90 minutes. The Mayenne is popular with Parisians as a location for second homes as the high-speed train from the capital takes just 80 minutes. There is an excellent service from London to Laval but from then on there are very few buses, taxis are inordinately expensive, and you are stuck unless you hire a car. Nor is there a country bus system. Once you are installed at your property it is difficult to get about unless you have a car. But the property prices are among the lowest in France.

The **Aquitaine** region in southwest France consists of the *départements* of Pyrénées-Orientales, Landes, Gironde, Lot-et-Garonne and Dordogne. On the coast near the Spanish border around Biarritz, as long as you're not very close to the city of Biarritz itself, prices are reasonable. For example a renovated farm-

train from London to Le Mans could take you between 5 and 6½ hours depending on the time of day.

Unless you are hiring a car at your destination it is vital to thoroughly check out the public transport options to your proposed property, as these can be surprisingly limited outside main towns. For the Mayenne area, for example, there is an excellent train service from London to Laval, but then there are very few buses and taxis are inordinately expensive.

Going by rail to France can often work out considerably cheaper than going by air, especially at popular times. The standard rail fare from London to Nice is £114 return, and although the mushrooming band of bargain airlines advertise enticingly low fares, a Friday afternoon flight from London to Nice, returning on Sunday afternoon, currently varies from around £230 to over £300 return with so-called low-cost airlines.

The author was recently foolish enough to take a British train on a Sunday from London's Waterloo to Southampton, which, because of cancellations, staff shortages, leaves on the line and similar catastrophes took five hours. Yet a five-hour train journey from London Waterloo to France takes you to destinations such as Rouen in northern France, Le Mans in western France and Orléans near the centre.

A good area to be looking at for property at around 5 hours from London is the Loire valley. It has temperate weather and there's a great variety of properties at good prices. From around 6 hours from London you're looking at Caen, Le Havre, Valence, Epernay, Dijon, Poitiers, and Avignon. Train journey times averaging around 7 hours from London allow buyers to cast their nets as far as Grenoble in eastern France, and Clermont-Ferrand in central France. The 7-hour service to La Rochelle gives access to the Charente-Maritime to the south and the Vendée to the north.

house with land would be around £100,000. Moving northwards, the Gironde offers stunning countryside and plenty of space as well as efficient transport, good schooling, a vibrant cultural life and the city attractions of Bordeaux. Considerably cheaper than the Dordogne, and populated by far fewer British people, it is an area popular with writers, artists and publishers, and some British buyers are taking on vineyards in the region. The Gironde's geographical position gives it an Atlantic climate – cold and windy at times, with quite severe winters.

Both the Pyrénées and Atlantic coast are easily accessible from Bordeaux, the fifth-biggest city in France. The climate is good and access is easy, with a TGV train service and choice of airlines flying to its good airport.

Much of Bordeaux has resembled a building site in the last few years, the result of an over-ambitious regeneration plan for the riverbank and centre. This has caused the town to be undervalued compared with similar-sized cities elsewhere in France in recent years, although prices should rise once the regeneration project is completed. Town houses in the city currently start at around £200,000, and £300,000 gets you a fabulous home.

Entre-deux-Mers, east of the city, is a good region for country living. It is beautifully hilly with vineyards and very little new development likely. A good five-bedroom house here is around £500,000.

The **Midi-Pyrénées** region (Gascony) consists of the *départements* Haute-Garonne, Ariège, Hautes-Pyrénées, Gers, Tarn-et-Garonne, Lot, Aveyron and Tarn. The Midi extends from the Pyrenees to the Alps and enjoys a hot and dry climate, except for springtime, when there tends to be heavy rainfall.

The increasingly popular department of Gers is rich in rolling green countryside and, being heavily agricultural and sparsely populated, is delightfully unaffected by modern development and free from traffic and mass tourism. It's dotted with ochre-coloured farms with terracotta roofs and fortified towns and villages with galleried arcades and market squares. Gers enjoys a temperate climate with mild winters and long summers and is close to some of France's principal wine-growing regions and skiing resorts in the Pyrenees.

Locally there are concerts and music festivals, golf and many other leisure activities to enjoy. Auch, the capital of Gers, has pedestrian shopping streets, pavement cafes and restaurants and a notable absence of heavy traffic or industrial development.

Housing still offers excellent value for money. There's a wide range of building styles to be found, including large farmhouses, elegant manors, country houses and historic *châteaux*. Many date from the late 18th century. Good examples of five- or six-bedroomed properties start at around the £300,000 mark, but far cheaper properties abound in the region, and something like a three-bed village house with a terrace garden is relatively easy to find for under £130,000.

Gascony is bordered by excellent roads, and international airports and the nearest TGV rail stations are at Toulouse, Tarbes, Pau and Bordeaux. The direct air links now make it feasible for weekend visits from the UK.

Another department of the Midi-Pyrénées worth considering is the Tarn, east of Toulouse, which is now very easily accessible. Particularly in the area of Albi or Gaillac, the countryside is very beautiful with lots of vineyards and attractive stone houses, and you can easily get to the Mediterranean coast. A stone house in good condition is £90,000 or so, and you can still find village properties for £50,000.

If the climate is too dreary and unsettled and the British presence too great in Dordogne, perhaps the **South of France** (Provence-Alpes-Côte d'Azur) is for you: but you'll need a big wallet! Indeed, celebrities who have bought here include Elton John (Nice), George Michael and Joan Collins (St-Tropez). The south of France has a Mediterranean climate with mild winters and hot summers.

The Côte d'Azur (or French Riviera), largely encompassing departments Var and Alpes-Maritimes, has some of France's most expensive real estate, especially around Nice, Cannes, Antibes, Cap Ferrat, St-Tropez and St-Paul de Vence.

If the coast is too pricey, consider going northwards to neighbouring Alpes-de-Haute-Provence (or simply Haute-Provence). Although many British people drive through it on the way to the Côte d'Azur, the region remains fairly undiscovered. It boasts many of the advantages of Provence yet with lower prices and a far smaller British contingent. The climate (over 300 sunny days per year and very mild winters) and terrain are similar to that of Provence, with farmland and pine forests, but with the added ingredient of imposing mountains as well. Properties vary from pretty wooden ski chalets to old stone houses and some new build too. Prices have risen by nearly 50 per cent between 2002 and 2004, pushed up by French buyers who can't afford the coast.

The **Languedoc-Roussillon** region west of the Côte d'Azur consists of the *départements* of Aude, Pyrénées-Orientales, Hérault, Gard and Lozère. It is for those wanting to be near the Mediterranean but who do not want to pay St-Tropez prices. Pretty, old houses in hilltop villages an hour or so from the sea can be picked up for about £80,000. Although Languedoc has hot, dry summers, the winters are much colder than on the Côte d'Azur and snow is often present into May in the mountainous regions inland.

Property prices: On a general level, French property prices have risen by 50 per cent from 2000 to 2004. According to **www.primelocation.com**, in 2004 the average cost of a three-bedroom property was £107,000 in the Pays de la Loire, £113,500 in Burgundy, £142,000 in Brittany, £175,000 in Midi-Pyrénées, £200,000 in Languedoc-Roussillon, £386,000 in Rhône-Alps, £598,500 in Provence and £648,000 in the Ile de France (the area around Paris)

Prices continue to rise steadily in many areas and are, increasingly, putting properties out of the reach of many, especially in cities and coastal areas. In the Côte d'Azur, prices rose by 9 per cent in 2003, and the average property there is now £232,000. During the same period, prices rose 12 per cent in 2003, pushing the average price to £161,000. In Paris, prices rose by 14 per cent in 2003 alone. But prices are generally still way below those in the UK. For example, in March 2004 British-based agents Domus Abroad were selling a £161,000 four-bedroom 1850s house in a tranquil village 100km from Caen with four reception rooms set in 3.5 hectares (8.6 acres) with an attic ripe for conversion.

Inexpensive areas today now include Aveyron, a mountainous region two hours' drive from Toulouse (Ryanair flies to Rodez for here) and Limoges in central France and northern Auvergne, where properties in good locations are still available for under £50,000. EasyJet and Ryanair services have made £20,000 small town houses at Limoges in forested Limousin accessible. East of here the Creuse region is rich in bargains, with cottages and small farms from £30,000, while to the northeast Allier in the Auvergne is cheaper still.

Normandy still has some bargains too. A good area to focus on is the Calvados area in lower Normandy. Brittany still has some houses for renovation for sale at under £40,000. Between £40,000 and £80,000 two- and three-bedroom cottages with gardens and habitable village houses and apartments in good locations, such as near lakes, are available. From £75,000 to £150,000 you can choose between newly built four-bedroom houses and larger resale properties often requiring some remedial work. From £150,000 to £300,000, beautiful period stone houses with outbuildings, great views and land become available, as do newly built luxury homes. The £300,000 to £600,000+ price bracket gives you the choice of manoirs, châteaux, country estates and exceptional old stone-built houses. Properties in towns like Dinan, Dinard and St Malo are especially pricey. In Nice, Antibes and Cannes £250,000 would generally only get you the most basic apartment.

Property prices in Poitou-Charentes generally range from under £40,000 to renovate, around £60,000 to £80,000 for something habitable and from £100,000 for an impressive property that is completely ready to move into.

Legal restrictions: There are no legal restrictions for foreigners.

Finance

Currency and exchange rate: Euro (€); £1 = €1.50

Local mortgages: French lenders require proof of income and a list of monthly outgoings. Most loans are on a repayment basis and granted on the basis that life cover is also arranged. Unlike in the UK, remortgaging is relatively rare. Credit Agricole is the largest French lender by far.

Numerous British lenders have set up shop in France in response to demand. Abbey , which has 10 branches in the country, saw mortgage demand in France rise by 42 per cent in 2003. It arranges loans of up to 85 per cent of the cost of the property.

The buying process: French property law is based on the *Code Napoléon*, introduced in 1804, and it shares similarities with the Scottish conveyancing system.

French estate agents (*agents immobiliers*) are regulated and subject to codes of practice. Sellers generally do not enter into exclusive contracts with agents and the same property may be with several agents at different prices and attracting differing fees. Therefore, look around first to see if you would get a better deal using a different agent. Note that in France it is also common for people to sell privately (*de particulier à particulier*) or 'PAP') via newspapers and websites. Assume that any figures agents suggest for renovation are likely to be far below the true cost.

Make sure that the agent is professionally qualified and in possession of a current permit (*carte professionnelle*) issued by the *préfecture*. Ideally the agent should be a member of the main trade association, FNAIM, but this is not absolutely necessary.

Agents may try to get you to sign a contract to view (*mandat*) but try not to sign this, as if you see the same property with another agent and then buy it, the first agent will claim compensation.

The vendor is not legally obliged to point out any problems with the property and any structural defects found after the contract has been signed are the responsibility of the buyer. Therefore, it can make sense to commission a survey. French ones (*experts immobiliers*) tend to specialise in one property type, such as industrial or residential, so it is important to make sure you have the right one. A growing number of British surveyors well versed in French property are becoming established in France.

Owing to the complicated inheritance laws (*see* p.221), before committing yourself, you need to decide whether to buy the property in your name or your child/ren's name/s if applicable. There are various advantages and disadvantages to each and it is possible your heirs may have to pay inheritance tax at well over 60 per cent if you make the wrong choices. A suitably qualified lawyer or legal adviser should advise you of the most advantageous option.

Property purchase in France involves using the services of one of the nation's 7,800 notaries (*notaires*), who is a lawyer trained in property, family and corporate law. They are employed by the government to collect taxes payable to the state and ensure that the sale is legal, that the title to the property is valid and that the contract represents the agreement reached between the buyer and seller. *Notaires* increasingly act to a limited extent as estate agents as well.

The *notaire* will handle the conveyancing (*cession*) in the period between signing the preliminary agreement and the final deed of sale, the *acte de vente*. This usually takes about three months.

Use of a *notaire* is obligatory and almost always prevents any subsequent legal problems following a property purchase. You should also have your own lawyer to represent your interests.

Once the purchase price of the property has been decided, both buyer and seller sign the preliminary agreement, a legally binding document called the *compromis de vente*, which is comparable to 'exchange of contract' in the UK. There are variants of the *compromis*, including the *promesse de vente*, *offre de vente*, *offre d'achat* and *échange de lettres*.

The preliminary agreement contains such details as the full names and marital status of vendor/s and purchaser/s, the agreed purchase price of the property, the method of payment and any extra costs, which could include registration taxes and any agency fees. The agreement usually includes the proposed completion date, when the final payments will be made, along with a deadline for completion. Agreement over payment for any necessary repair work should be made between the buyer and seller at this stage.

Explain to the *notaire* exactly what you intend to do with the property, for example, use it as a holiday home, for permanent residence, or to convert. Clarify everything you are buying and if there is a plot of land, confirm that it is included in the sale. Clarify rights of way.

If you wish to buy the property in a trust or company name to avoid French inheritance tax, be aware that you will pay 3 per cent French tax annually.

If the property is being bought using a mortgage, this must be included on the *compromis* as a conditional clause on which the sale is dependent. Other common conditional clauses are for obtaining planning permission, receiving acceptable survey results or confirmation of a tenant's vacating the property.

When the preliminary agreement has been signed (either in the estate agent's offices, the *notaire*'s office or by post) the property is taken off the market. There is a seven-day 'cooling off' period to ensure that both parties wish to proceed with the sale before the deposit is paid to the *notaire* or estate agent, which is typically 10 per cent of the purchase price, and 5 per cent for new build. An agent is required to be bonded to hold funds on a client's behalf and must display the amount of his financial guarantee (*pièce de garantie*).

At this stage, the buyer either decides to use the vendor's *notaire*, who is supposed to be neutral, or appoints his or her own also or, instead, uses a UK solicitor experienced in notary practice. It is highly recommended that the buyer employs their own lawyer to scrutinise the sale and protect their own interests.

If the buyer decides to cancel the sale after paying the deposit, the vendor keeps the deposit unless the sale cannot go ahead for reasons out of his/her control, for example if the mortgage is declined or the *notaire* finds problems with the title.

The *notaire* checks such things as the identification of the property, buyer/s and vendor/s, their place/s and date/s of birth, the legal right of the vendor to sell, that there are no outstanding loans or mortgages on the property, any planned restrictions or developments that would adversely affect the property, rights of way, common spaces, details of leases where a property is sold with a tenant in place, etc. The *notaire* ensures that the buyer is able to pay the purchase price, and registers the mortgage, if there is one, at the land registry (*conservation des hypothèques*).

The land registry then grants a certificate of free title and the local authority provides a *certificat d'urbanisme*, which declares the existing use of the land and any administrative restrictions or requirements imposed.

As long as everything is in order, the signing of the final deed of sale, the *acte de vente* (or *acte authentique*) drawn up by the *notaire* then takes place in his office. Buyers and sellers unable to attend can give power of attorney (*procuration*) to a relative, friend or clerk at the *notaire*'s office.

Before the acte is signed, the balance remaining for the property is paid to the vendor and the *notaire*'s fees, any outstanding loans or mortgages and estate agent's fees are also paid. Upon signing, the purchaser is responsible for third party insurance and property taxes.

Costs of buying: Many Britons do not realise that it is often the buyer rather than the seller who generally pays the estate agent's fee in France, and this can run into thousands of pounds. If they are included in the purchase price the letters 'FAI' are included in descriptions. *Notaires* also often act as estate agents. In this case their fees are 5 per cent up to €46,000 and 2.5 per cent above that, plus VAT.

There are also various taxes and a *notaire*'s fee, and prospective buyers, especially those on a tight budget, should be aware of all these extra costs before embarking on a purchase.

There are transfer taxes (stamp duty) at 7.5 per cent of the purchase price. VAT of 19.6 per cent is payable on new properties or the first sale within five years of completion. When VAT is due, the transfer tax is reduced to 0.6%. The *notaire*'s fees, paid for by the purchaser, include such things as costs for requests for personal identification documents and planning information, and vary from 0.987% to 5.98% of the purchase price.

If you are taking out a mortgage, the *notaire* administers an extra charge for registering the lender's charge with the land registry.

Is property a good investment? Long perceived by the British as a country with undervalued properties, France is now changing, and some areas are in the grip of rampant house price inflation in some areas. In 2002 prices rose by an average of 7 per cent overall, and 11 per cent in 2003. The days of the fabled wreck for the price of an old Citroën are long gone.

Investors reliant on letting to fund their purchase should note that France has recently suffered a 20 per cent downturn in tourism and many British buyers are finding that the *gîtes* they enthusiastically bought a few years ago in expectation of high occupancy rates remain empty.

There are no restrictions on holiday letting, although tax is payable by non-residents on the income derived from letting.

For those wishing to own a property through an offshore company to avoid local taxes and inheritance laws, the Inland Revenue in the UK has, in 2004, given notice that homes owned through a company structure may be taxed as a benefit in kind. The charge would be based on an assumed value for the property and, therefore, the more it is thought to be worth, the higher the amount to pay. The Inland Revenue would assume a rateable value for the first £75,000 and charge what it calls the interest on beneficial loans on any excess amount. The rate is currently 5 per cent.

Leaseback: The French government introduced the '*résidence de tourisme*' tourist leaseback scheme in the 1970s to encourage investment in the tourism sector. Many new developments adhere to the scheme, offering leaseback arrangements where the government waives the 19.6 per cent VAT charge and, in return, you give up some rental rights for a set period, which is usually around 11 years. You are typically allowed, during this period, to use the property for six weeks each year. Such arrangements should be carefully checked so that you are absolutely sure you will have vacant possession and no encumbrances at the end of the agreed term.

Selling: Capital gains tax of 33.5 per cent is payable on profits made on the sale of a home that has been owned for less than two years, and the percentage is reduced in subsequent years.

Inheritance tax: This is paid by individual beneficiaries rather than the estate, the rate payable, of between 5 and 40 per cent, dependent on the relationship between the beneficiary and the deceased.

Living in France

France enjoys political stability, a high standard of living and a low cost of living compared with most of the EU. Except in rural areas, where rates are low, crime is at a similar rate to other European countries and has increased in recent years. Medical facilities are of a very good standard and there is a successful national health scheme for those making social security payments and retirees.

Income tax is comparatively low (ranging from 10.5 to 54 per cent), but this is tempered by a high social security rate. Property tax (*taxe foncière*) is paid annually, based on the assessed rental value as calculated by the land registry, and can vary greatly from region to region. A further, smaller residential tax (*taxe d'habitation*) is payable by whoever lives at the property on 1 January.

Wealth tax of between 0.5 and 1.8 per cent is payable on assets of more than €760,000. If you are domiciled in France, the value of your estate is based on your assets worldwide; if you are resident in France but not domiciled there, the value of the estate is based on your assets in France only.

Work permits are not required for EU nationals but are difficult to obtain by others. Obtaining a residence permit is now a formality for EU nationals, although those not working need to have sufficient financial resources to live in France without employment. Visitors may remain in the country for up to 90 days at a time although a number of nationalities require a visa to do so. Non-EU nationals must apply for a long-stay visa (*visa de long séjour*) if they wish to stay for more than 90 days.

Further information

- **France: t** (00 33)
- **French Tourist Board,** 178 Piccadilly, London W1J 9AL, UK, **t** 090 6824 4123; **www.franceguide.com.**
- **French Embassy,** 58 Knightsbridge, London SW1X 7JT, UK, **t** (020) 7201 1000; **www.ambafrance.org.uk.**
- **French Embassy,** 4101 Reservoir Road, NW, Washington, DC 20007, USA, **t** (202) 944 4000; **www.info-france-usa.org.**

Estate agents

- **www.buyfrenchproperty.com**: properties for sale, advice and links covering finance, removals and legal matters.
- **Abbey France, t** (UK) 0800 44 90 90, **t** (France) 320 18 18 18; **www.abbey.com**. Provides bilingual mortgage advisers and has a free guide to buying property abroad.

Bordeaux region

- **Francophiles** (UK), **t** (01622) 688165; **www.francophiles.co.uk**.
- **Latitudes** (UK), **t** (020) 8951 5155; **www.latitudes.co.uk**.
- **European Property and Estate** (France), **t** 555 09 99 59; **www.epestate.com**.
- **French Property Services** (France), **t** 557 54 06 19; **www.french-property-services.com**.
- **Sarl Voilà** (France), **t** 553 80 72 13; **www.sarlvoila.com**.

Charente

- **Domus Abroad** (UK), **t** (020) 7431 4692; **www.domusabroad.com**.
- **Eclipse Overseas** (UK), **t** (01425) 275984; **www.french-property.com/eclipse**.
- **North and West France Properties** (UK), **t** (020) 8891 1750; **www.all-france-properties.com**.
- **VEF** (UK), **t** (020) 7515 8660; **www.vefuk.com**.
- **Cognac Property Services** (France), **t** 668 53 12 81; **www.cognacproperty.com**.

Charente-Maritime

- **Eclipse Overseas** (UK), **t** (01425) 275984; **www.french-property.com/eclipse**.
- **Agence Delille** (France), **t** 546 47 02 45; **www.agence-delille.com**.
- **Baguelin Immobilier** (France), **t** 546 84 86 51; **www.baguelin-immobilier.com**.
- **Century 21** (France), **t** 546 07 64 13; **www.century21france.fr**.
- **Turpin Immobilier** (France), **t** 546 56 02 03; **www.turpinimmobilier.com**.

Gascony

- **Purslow's Gascony** (France), **t** 562 67 61 50; **www.purslowsgascony.com**.

George East's tips for buying in France

George East has written numerous humorous and informative books about his experiences of buying property in France with his wife Donella. The first of the popular series, a restoration comedy called *Home and Dry in France*, was quickly followed by *Réné and Me*, *French Letters*, *French Flea Bites*, *French Cricket* and *French Kisses*. They rapidly won over a sizeable army of devotees. All six books plus new title *French Lessons*, being published in October 2004, are available for £7.99 each from La Puce Publications (**t** (UK) 02392 468181; **www.la-puce.co.uk**). These are Geroge's top tips:

• Decide on the sort of property you really want at an early stage. In my experience, and as any French property estate agent will tell you, most people end up buying an entirely different type of property from the one they originally thought they were looking for. Couples often go over the Channel afire with the idea of living in isolated splendour in a restored farmhouse or derelict château, but sensibly opt for a more realistic village property with much less to spend on restoration, no huge area of land to worry about keeping in order, and neighbours to get to know who can keep an eye on your investment while you're away.

• Set a price limit and try to stick to it. It's so tempting to go over budget when you see what just a few thousand more pounds will buy. It may be a sensible move to spend more on a property which is fully restored, but you should definitely beware the siren call of a ruined castle with bags of potential costing less than your modest home in the UK. And don't forget all the 'hidden' costs, like the fees and taxes you, as the buyer, will have to pay when you find your dream home. They may well not be included in the asking price.

• Don't underestimate the cost and challenge of restoration. You may think you're a master builder because you can put a shelf up safely, but have you ever fitted an entire new roof including rafters, or installed a septic tank? The cost of

Mayenne

• **Mayenne Properties** (France), **t** 243 04 36 80; **www.mayenneproperties.com**.

Provence

• **Latitudes** (UK), t (020) 8951 5155; **www.latitudes.co.uk**.

• **Hamptons International** (France), **t** 492 04 11 70; **www.hamptons.co.uk**.

• **Propriété 'Direct' France** (France), **t** 140 07 86 25; **www.pdfparis.com**.

Tarn

• **Agence Climex** (France), **t** 561 25 94 94; **www.climex.immo.com**.

skilled labour can be even higher in France than in the UK, and communications can be difficult if your restaurant French can't cope with telling a plumber you'd rather have the sink unit in the kitchen than the sitting room. Materials cost more in France, too.

• Think very carefully about the downside of sharing the cost of your dream home with friends. The idea of halving the outlay and running costs by buying a property with another couple may seem a perfect proposal, but just wait till you get to the nitty gritty of what colour and style the curtains should be, let alone what sort of property you want, and where it will be.

• View your potential purchase in the winter, at least a dozen times, and in the sober light of day. I know people who bought their home in France after just one viewing visit, and lived to regret it. The story about falling in love with a place and buying it on sight sounds fine, but love is blind, and all those little problems like deathwatch beetle and subsidence can be missed if you are full of enthusiasm or red wine.

• Be sure your partner really shares your vision and dream. You may start off thinking that you both agree on exactly where you wish to buy and what you want from a holiday or retirement home, but are you sure? All too often in my experience, one partner will agree to the other's fantasies to keep the peace, and the truth will emerge only when it is too late.

• Remember that your property will usually take much longer to sell than it did to buy. Unlike in the UK, it can take two years or more to sell your French property if you need to. Buyers are spoiled for choice, and may not share your idea of a perfect holiday home.

• Take your time. It's so easy to settle quickly for what looks like a perfect holiday home at a crazy price. There may well be an even better buy just around the corner, and besides, looking is part of the fun!

Alps

• **Alpine Apartments Agency** (UK), **t** (01544) 388234; **www.alpineapartmentsagency.com**. Specialises in the French Alps, Swiss and Italian borders, the lakes near Geneva and Annecy.

• **Investors in Property** (UK), **t** (020) 8905 5511; **www.investorsinproperty.com**.

Haute-Provence

• **Eclipse Overseas** (UK), **t** (01425) 275984; **www.french-property.com/eclipse**.

• **Francophiles** (UK), **t** (01622) 688165; **www.francophiles.co.uk**.

• **VEF** (UK), **t** (020) 7515 8660; **www.vefuk.com**.

Paris

- **Paris Property Options** (UK), **t** (01424) 717281.
- **Knight Frank** (France), **t** 143 16 88 88; **www.knightfrank.com.**
- **Philip Hawkes** (France), **t** 142 68 11 11; **www.luxuryrealestate.com.**
- **Propriété 'Direct' France** (France), **t** 140 07 86 25; **www.pdfparis.com.**

Schools for English-speaking pupils

- **International School of Paris**, 6 rue Beethoven, 75016 Paris, France, **t** 142 24 09 54; **www.isparis.edu.** Co-educational, 3–18 years.
- **Bordeaux International School**, 53 rue de Laseppe, 33000 Bordeaux, France, **t** 557 87 02 11; **www.bordeaux-school.com.** Co-educational plus boarding, 4–18 years.

Books

J. Kater Pollock, *Buying and Renovating Property in France* (Flowerpoll, £8.95).

David Everett, *Buying and Restoring Old Property in France* (Robert Hale, £10.99).

David Ackers, Jerome Aumont and Paul Carslake, *How to Renovate a House in France* (Ascent, £25).

Mark Igoe and John Howell, *Buying a Property: France* (Cadogan Guides/Sunday Times, £12.99)

Germany

Why buy here?

Pros: Few British people choose to relocate or buy a second home in Germany, for a variety of reasons. It is not known for its sunny beaches or scorching climate, there is a language barrier as well as an uneasy history between the two countries, and few Britons visit it as tourists. Yet it boasts spectacular scenery, from gorgeous lakes and mountains to pretty, unspoilt countryside, a beautiful Baltic coastline, culture-rich towns steeped in history and vibrant, ultra-modern cities like Munich and recently transformed Berlin.

Outdoor types keen on walking and cycling will love Germany, which is full of trails and bike paths. It is also a haven for skiers.

Cons: It can take time to integrate, and German people generally, like much of those in the north of Europe, are not the most open on the continent.

There have been disputes over ownership of some older properties in former Eastern Germany and, therefore, it is especially important to be completely clear about ownership there before committing yourself to purchasing. Furthermore, the quality of building in the east can be poor.

Bear in mind that if you choose a detached home in a ski resort, heavy snowfall may greatly impede access, winters can be hard and long, and you may require someone to visit your property regularly to clear the snow and check the central heating. Uncleared snow can result, once the temperature has risen and it re-freezes, in a glacier around the property.

Access: Inexpensive direct flights from the UK are run by a large number of carriers, including easyJet, Ryanair, GermanWings, Hapag-Lloyd Express and Air Berlin, with single journeys from as little as £19.

Property

Types: Many Germans rent apartments in city suburbs but the properties most likely to be of interest to foreign buyers are either city-centre apartments or houses located in the pretty rural areas. The best value for money is to be found in the former East German states, and properties in need of restoration.

Where to buy: Berlin has been transformed in recent years and is an exciting, vibrant city. Around the cosmopolitan city of Munich you have the proximity of the mountains as well as Austria, Italy and Switzerland. More enterprising buyers may like to investigate pretty, culture-rich towns like Weimar and Erfurt. The areas around the lakes are ideal for walking and cycling. Popular areas include the Rhine and Mosel valleys, Bavaria and the Black Forest. For skiing, the resorts of the German Alps are ideal.

Property prices: Property in Germany rose by a sober 0.5 per cent or so overall in 2002 and 2003, no doubt a reflection of the country's economic troubles in recent years. Prices are generally highest in the south and here there are many more buyers than properties, which leaves little room for haggling or a relaxed purchase. To make things even more tricky, many vendors do not use agents as they know they will be able to sell quite easily themselves.

Prices in and near the most popular cities, such as Berlin and Munich, are relatively high. In a sought-after suburb of Munich like Pullach, for instance, expect to pay something like £500,000 for a spacious two-bedroom flat, although large houses further out at the River Wurm go for not much more.

Legal restrictions: There are no legal restrictions for foreigners.

Finance

Currency and exchange rate: Euro (€); £1 = €1.50.

Local mortgages: German lenders generally require a larger deposit than UK ones and mortgages are less flexible and varied than UK ones.

The buying process: Property sales are overseen by a government-appointed public notary or conveyancing lawyer, who carries out formalities, certifies the purchasing contracts and registers the title deed at the land registry.

Costs of buying: There is a transfer tax (*Grundwerbsteuer*) of 2 per cent of the purchase price. The estate agent's fee is comparatively large, as much as 6 or 7 per cent, and may be split between buyer and vendor. The notary's fee averages around 1.25 per cent.

Is property a good investment? Property in the booming major cities, popular resort areas and property suitable for refurbishment are the best bet. There are no restrictions on holiday letting.

Selling: Income tax is payable on the capital gains made on property sold within two years of purchase.

Inheritance tax: Inheritance tax ranging from 7 to 50 per cent is payable, depending on factors such as the relationship between the deceased and the beneficiary and the value of the property. Non-residents of Germany are only required to pay inheritance tax on property within Germany.

Living in Germany

Germany enjoys a high standard of living and a cost of living similar to the UK, France and Belgium. The crime rate is low; indeed, Munich was recently voted the safest city in Europe, although unification has caused rates to rise in recent years. Medical facilities are very good, and for those paying social security, treatment is free.

Although differences in climate inevitably occur in a country as large as 356,844 square km/138,000 square miles, Germany has a mild, temperate climate, with occasional periods when it can be very hot or cold.

As well as the official language, German, English is quite widely spoken, especially in the western half of the country. Though it is politically very stable, reunification in 1990 caused widespread economic and social difficulties, which are gradually being resolved.

Income tax ranges from 22 to 53 per cent and local authorities levy a land tax (*Grundsteuer*) of 0.5 to 1.5 per cent of a property's assessed rentable value.

Residence permits are a formality for EU citizens although sufficient income to support oneself is required by those not working. Work permits and visas are required by non-EU nationals, while visitors can stay for 90 days.

Further information

- **Germany: t** (00 49)
- **German Tourist Office**, PO Box 2695, London W1A 3TN, UK, **t** (020) 7317 0908; **www.germany-tourism.co.uk.**
- **German Tourist Office**, Chanin Building, 122 East 42nd Street, New York NY 1068-0072, USA, **t** (212) 661 7200; **www.germany-tourism.de.**
- **German Embassy**, 23 Belgrave Square, 1 Chesham Place, London SW1X 8PZ, UK, **t** (020) 7824 1300; **www.german-embassy.org.uk.**
- **German Embassy**, 4645 Reservoir Road, NW, Washington, DC 20007, USA, **t** (202) 298 4000; **www.germany-info.org.**

Estate agents

- **Casa Dimen** (Germany), **t** 4086 5995.
- **Engel and Volkers** (Germany), **t** 8964 98860; **www.engelvolkers.com.**

Schools for English-speaking pupils

- **Berlin British School**, Dickensweg 17–19, 14504 Berlin, **t** 3030 42204; **www.berlinbritishschool.de.**
- **Black Forest Academy**, Postfach 1109, N79396, Kandern, **t** 7626 91610; **www.bfacademy.com.** Co-educational, 6–19 years.
- **Dresden International School**, Goetheallee 18, 01309, Dresden, **t** 3513 400428; **www.dresden-is.de.** Co-educational, 3–18 years.
- **European School Munich**, Elise-Aulinger 21, D-81739, München, **t** 8963 02290.
- **Independent Bonn International School**, Tulpenbaumweg 42, D5300, Bonn, **t** 228 323 1666; **www.ibis-school.com.** Co-educational, 5–13 years.

Gibraltar

Why buy here?

Pros: If you like a touch of Britishness coupled with the advantages of a Mediterranean climate of hot summers and mild winters, Gibraltar, being a British dependent territory and crown colony since 1713, delivers on both counts. It is also full of historical interest and charm.

At the meeting place of the Mediterranean Sea and Atlantic Ocean, this small enclave (population 27,000 and just four square miles) is dominated by the

427m/1,400ft Rock of Gibraltar, home of the colony's 300 Barbary apes. Its location, at the tip of southern Spain and just 20km/12 miles north of Africa, is ideal for jaunts to both Spain and Morocco.

Cons: There have been years of friction with Spain over ownership of the colony. There can be long delays at the Spanish border for those leaving or entering Gibraltar. There is always the slight possibility that Spain will close the border, as it did in the 1980s.

Access: There is a good choice of direct flights both to Gibraltar and neighbouring southern Spanish airports.

Property

Types: Gibraltar's period property boasts an attractive mix of Maltese stonemasonry, Neopolitan *jalousies*, 18th-century wrought-ironwork and Portuguese tiling. However, very little old property becomes available and the main market is in properties in newly built apartment blocks. In recent years, former boatyards have been transformed into marinas and former naval and military buildings, including military barracks and officers' quarters dating back to 1760, have been redeveloped into imaginative apartment complexes.

Where to buy: The principality is so small and, with not a huge choice of properties to choose from, most areas are good.

Property prices: Prices of residential property have almost doubled over the past decade. Prices are comparatively high owing to the lack of building land available, although periods of uncertainty that flare up caused by British–Spanish tensions over the colony tend to help keep prices down.

A two-bed resale flat would be in the region of £65,000–£85,000 , while a small leasehold apartment in a new development is likely to cost in excess of £100,000, more typically £150,000 plus. In Spain, in contrast, £150,000 would get you a house with a garage and garden. Many of the luxury schemes have £500,000 apartments and the occasional villa nudging the £1 million mark.

Legal restrictions: There are no restrictions on foreign ownership.

Finance

Currency and exchange rate: The official currency is the pound sterling (£) although there is also a Gibraltarian pound set at the same rate. Euros (€) are also accepted widely, although the exchange rate may not be as good as in neighbouring Spain.

Local mortgages: Branches of British lenders, such as Barclays Bank and the Norwich and Peterborough Building Society, are present in Gibraltar, offering good rates of borrowing.

The buying process: This is very similar to the British system, although a local lawyer should be used.

Costs of buying: Stamp duty is 1.26 per cent of the purchase price, and there are nominal land registry and land title fees. Conveyancing fees average 0.5 to 1 per cent of the purchase price.

Is property a good investment? Gibraltar's small size, coupled with an enduring sizeable number of people who wish to live there, ensures that the market is likely to stay buoyant. There are generally no holiday letting restrictions and the letting season is year-round, unlike Spain, with a strong company-let market. Yields in recent years have hovered around 7 or 8 per cent.

Selling: There is no capital gains tax.

Inheritance tax: This is on a sliding scale from 5 per cent to a maximum of 25 per cent on estates valued at over £100,000. Estate duty for non-residents is levied on Gibraltarian property, although this is waived on properties valued at under £100,000 that are passed to a surviving spouse or children. Property can be owned through an offshore company so that inheritance tax is avoided.

Living in Gibraltar

Although Gibraltar is self-governing, a British-appointed governor representing Britain exerts executive authority and the UK is still responsible for defence and foreign policy. There are around 7,000 expatriates, including many ex-service people who returned after living on the island when it was an important military base.

English is the official language, although native Gibraltarians, of whom there are 20,000, also speak Spanish. Residents are swamped by visitors: 7.5 million of them descended on Gibraltar in 2002.

The British feel is not only seen in the presence of British bobbies and bright red post- and telephone-boxes – the tacky souvenir shops along the main drag, Main Street, have been replaced by familiar UK retailers, such as Tesco, Top Shop and Marks & Spencer.

Gibraltar boasts a Mediterranean climate. The temperature averages 19–27°C/66–81°F in summer and 11–15°C/52–59°F in winter.

The cost of living is low and similar to that of Spain. The crime rate is also low, although the smuggling of drugs and tobacco into Spain is widespread. Medical facilities are good, and free to those who pay towards social security. EU visitors have reciprocal health agreements.

Income tax varies from 20 to 50 per cent. EU residents do not require permission to live or work in the colony, but need to have sufficient living expenses and if planning to work need to find employment in the first six months. Work and residence permits for non-EU nationals are difficult to obtain.

Further information

- **Gibraltar: t** (00 350)
- **Gibraltar Tourist Board**, 4 Arundel Great Court, 179 Strand, London WC2R 1EH, UK, **t** (020) 7836 0777.
- **Gibraltar Information Bureau**, 710 Madison Offices, 1155 Fifteenth Street, NW, Washington, DC 20905, USA, **t** (202) 542 1108.
- **Newcastle Building Society Gibraltar** (Gibraltar), **t** 42136; **www.newcastle.co.uk**.

Estate agents

- **Norwich and Peterborough Estate Agents** (Gibraltar), **t** 48532.
- **RLS Homes** (Gibraltar), **t** 71111.

Greece

Why buy here?

Pros: Sun-drenched Greece offers sandy beaches, azure seas, olive groves, white-washed villages, the friendliest of people, carpets of beautiful spring wild flowers and sleepy tavernas.

It is becoming increasingly popular in recent years with buyers searching for a bargain. Fortunately much of the country remains unspoilt and it is considerably less built up than Spain.

While many parts of the Med sport ill-conceived developments that destroy past paradises, Greek planning regulations preserve archaeological sites and limit building density and the use of agricultural and forestry land, which continues to deter mass development.

You can also be assured many more hot days each year than in France – indeed, over 3,000 hours per year. Many people have been inspired to visit and live in Greece by the success of films and books like *Shirley Valentine* and *Captain Corelli's Mandolin*.

Cons: But before you book that flight over the Med with cheque book in hand, be sure you know what costs may be involved in making the property habitable. Greek property is certainly usually a fraction of British prices, but if the 'bargain' home you're buying to renovate has no water, electricity or drainage, hasn't been lived in since the Beatles first hit the charts, and is situated at the top of a steep hill with no road in sight, holidays at a muddy Cornish camping site in a caravanette costing the same amount may quite rapidly seem more attractive.

Local unskilled labour is in short supply and illegal workers from Albania and other Balkan states are common.

Being in the northern hemisphere, Greece does not escape cold winters, especially the further north you go, and in many parts it is too cold for swimming or sunbathing at Easter time. Central heating is essential if the property is to be used year-round.

To the non-linguist, the Greek language and alphabet can be a formidable challenge to conquer, although English is quite widely spoken. Politically, Greece has been rather volatile in recent decades with weak governments, scandals and tensions with Turkey over Cyprus among other things. Lastly, if you are considering buying an apartment in Athens, bear in mind that you'll probably require an aqualung as Athens suffers the highest pollution levels in Europe.

Access: There are plenty of flights each week to Athens to choose from, and the flight time from London is around 3½ hours. Luckily, more and more islands now have year-round direct flights from the UK including Corfu, Kos, Rhodes and Zakynthos. From May to October there are numerous charter flights from Gatwick, Luton, Glasgow, Cardiff, Newcastle, Manchester and Belfast to many of the islands.

Property

Types: A great variety of properties, including seaside villas, old village properties and old stone houses ripe for renovation, are available. New developments are sprouting up in many areas, with off-plan new-build apartments and villas a-plenty.

Where to buy: Many Britons who buy in Greece flock to the romantic **islands** where picturesque wrecks in need of complete renovation start at just £5,000. With more than 2,500 islands sprinkled around its coastline, Greece has an isle for everyone. Whether you want sophisticated restaurants and wild nightlife or a quiet, sleepy spot to laze away the days, you can buy a property on a Greek island for a fraction of its British equivalent. Yet the rebuilding and renovation costs can be astronomical and, especially in remote areas, are unlikely to be a good investment. Bear in mind that in winter it may be wet and windy, the tavernas may be closed and flights and ferries reduced to skeleton services. A long ferry trip after a long flight from Britain to Athens can make weekend visits impractical.

The most popular islands, such as Crete, the Cyclades (including Paros, Ios, Naxos and Mykonos), the Ionian islands (e.g. Corfu, Zakynthos and Paxos) and the Dodecanese (for example Kos and Rhodes), are the most well known and loved by Brits. Skopelos boasts a picturesque harbour and pine forests.

Think again before buying on one of the smaller islands. Although many are easily accessible during the summer months, during the winter when the tourists have disappeared and the tavernas may be closed, the direct flights may have stopped and the ferry boat may call just once a week if it hasn't been suspended during bad weather.

If you want a sizeable home in good condition with a generous slice of land, £50,000 would easily cover it on Greece's largest island, **Crete**. Many overseas property regions that can boast a warm climate the whole year round tend to be pricey but in terms of variety, beauty and climate, as well as value for money, Crete is hard to beat. You tend to get more for your money in Crete than on the mainland and islands of Spain, France and Italy, and in Portugal. And because it is at the crossroads of Europe, Asia and Africa, it tends to be hotter, too.

Surprisingly large properties ready for renovation are often available for under £20,000. If major building works seem too much of a headache, fully furnished one-bed apartments only metres from the sea with terraces and lovely views typically start at around £35,000. £40,000 could easily get you a two- or three-bedroom refurbished home quite near the sea. At a village like Koutsounari, southeast of the island, you could get a small villa ready to move into under a kilometre from the beach with a terrace and sea views for under £45,000. At the old traditional village of Pano Elounda, spacious homes (five rooms or more) near the sea needing restoration are commonly availalable for under £60,000.

One reason prices are low is because there is a lot of old stock available. Planning laws are strict so there's little new build compared with, say, Spain and Portugal. Crete appeals to people wanting a quiet unspoilt village rather than an apartment complex with a pool.

Crete is the most southerly Greek island and the fifth largest island in the Mediterranean. Winter is generally mild, with snowfall only on the high mountain range that crosses the island from west to east. Being large, it can offer both wilderness and wildness, with deserted beaches as well as vibrant nightlife. There are traditional holiday resorts full of shops and restaurants with water sports, other entertainments and glorious beaches as well as its typical sleepy villages.

The **mainland** may not sound as romantic as the islands but access can be far easier.

The Methana peninsula in the **Saronic Gulf** is an excellent choice for a holiday home abroad as here you will still find the tranquillity, scenery and relaxed way of life of the Greek islands but within easy distance of Athens by car, ferry and hydrofoil. The peninsula, untouched by mass tourism, is dominated by spectacular mountains dotted with little villages. At Vromolimni for example, on the edge of Methana town and a kilometre from the port, beach and marina, old stone houses requiring renovation, with good-sized gardens and lovely views, regularly sell for under £30,000.

The region is typified by whitewashed buildings, narrow alleys and a backdrop of magnificent mountain scenery, fertile plains and rocky coves. A two-bedroom house with a swimming pool located in a former fishing hamlet laden with pine trees, clear sea waters and golden sands recently sold for £110,000.

Only a narrow strip of water separates the dramatic hills of mainland Greece from the tiny island of **Poros** in the Saronic Gulf. A one-bedroom traditional town house on the waterfront in Poros town will cost around £120,000. Here you can watch the yachts sail by between swimming and enrolling in the water-ski school. The town is clustered with traditional whitewashed houses and boasts a good market and some of the best restaurants in the Gulf.

The **Peloponnese** peninsulas south of Athens have plenty of fine old properties to restore. The mountainous Pelion peninsula is rich in forests and skiing is possible in the winter. The Peloponnese provides the best the country can offer: empty beaches, beautiful mountainous scenery, fewer crowds and easy access to Athens. Increasingly, wealthy Athenians, foreign ambassadors and diplomats are buying summer retreats to escape the summer heat at the exclusive resort of Porto Heli on the island of Argolis in the east Peloponnese. Because of this, the town does not become saturated with tourists and for sailors its lovely sandy bay offers calm waters in which to drop anchor. One-bed apartments here start at around £60,000.

Property prices: Two- and three-bedroom homes in seaside locations and old village properties for under £50,000 are still widely available. A remote old stone house in need of renovation may be under £10,000 and inland properties are generally far cheaper than on the coast. A three-bedroom apartment on an island will typically cost from around £80,000, with an extra £12,000 or so for a swimming pool.

Legal restrictions: None.

Finance

Currency and exchange rate: Euro (€); £1 = €1.50.

Local mortgages: Mortgages are generally only available to Greek residents and, therefore, a loan abroad is usually the best option.

The buying process: The system is similar to that in countries such as Spain, Portugal and Malta, with a notary public appointed to ensure that there are no encumbrances.

You will need to open a Greek bank account, which must remain in credit and will require a Greek tax code number from the local tax office to demonstrate that you do not owe any Greek income tax. You may require clearance to buy from the Frontier Territory Committee.

A lawyer experienced in Greek conveyancing is required to establish exactly who owns the property, whether it is one owner or several family members, all of whom have to grant permission to sell. He/she has to ensure that the property is free of debts. If the property is newly built or being bought off-plan (before construction – *see* p.196) the lawyer should ensure that the required planning permission has been obtained. Government permission is sometimes required by foreign persons wishing to buy in some areas. Your lawyer should ideally be fluent both in Greek and English.

A deposit of 10 per cent is usually paid (sometimes as much as 30 per cent) after the agreement to buy has been signed. This agreement is usually made in the presence of a notary public, who will check that formalities are in order and that the property has a clear title. Another requirement is that the origin of funds used to buy the property must be declared to the Bank of Greece using an official importation document.

The agreement should include full details of the purchase price as well as the completion date. The agreed price should be fixed for a minimum of three months as, under Greek law, if the vendor reneges on the agreement or attempts to raise the price, they must return twice the value of the deposit. If the sale collapses because there are problems out of your control such as over title or resulting from the search, the vendor is required to return your deposit. If you, as the buyer, do not go ahead with the purchase, you lose your deposit.

Your lawyer will organise payment of any local taxes and register the property deeds with the registry of mortgages (the land registry) as freehold. After signing the contract you should allow at least three weeks for an ownership certificate to be issued by the land registry.

Costs of buying: The cost of buying is higher than in the UK and can add as much as a fifth to the cost of the transaction.

Fees include a transfer or purchase tax based on 9 to 13 per cent of the officially estimated price of the property. Land registry fees are 0.3 per cent of the assessed value of the property and there are extra small stamp duty fees. The notary's fees are usually around 1 to 2 per cent of the value of the property. The lawyer's fees average about 1.5 per cent of the property's value.

Annual property taxes are also payable at around 0.25 per cent of the declared value of the property, which cover the cost of local services. There are no restrictions on letting.

Is property a good investment? The Greek property market has tended to be on a bit of a rollercoaster of late – in 2002 prices rose by an average of 15 per cent, while in 2003 the figure was just 3.5 per cent – but there are still plenty of properties available that are very keenly priced, in need of realistic renovation and suitable for healthy rentals.

Selling: Capital gains tax should not be an issue, as property gains by individuals are generally not taxable.

Inheritance tax: Inheritance tax is based on the value of the bequest and the relationship of the donor and recipient. Rates vary from 25 to 60 per cent.

Living in Greece

Greece enjoys a low cost of living compared with most EU states, although Athens is exorbitantly expensive. Income tax ranges from 5 to 45 per cent and an annual tax return has to be filled out by property owners even if they are resident and paying tax in the UK. There is an annual property tax of 0.3–0.8 per cent on properties officially valued at €205,000 or more.

Crime is quite low and Greece has reciprocal health agreements with many countries, although the national health service is variable in different regions (almost non-existent on some islands) and under stress, so private health insurance is recommended.

Further information

- **Greece: t** (00 30)
- **Greek Embassy**, 1a Holland Park, London W11 3TP, UK, **t** (020) 7229 3850; **www.greekembassy.org.uk**.
- **Greek Embassy**, 2221 Massachusetts Avenue, NW Washington, DC 20008, USA, **t** (202) 939 5800; **www.greekembassy.org**.
- **Greek Tourist Office**, 4 Regent Street, London W1R 0DJ, UK, **t** (020) 7734 5997.
- **National Greek Tourist Office**, 645 Fifth Avenue, Olympic Tower, New York, NY 10022, USA, **t** (212) 421 5777.

Estate agents

- **Crete Property Consultants** (UK), **t** (020) 7328 1829; **www.fopdac.com**. Well-established British-based agency specialising in period homes often in need of renovation.
- **Halcyon Properties** (UK), **t** (01323) 891639; **www.halcyon-properties.co.uk**. Greek and Cypriot specialist property consultants.
- **Crete Homes** (Greece), **t** 28410 28804; **www.crete-homes.com**. Established agents with a good choice of stone-built properties, villas and apartments.
- **Euroland Crete** (Greece), **t** 28250 32557; **www.euroland-crete.com**.
- **Ktimatoemporiki Real Estate** (Greece), **t** 28210 52981; **www.ktimatoemporiki.gr**.

- **O'Connor Properties** (Greece), **t** 27210 96614; **www.oconnorproperties.gr**.
- **Pelion Properties** (Greece), t 24210 87610; **www.pelionproperties.com**. Specialises in the booming Pelion region north of Athens.

Schools for English-speaking pupils

- **Athens College**, PO Box 5, Psychio, Athens; **www.haef.gr**. Co-educational secondary school.
- **Campion School**, Athens, PO Box 67484, Pallini, 15302, **t** 210 607 1700; **www.campion.edu.gr**. 3–18 years.
- **Pinewood – The International School of Thessaloniki**, PO Box 21001, 555 Pilea, Thessaloniki, **t** 2310 301 221; **www.pinewood.gr**. Co-educational for 3–19 years.

Hungary

Why buy here?

Pros: Until 2002 there was a government ban on overseas ownership, but the relaxation of this rule has opened up a spectacularly low-priced property market for foreign buyers in this hub of central Europe located between Vienna and the Balkans.

Hungary has a fast-growing economy coupled with a long history of pre-Communist-era private ownership. Its capital, Budapest, straddles the River Danube and with its wealth of culture, grand Habsburg-era boulevards and elegant cafés is an increasingly popular city destination.

As with most Eastern European countries, there are potential pitfalls in the buying process and it is vital that your lawyer ensures that the vendor is registered at the land registry as the legal owner.

Cons: The language in this country takes a considerable effort to master.

Hungary's history has left a legacy of inferior infrastructure in places although this is improving all the time.

There is not the choice of low-cost airlines that neighbouring countries enjoy, though this may improve.

Access: There are daily 2½ hour flights from London to Ferihegy Airport, Budapest. Malev Hungarian Airlines and British Airways have flights from under £130 return, while bargain carriers such as easyJet have cheaper deals.

Property

Types: These vary from apartments and villas in new-build developments to larger, older, more run-down rural properties.

Where to buy: Compact, vibrant Budapest is, unsurprisingly, seeing the largest growth in prices. The best areas to buy in are in the inner-city areas that still await full gentrification, such as districts VI, VII and XI, the latter being Hungary's answer to Soho.

Around Lake Balaton, south of the capital, spa towns like Sarvar, Balf, Gyula and Zalakaros are particularly good places to buy.

Property prices: Hungary's having joined the European Union in 2004 is not expected to precipitate a full-scale property boom. Even so, prices in Budapest have been rising rapidly recently. In 2004 on the Pest side a central two-bed apartment may be £140,000 or so, although properties can still be bought for under £50,000. On the hilly Buda side, properties are mainly houses, and a luxury four-bed house with pool would be over £400,000.

Outside Budapest prices are generally spectacularly low. For example, a two-bedroom villa with a 300ft garden was sold in early 2004 to a British buyer in the large town of Nagykanizsa, a big town about 10 miles from the Croatian border, for £10,000, nearby stream included.

Properties on the shores of Lake Balaton range from around £20,000 to £70,000 for a small house, and for the same amount you could get a three- or four-bedroom home in outlying villages.

Local mortgages: At present loan interest rates are very high in Hungary, at between 10 and 14 per cent and for a maximum of 50 per cent of the value of the property, so it is better to raise finance in the UK.

Legal restrictions: You need to set up a local company to buy property here, and this can usually be arranged by the estate agent or property consultant. The company is subject to tax in Hungary but also corporation tax has to be paid in the UK on any company profits, i.e. when you sell, or receive rental income. Currently UK corporation tax is 23.75 per cent on profits of between £10,001 and £50,000. However, tax paid on the property overseas can usually be offset against your British tax bill.

Finance

Currency and exchange rate: Hungarian Forint (HUF); £1 = 365 HUF

The buying process: There are no residence requirements for foreign purchasers. After the offer to buy has been accepted and contract signed, the buyer, if foreign, puts down a 10 to 20 per cent deposit and applies for a buying permit from the local council. If the permit is refused, the deposit is forfeited. Alternatively, foreign buyers are required to form a property company, or they can pay a local agent to carry out the process on their behalf.

Unlike in Britain, the same lawyer will act for both buyer and seller. It is recommended that the property is surveyed, as many Hungarian homes have numerous defects.

Costs of buying: Stamp duty, legal costs and estate agency fees average around 10 per cent of the purchase price.

Is property a good investment? Hungary enjoys low inflation and low unemployment. Joining the European Union in 2004 will almost certainly result in an even more stable economy and currency, although the euro is unlikely to be adopted before 2007.

If you are planning to let out a property, bear in mind that rental income is taxed at 20 per cent. Rental yields in Budapest are currently around 8 per cent, which is better than in the UK. Beware investing in the more exclusive homes as these are the most likely to be over-supply, resulting in lengthy rental voids.

Selling: There is currently no capital gains tax but an increasing likelihood that it will be reintroduced.

Inheritance tax: The rate is progressive and depends on the relationship between donor and recipient.

Further information

- **Hungary: t** (00 36)
- **Hungarian Tourist Board,** 46 Eaton Place, London SW1X 8AL, UK, **t** (020) 7823 1032; **www.hungarywelcomes-britain.com.**
- **East European Property Secrets, www.easteuropeanpropertysecrets.co.uk.**
- **British Consulate** (Hungary), **t** 1 266 2888. Can provide a list of reliable English-speaking lawyers.

Estate agents

- **Hungary Property, t** (UK) (01293) 541667; **www.hungaryproperty.net.**
- **www.casaro-hungary.com** and **www.viviun.com**: Hungarian property for sale.
- **Avatar International, t** (UK) 08707 28 28 27; **www.avatar-international.com.**

Ireland (Eire)

Why buy here?

Pros: The Republic of Ireland boasts a largely unspoilt landscape of rolling hills, windswept moors, lush green farmland and lakes, and is heaven for both the pub-goer and outdoor sports enthusiast. The easy-going lifestyle and low population make for a real contrast to the hectic ways of much of the UK.

Cons: You don't come to Ireland for the weather: its climate is similar to that of Britain, i.e. generally cool and changeable with plenty of rain. Winters are cold and summers warm.

Access: There are scheduled services from the UK operated by British Airways, Aer Lingus and British Midland. Two budget airlines run frequent flights from UK airports to Ireland. Ryanair flies to Derry, Cork, Dublin, Shannon and Knock. EasyJet flies to Belfast – a one-hour drive to the border with the Republic of Ireland. Stena Line's HSS ferry service goes from Holyhead to Dun Laoghaire near Dublin in 99 minutes.

Property

Types: Properties vary from expensive estates and period homes to pretty, rural cottages and farmhouses as well as many less attractive modern bungalows and houses.

Where to buy: Anywhere close to an airport is popular because of the frequency and price of budget flights. West Cork, Dublin and Donegal are the principal areas where Britons buy, according to local estate agents. Actor Jeremy Irons, Carol Vorderman and film producer Lord Puttnam have homes in west Cork. Cork, Kerry and Waterford are enduringly popular, as are the southern and western coasts, which are near an airport.

Galway is a good base: Galway city has a thriving arts scene, nightlife and plenty of restaurants and bars, and a short drive takes you to the stunningly beautiful landscapes of Connemara. Dublin has a similar boast: the nightlife is great but in 15 minutes you can be in some of Ireland's most beautiful countryside. Athlone is another area worth considering. Pockets of Athlone city, midway between Dublin and Connemara, have lively bistros, restaurants and bars.

Property prices: The geography and property types in the Republic of Ireland share many similarities with Scotland, but price is not one of them. While you can pick up neglected cottages in Scotland surprisingly easily for under £50,000, Eire has, in recent years, been experiencing a property boom that has led to hefty price hikes. Property prices overall doubled from a rise of 7.5 per cent in 2002 to 15 per cent in 2003.

In the late 1990s prices in Dublin rose by 165 per cent in five years, but since then things have cooled. In the Killiney Bay area of Dalkey just south of Dublin, prices topped £5 million for the best properties in 2000. A number of stars have homes there, including Bono, Van Morrison, Elvis Costello, Enya, Jack Nicholson, Chris de Burgh and Damon Hill.

Newly built homes are relatively cheap compared with British prices, but period homes are generally substantially more expensive. For example, a six-bedroom Georgian home set in a few acres of land in west Cork would be in the region of £2 million, which is considerably more than a similar house in a desirable southern English coastal area.

Properties built on the seafront and on coastal hills are rising in cost more rapidly as these are often sought-after locations and there are more building restrictions than before.

Dublin is expensive, and one-bedroom apartments typically start at over £100,000. You get much more for your money in rural areas, of course, and, away from the fashionable areas, detached houses are available for under £70,000, with cottages to renovate from half that.

At picturesque Clonmacnoise, Athlone, older-style cottages set in large gardens were still available for under £80,000 in early 2004, but this is certainly a rarity. A five-bed rural property in the popular area of Curramore would be around £250,000.

Legal restrictions: There are no legal restrictions.

Finances

Currency and exchange rate: Euro (€); £1 = €1.50

Local mortgages: Fifteen-year mortgages of up to 90 per cent are widely available from Irish banks. Stamp duty of 0.1 per cent is payable on loans over €25,316.

The buying process: This is similar to the process in England and Wales, with exchange and completion typically taking place two months after both parties have signed the preliminary contract.

Initially the buyer pays a 5 per cent returnable booking deposit to take the property off the market. Then the buyer pays a 10 per cent non-returnable deposit, with the balance paid on completion. Gazumping is rare.

One difference from the British market is that estate agents have lists of property that are for private sale and where the vendor does not want the transaction to become public.

Costs of buying: Costs include stamp duty on second-hand homes on a scale from zero per cent on properties up to €127,001 to 9 per cent on properties over €632,911, legal fees from 1 to 1.5 per cent of the purchase price, survey costs and deed registration. Land registration costs between about £90 and £450. Stamp duty is not payable by first-time buyers or buyers of new homes.

Is property a good investment? Yes: there is still much scope for Ireland's developing property market. Recent buyers of property in Dublin have reported 35 per cent price increases in three years.

Selling: Capital gains tax is 20 per cent, and gains made from the sale of a principal residence are exempt.

Inheritance tax: There is an inheritance tax, known as capital acquisition tax, at 20 per cent.

Living in Ireland

Despite the problems that have occurred in Northern Ireland, the Republic of Ireland is politically very stable and relatively unaffected. The crime rate is comparatively low and medical facilities are good, with a national health scheme for residents paying social security as well as the retired.

The cost of living is relatively high. Pensioners receive a high number of benefits including free healthcare, public transport and telephone rental and various allowances for clothing and fuel.

Householders are charged for refuse collection, which varies from a nominal charge to over £450 per year depending on location.

Non-residents are taxed on income earned in the Republic. Income tax ranges from 20 to 44 per cent, and writers, artists and sports people are exempt from paying tax on some earnings.

Visitors to Ireland can stay for three months without formalities. Residence permits for EU nationals, obtainable from the Department of Justice, are generally easy to obtain.

Further information

- **Republic of Ireland: t** (00 353)
- **Irish Embassy**, 17 Grosvenor Place, London SW1X 7HR, UK, **t** (020) 7235 2171.
- **Irish Embassy**, 2234 Massachusetts Avenue, NW, Washington, DC 20008, USA, **t** 202 462 3939; **www.irelandemb.org**.
- **Department of Justice**, 72–76 St Stephen's Green, Dublin 2, Ireland, **t** 1 602 8202.
- **Irish Auctioneers' and Valuers' Institute**, 138 Merrion Square, Dublin 2, Ireland, **t** 1 661 1794; **www.ipav.ie**.
- **Irish Tourist Board**, 150 New Bond Street, London W1Y 0AQ, UK, **t** (020) 7493 3201; **www.tourismireland.com**. The tourist board has various free publications.

Estate agents

All are based in Ireland.

General

- **www.ascotfirst.com**. Over 6,000 properties can be viewed.
- **Michael H. Daniels and Co.**, **t** 253 9145; **www.michaelhdaniels.com**. Nationwide listings.

Galway

- **Spencer, O'Toole**, **t** 91 552999; **www.spentool.com**.
- **Colleran Auctioneers**, **t** 91 562293.

Wexford

- **Re/Max Southeast**, **t** 53 21977.

Waterford

- **Jack Flanagan**, **t** 58 41496; **www.flanaganauctioneers.com**.

Wicklow

- **Dooley Poynton**, **t** 404 62292; **www.wicklowproperty.com**.

Athlone

- **Re/Max**, **t** 90 649 3135; **www.remax.ie**.

Cork

- **Celtic Properties**, **t** 275 2290; **www.celticproperties.com**.
- **Charles McCarthy Estate Agents**, **t** 282 1533; **www.charlesmccarthy.com**.
- **Ganly Walters**, **t** 1662 3255; **www.ganlywalters.ie**.
- **Hamilton Osborne King**, **t** 2142 71371; **www.hok.ie**.
- **Henry O'Leary Auctioneers**, **t** 233 5959; **www.hol.ie**.
- **Jackson Stops**, **t** 1633 3777; **www.jacksonstops.ie**.
- **Leonard Estates**, **t** 91 565853.
- **Sheehy Brothers**, **t** 214 772 338; **www.sheehybrothers.com**.

Italy

Why buy here?

Pros: Romantic Italy, with its rich heritage, attracts arty, literary types, and lovers of beautiful countryside and wonderful food and wine. It has some stunning cities, lively towns and very pretty villages as well as a varied coastline.

Cons: Like France, the weather can be uncertain and winters freezing in many areas. Some parts of the country are prone to earthquakes and flooding. More expensive and harder to reach than Spain and France, it suffers from over-complex bureaucracy and higher levels of inefficiency in day-to-day life.

Access: The expansion of Perugia airport and Ryanair's cheap service to Ancona have opened up the unspoilt, beautiful, mountainous Marches on the Adriatic coast, where property prices are significantly lower than in Tuscany and Umbria. Charter flights to nearby Rimini also run in summer. Italian cities are also well served by the bargain air carriers, including Rome, Pisa, Genoa, Turin, Naples, Venice, Brescia, Treviso, Bologna and Milan. Parma airport will also become a budget destination in 2005.

Access to the Lake Como area is easy and there are two airports in Milan as well as ones at Linate and Malpensa. Many cheap flights are available.

Property

Types: Unlike Spain, where comfortable new villas are the norm, in Italy the second-homers tend to search out characterful older properties. New-build developments are a rarity. Much of the coastline has been marred by overdevelopment, although some areas, such as Tuscany, have been somewhat protected by controls on new development and strict guidelines concerning restoration of existing properties. Inland, however, many towns and villages remain unspoilt and the best buys are old village and country properties in need of restoration. All properties in Italy are freehold.

Where to buy: Most foreign buyers opt for areas north of Rome such as Tuscany, Umbria, Lombardy, Veneto, Liguria and Le Marche. The Italian Lakes and Riviera and northern Adriatic coast are other especially popular regions.

The less-prosperous south of the country has yet to be discovered by British buyers and, although the property market infrastructure is less developed here, adventurous purchasers are likely to be well rewarded with comparative property bargains.

Tuscany remains the top choice for many in Italy, being close to beautiful countryside, mountains and sea and within a manageable distance from Pisa and Florence airports. On most people's wish list is the typical Tuscan farmhouse with plenty of land, known as a *colonica*. They don't come cheap and a typical small rural house here will cost around £250,000. Celebrities who have bought here include Sting, Bryan Ferry and Paul Smith. John Mortimer rents here every summer. Tuscany is not the place to look if you want value for money, but the north is cheaper than the south.

Many aspirants to Tuscany, but without wallets to match, have instead focused on the charming region of **Umbria**, to such an extent that having a good choice that is value for money is something of a rarity now.

What everyone tends to want, the bargain traditional farmhouse in need of restoration in an acre of land, has practically dried up now in Tuscany and Umbria. It is better to look at the significantly quieter, much cheaper area of **Le Marche**, east of Umbria, as there are many more houses available there. You could buy a four-bed house with an acre of land to do up here for £80,000 – and the improving road network and expansion of Perugia airport makes it less daunting to reach.

Bound by the Apennine mountains on one side and the Adriatic sea on the other, the property market of Le Marche is more like that of Tuscany a couple of decades ago, with plenty of properties still available to restore and, therefore, relatively low prices. Particularly unspoilt, it boasts an admirable coastline. It is culture-rich, too, with ancient historical cities like Urbino, the Florence of the Marches region, and attractive towns like Ascoli Piceno. Buyers are especially looking at properties within easy reach of the Sibillini mountains (for winter skiing), which are also convenient for the coast. What the region does not have, which Tuscany does, is easy access to Rome, Lucca, Siena and Florence. But this can be a blessing in disguise as the area is likely to stay unspoilt for longer.

Many foreign buyers priced out of Tuscany look to the pretty region of **Liguria**, the Italian Riviera, on the Mediterranean. Liguria is rich in property bargains and far less commercialised than, say, France's Côte d'Azur.

Property on the coast itself tends to be expensive, although better value than its French counterpart. There are some gorgeous towns, such as San Remo and Portofino (which some people find almost too pretty and geared to the tourist).

Inland it has lots of olive groves and hills going back from the sea and it is an easy driving distance from Monaco and Milan. Its main city is Genoa. Villas requiring full renovation are currently under £50,000; those needing no more than redecoration and updating are selling for around £100,000, while recently renovated ones are fetching more than £200,000.

The northern parts of Italy around the **Lombardy lakes** are another good source of comparatively inexpensive Italian property. A two-bedroom house is easily obtainable for under £75,000 in villages near the lakes. Inexpensive flights are available to the area. The area has the added advantage of beautiful summer weather and mild winters, and is close to the ski slopes for lovers of winter sports.

The northeastern region of the **Veneto** and around the beautiful **Dolomite** mountains, which form the southeastern part of the Alps, around Trentino and Lake Garda in northern Italy, offers both winter skiing and summer sun-lounging. Well away from the package holiday hotspots, this region boasts fashionable ski resorts such as Madonna di Campiglio (favoured by celebs like Michael Schumacher), numerous gorgeous lakes, and its residents enjoy the longest average lifespans in Europe. Prices are comparatively low, but have been rising quite rapidly of late.

At the top end of the market, a lakeside villa will set you back over £1 million, but terraced houses with a view of Lake Garda can be bought for a third of that. Apartments in complexes with a communal swimming pool in a lakeside town like Riva del Garda start at around £100,000.

The region boasts numerous culture-rich towns and cities including Trento, with a very attractive piazza, fabulous Venice and historic, stylish, yet laid-back, Verona. Access is easy, with good air, road and rail connections, including Ryanair flights to Brescia and Treviso, and easyJet, British Airways and Alitalia routings to Venice and Verona.

Prices generally plunge even further in southern Italy. **Calabria**, for example, is becoming increasingly popular with holidaymakers yet few British buyers consider buying in this gloriously unspoilt corner. For this reason the infrastructure for buying a property is less developed here for overseas purchasers. Bear in mind that access is not as good as in more northern regions, although the wonderful homes on offer – with price tags to match – can amply compensate for this. You could also look at **Puglia**.

Despite almost 40 years of the world's glitterati jetting and cruising into the Costa Smeralda in **Sardinia**, this beautiful Italian island has not kept pace with the Côte d'Azur, the Algarve and the Costa del Sol in terms of exposure and numbers of visitors. Sardinia is rather exclusive and beautiful with wonderful beaches, and the coastline hasn't been spoilt. Many people would rather buy in Sardinia in preference to the over-developed areas of the Mediterranean mentioned above, if only they knew about it. The Costa Smeralda boasts excellent golf courses and for sailors there are many beautiful islands to visit and beaches to discover, accessible only from the sea and away from other people. But it doesn't come cheap. A three-bedroom villa with a swimming pool overlooking the sea at Costa Smerelda typically costs in excess of £500,000.

Leave Sardinia and the price of island property plunges. The small island of Isola Piana off Sardinia, for example, has properties for under £50,000. Isola Piana is ideal for anyone wanting to get away from it all. It has a doctor's surgery, church, restaurant, bar, pizzeria, two tennis courts, two swimming pools and a small marina. For main shopping you'd need to take a boat across to Sardinia.

Beach-house hunters should also consider **Sicily** – its architectural wealth gives it added value, and prices are still very low. Many foreigners own homes near Taormina and Syracuse.

Property prices: In most parts of London £100,000 does not buy even a tiny studio flat, but focus on Italy and you can take your pick from a fabulous range of villas, rustic farmhouses, village houses and beachside apartments.

Prices may have shot through the roof in many parts of Umbria and Tuscany (although around Lucca you can still obtain picturesque small village houses requiring restoration from about £60,000), but look eastwards to Le Marche (or the Marches) and property is much better value.

It is still possible to buy a four-bed house with an acre of land to renovate in Le Marche for under £80,000. Properties recently available in Le Marche include a £70,000 watermill with 11 rooms to restore plus large old outbuildings with exposed beams, and for £90,000 a two-bedroom habitable farmhouse near the sea. Four-bedroom farmhouses for restoration with an acre of land in Le Marche are sometimes available for as little as £60,000, a fraction of the typical £250,000 or so you would pay in Tuscany. Inland, in the Macerata area, ruins start at around £15,000 with habitable homes from under £50,000.

Small rustic houses in the Veneto and Dolomites region are available from about £40,000. Prices plunge in southern Italy generally. For example, you could pick up an apartments here for under £15,000.

Sardinia is not cheap. For around £250,000 you would get something like a three-bedroom semi-detached house away from the sea in the typical Sardinian style in the exclusive Porto Cervo district of the Costa Smerelda. Sicily is cheaper.

If you are looking for city apartments, there are few bargains in the north. A restored apartment in the centre of Milan costs up to £4,000 per square metre, making it the nation's most expensive real estate – you could easily pay £80,000 for a studio apartment well outside the centre; in the centre it could cost more like £170,000. Canalside apartments in Venice will fetch between £2,000 and £4,000 per square metre. Rome is about a third cheaper, though location within the city is everything – a three-bedroom flat near the Trevi fountain could easily cost £600,000.

Legal restrictions: Planning restrictions on old properties can be very strict, so check the extent of these thoroughly before committing to buy.

Finance

Currency and exchange rate: Euro (€); £1 = €1.50

Local mortgages: Loans are generally repayment mortgages in euros of between 5 and 25 years and up to 80 per cent of the purchase price. Loans must be paid off by the applicant's 70th birthday. Proof of income and outgoings are required and assumed rental income is not taken into account. Funds imported to buy property in Italy should be officially registered by your Italian bank.

The buying process: When you have found a suitable property, the first thing to do is employ a surveyor (*geometra*) to survey the property. For added protection it is advisable only to use estate agents registered with their local chamber of commerce.

A notary (*notaio*), an independent public official, presides over the sale of property in Italy. Although they are independent, buyers should instruct their own independent, English-speaking lawyer (*avvocato*) who is familiar with the Italian conveyancing process. He/she will carry out searches to ensure that the property is unencumbered, i.e. that there are no outstanding financial liabilities, which in Italy would become the new buyer's responsibility. In rural areas it is common for a property to be owned by several family members and all must agree to the sale.

The vendor may then require a 'buying proposal', legally committing the purchaser to buy but leaving the vendor free to consider other offers.

When both parties have agreed on the purchase price, a preliminary contract, legally binding for both parties, is drawn up by either the estate agent, vendor or a lawyer and signed by both parties. This contract, known as a *compromesso di vendita, contratto preliminare di vendita* or *promessa di vendita*, usually discourages gazumping and sets down the terms and conditions of the sale including the price, completion date, financial details, a description of the property, a guarantee from the vendor and possibly other clauses.

Before signing, the surveyor should have assured the buyer that the property is sound and conforms with local planning laws and building regulations.

The sale must be completed within the time limit stated, which is typically anything from a couple of weeks to more than four months and averages around two months.

A deposit (*deposito di garanzia or caparra penitenziale*) of between 10 and 30 per cent of the purchase price is in most cases paid to the notary by the buyer. The buyer loses this if he doesn't go through with the purchase, while the vendor loses twice the deposit if he drops out. The buyer's lawyer should ensure that the deposit is not described as a *caparra confirmatoria* as this gives the seller the right to take legal action against the buyer should he pull out.

A declaration of value of the property is required to ascertain the rate of registration tax to pay (*imposta di registro*), which is set at 4 per cent for new properties, 11 per cent for other residential properties and 17 per cent for agricultural land. Your lawyer should be involved in checking the value set. Properties are often undervalued to avoid capital gains tax.

Buyers are also required to obtain an Italian tax code number (*codice fiscale*) before completion.

When the final contract, the *rogito*, is ready, completion is made before the notary. The deed or conveyance of transfer (*scritta privata* or *atto di compravendita*) is signed by both parties or their legal representatives. The notary registers the deed of sale with the land registry (*registro immobiliare*) and issues a certified copy to the buyer. At the time of completion, the balance owing as well as any relevant fees and taxes are paid to the notary.

About two weeks later the buyer should obtain a copy of the deeds from the notary's office and a form to give to the local police to notify them of the purchase.

Costs of buying: Property taxes depend on the assessed value, which is open to negotiation. These consist of a purchase/registration tax of 3 to 4 per cent for Italian residents and 10 per cent for buyers of second homes. Notary fees (fixed, according to purchase price) are about 3 per cent of the purchase price. There is a stamp duty of between 4 and 17 per cent. In addition there are valuation, survey, document and search fees. Usually both vendor and purchaser share the agent's fee, which can vary widely.

Is property a good investment? Despite high prices in many regions, property is on the whole a very good investment, especially in the major cities and resort areas. Overall, Italian property prices have been rising steadily, if not dramatically, in recent years and there's no reason why this should not continue. Properties near the mountains and lakes, such as the Dolomites, have year-round appeal, from skiing in winter to sun in the summer, a boon for those considering letting. There are no restrictions on holiday letting.

Selling: There is no capital gains tax payable on properties.

Inheritance tax: Inheritance tax varies between 3 and 33 per cent but has been abolished on legacies to family members.

Living in Italy

Italy enjoys a temperate climate characterised by hot summers and cold winters, although the climate is milder on the Italian Riviera and the islands.

The cost of living is about a third lower than that of the UK, except in cities, where there is little difference. Italy has a quite good health service, although it is overstretched, as in many European countries. Politically, it is relatively unstable compared with much of Europe and the crime rate varies considerably, but overall is not exceptional for Europe.

All income from letting has to be declared to both the Italian and UK authorities. If you are a non-resident, the Italian authorities are only concerned with income that has originated in Italy. Connected expenses such as repairs, local taxes and management expenses can be offset against tax. In Italy you are taxed on this income at from 19 to 46 per cent depending on the net income you receive. If you are also declaring your income to the UK authorities, any taxes you have paid in Italy are deducted from your UK tax liability.

There is also an annual community tax payable on the notional value of your property, whether rented out or not.

Visitors may stay for 90 days, while residence permits are valid for a year and renewable annually. Non-EU nationals require a work permit, which can be difficult to obtain.

Further information

- **Italy: t** (00 39)
- **Italian State Tourist Board**, 1 Princes Street, London W1B 2AY, UK, **t** (020) 7408 1254; **www.enit.it.**
- **Italian Tourist Board**, Suite 1565, 630 Fifth Avenue, New York, NY 10111, USA, **t** (212) 245 4822.
- **Italian Embassy**, 14 Three Kings Yard, Davies Street, London W1Y 2EH, UK; **t** (020) 7312 2200; **www.embitaly.org.uk.**
- **Italian Embassy**, 1601 Fuller Street, NW, Washington, DC 20009, USA, **t** (202) 328 5500.
- **Italian Consulate General**, 38 Eaton Place, London SW1X 8AN, UK, **t** (020) 7235 9371.
- **Visa information service** (UK), **t** 0900 160 0340.
- **Tourism information service** (UK), **t** 0900 160 0280.

Estate agents

- **Brian A. French and Associates** (UK), **t** 0870 730 1910, **www.brianfrench.com.**
- **Casa Travella** (UK), **t** (01322) 660988; **www.casatravella.com.**
- **Knight Frank International** (UK), **t** (020) 7629 8171; **www.knightfrank.co.uk.**
- **Piedmont Properties** (UK), **t** (01344) 624096.
- **Green Umbria** (Italy), **t** 0759 426500; **www.greenumbria.com.**
- **Tuscan Enterprises** (Italy), **t** 057 7740 623; **www.tuscanenterprise.it.**
- **www.marchepropertysales.com**

Schools for English-speaking pupils

- **American International School in Genoa**, Via Quarto 13/c, 16148, Genoa; **t** 010 386528. Co-educational, age 3–18.
- **International School of Como**, via per Cernobbio 19, 22100, Como, **t** 031 57 6186; **www.iscomo.com.** Small school, co-educational, 3–10 years.
- **International School of Milan**, 6 via Bezzola, Milano, **t** 02 409 10067.
- **International School of Naples**, Mostra d'Oltremore, 80125 Napoli, **t** 08 1721 2037. Co-educational, 5–17 years.
- **St George's English School**, Via Cassia-La Storta, 00123 Roma, **t** 06 308 6001; **www.stgeorge.school.it.** Co-educational, 3–18 years.

Lithuania

Why buy here?

Pros: Like Estonia, Lithuania is a lovely, if at times chilly, little Baltic state that joined the EU in May 2004. It is one of the least costly and least spoilt countries in Europe. It, too, boasts superb empty beaches, some splendid architecture and huge tracts of unspoilt countryside.

Property prices are very low due to low owner-occupation and years of a slow, problematic economy and a very troubled history, including years of Russian occupation. Yet EU membership will change this rapidly, with large-scale EU investment improving infrastructure and mortgage finance becoming increasingly available to locals, which will cause prices to shoot up. Early investors will be able to rent or sell at a good profit.

Cons: As with the other Baltic states, Lithuania and Latvia, investment here is more of a risk than in more familiar eastern European countries like Poland, Hungary and Croatia. Also, from October to March Lithuania tends to be very cold and dark. The language is another barrier for most people.

Access: There are regular direct flights to Vilnius, the capital, from the UK.

Property

Types: Despite the country's small size, there is a wide variety of property types, from city apartment blocks to tall merchants' houses, rickety, rambling, rural manor houses, wooden homes in the forests and chalets by the sea.

Where to buy: The capital, Vilnius, is very attractive and boasts a stately centre with plenty of vibrant cafés, restaurants and elegant buildings. The second city, Kaunas, is equally pleasant, with a vibrant main drag full of trendy bars and cafés charging 1970s prices.

Property prices: Since the end of Communism, most council houses have been sold off and now 85 per cent of property is privately owned. Foreign property speculators have been pushing up prices in recent years but in the capital you can still buy a two-bedroom flat for under £15,000, although it is likely to be in a rather grim 1970s Soviet apartment block. A two-bedroom house in Vilnius would start at around £20,000, with prices plummeting away from the capital.

Legal restrictions: None.

Finance

Currency and exchange rate: Lita (LTL); £1 = LTL 5.26

Local mortgages: The local mortgage market is way behind that of western Europe, so using lenders in your home country is recommended.

Is property a good investment? All indications are that it is. The *Economist* noted in July 2003 that Lithuania enjoyed the highest growth rate (6.7 per cent) in Europe the year before with booming exports, zero inflation, a rock-steady currency, shrinking unemployment and a budget surplus. Couple this with joining the EU and early investors in property in the country are likely to cash in.

Selling: There is no capital gains tax.

Inheritance tax: This is dependent upon the size of the estate and relationship of the deceased and the beneficiary.

Living in Lithuania

This small country, with a population of 3.6 million, has had an economy lagging way behind most European countries owing to its history as a Soviet republic.

The average earnings in 2004 were £2,712 and unemployment is officially 10 per cent but unofficially as high as 25 per cent. The cost of living is correspondingly low, with a beer around £1 a pint and an opera ticket under £10.

EU nationals working in Lithuania are entitled to Lithuanian benefits such as invalidity health care, unemployment benefit and a pension, although these are low: unemployment benefit ranges from £30 to £60 per month, for example. There are no housing benefits to speak of.

Further information

- **Lithuania: t (00 370)**
- **East European Property Secrets, www.easteuropeanpropertysecrets.co.uk.**

Estate agents

- **Bristol and Stone, www.bristolandstone.com.**
- **Ober Haus** (Lithuania), **t 5210 9700; www.ober-haus.ee.**

Malta

Why buy here?

Pros: Just a 3-hour flight from London, the central Mediterranean island of Malta (95 square miles) and its smaller sister islands Gozo (26 square miles) and Comino (1 square mile) have it all. Sandwiched between North Africa and Sicily, which is just 90km/60 miles away, this haven – half the size of the Isle of Wight – boasts long hot summers (25–34°C/77–92°F), mild winters (10–20°C/50–70°F) with an average five or six hours of sunshine daily, warm and friendly people, political stability, a low cost of living and very little crime.

Everywhere on the island is less than a 20-minute drive away, which is particularly attractive to Britons used to long journeys and heavy traffic. About 15,000 Britons own properties here.

Cons: With no natural resources to speak of, Malta's main industry is tourism. Even so, the beaches, dotted with limestone coves, can't really compare with those in Spain, though the sea is very clean, warm and clear and therefore excellent for diving, yachting and water sports.

It has no rivers or lakes and few green spaces but its culture is an enticing mix of Moorish, Spanish, British, Islamic and French. Because it was a British colony for 150 years (Malta gained its independendce in 1969) almost everyone speaks English, although there is also an official Maltese language that retains traces of Arabic.

Access: Air Malta, British Airways and other major international airlines operate regular scheduled flights between Malta and most major European cities. There are several flights daily from London alone. Cheap charter flights start at about £60 return.

Property

Types: For such a small island, a wide range of properties are available, from new apartments in holiday complexes to waterside villas and old sprawling farmhouses. Unfortunately, many apartment buildings are not particularly attractively designed.

Where to buy: While properties with a sea view or near the coast are expensive, the cheapest apartments are generally in touristic areas. You would have to go to the northern part of Malta, to Qawra, Buġibba, also Mellieħa, and St Paul's Bay, and on the southern part, Marsaskala, to get properties for the minimum amount. The property market has been boosted of late by a succession of bold development projects, including the huge Portomaso marina development in the parish of St Julian's. Prices at such developments are not cheap, but nevertheless tend to sell quickly.

Gozo, a 25-minute ferry ride from Malta, is high in demand from foreigners, as it is relatively untouched, as well as being smaller, quieter and greener than Malta, which is more commercial, although there are still some quiet, undeveloped villages.

There is a far smaller choice of properties at even smaller **Comino**. Two further tiny islands, Cominotto and Filfla, are uninhabited.

Property prices: At the time of going to press about £50,000 buys a one-bedroom apartment in a holiday complex with a communal pool, while two-bedroom, pretty, period town houses start at around £100,000. Houses and villas can easily exceed £700,000. A converted four-bedroom farmhouse with a sizeable garden and pool may set you back over £1.5m. Prices in Gozo are generally lower.

Malta joined the EU in May 2004, and this will almost certainly cause an increase in demand for property. Stamp duty was recently slashed from 17 per cent to 5 per cent. Maltese prices are flexible, so it's best to bargain hard for a good deal.

Legal restrictions: It is relatively easy for foreign nationals to buy in Malta. Even so, there are some restrictions. The Maltese government has set minimum values that foreign buyers can spend on a property. The requirement that overseas buyers obtain permission to buy from the Finance Ministry was waived after EU membership in May 2004 but foreign buyers must still spend a minimum of Lm30,000 (£47,500) on a flat or maisonette (including renovation costs) and Lm50,000 for a house or villa. Properties in need of renovation or in shell form can be purchased for lower amounts as long as the addition of the estimated cost of completion works plus the purchase price reach the Lm30,000/Lm50,000 thresholds. There are plenty of homes available at these prices, and properties in Malta tend to be very spacious when compared with other Mediterranean destinations.

Non-Maltese can only let a property if it is in a designated area like Cottonere or Tigne Point, or otherwise if it is a bungalow, villa or farmhouse with a swimming pool.

Finance

Currency and exchange rate: Maltese liri (Lm); £1 = Lm0.60.

Local mortgages: These are available but terms tend to be lower (usually 10–20 years), rates are generally higher and the loan to value percentage is lower than with foreign lenders.

The buying process: On acceptance of the buyer's offer, both vendor and purchaser sign a binding agreement known as a *convenium*, and the purchaser pays a non-refundable 10 per cent deposit, lodged with the agent or notary public. The agreement is usually valid for around three months.

The notary public makes the various legal checks and, once these are satisfactory, a deed of sale is drawn up and the balance for the property is paid to the vendor.

A property bought by a foreign national should, in theory, be sold only to a Maltese, although this law is usually relaxed. Non-Maltese buyers can normally only own one property in Malta, although there are exceptions in special designated areas.

Costs of buying: Fees incurred on buying include registration and search fees (£160 approximately), Ministry of Finance fees (£160 approximately), 1 per cent notary fees and a 5 per cent duty on documents. All property is sold freehold.

Is property a good investment? Property has proved to be a good investment, and there has been a steady 8 to 12 per cent increase in values each year since 1969. But in 2002 and 2003 average property values increased by around 20 per cent. Annual increases of half that are predicted over the next couple of years. Increased interest from Britons looking for an alternative to southern Spain and the anticipation of Malta joining the EU in 2004 have contributed to this rise.

Selling: When you come to resell there's always a strong a local market. The population is only around 375,000 but there are over 12,000 property transactions per year, which is very healthy.

Capital gains tax of 7 per cent is charged on the sale of property that has not been the owner's main place of residence for the previous three years.

Inheritance tax: Malta abolished inheritance tax in 1992 but there is a 5% transfer tax on property inherited in Malta. Note that if the recipient is a spouse, the transfer tax is levied on half of the value of the property.

Living in Malta

The cost of living is low and health and education standards are particularly high. There are reciprocal health agreements with the UK. There are no annual rates or property taxes. The roads do need updating and there are occasional water shortages.

Taxation for residents is low (currently starting at 15 per cent) and there are tax agreements with most Western European countries, Canada and Australia, which enable Maltese residents either to obtain exemptions from tax on certain income originating abroad, or to obtain tax relief in Malta.

Further information

- **Malta: t** (00 356)
- **Malta Tourist Office**, 36–38 Piccadilly, London W1V 0PP, UK, **t** (020) 7292 4900; **www.visitmalta.com**.
- **Maltese Consulate**, 2017 Connecticut Avenue, NW, Washington, DC 20008, USA, **t** (202) 462 3611.
- **Maltese High Commission**, 36–38 Piccadilly, London W1V 0PP, UK, **t** (020) 7292 4800.

- **Ministry of Finance**, St Calcedonius Square, Floriana CMR 02, Malta, **t** 21 236306.

- **Bank of Valletta**, BOV Centre, High Street, Sliema SLM 16, Malta, **t** 21 333084. Malta's leading bank.

- **HSBC Bank Malta**, Hexagon House, Spencer Gardens, Blata l-Bajda, HMR 12, Malta; **www.hsbcmalta.com**.

- **Air Malta**, 36–38 Piccadilly, London W1V 0PQ, UK, **t** (020) 7292 4949.

- **Association of Estate Agents in Malta**, PO Box 18, Sliema, Malta, **t** 21 343370; **www.maltaestateagents.com**.

Estate agents

All are based in Malta.

- **Dhalia Group** (Malta), **t** 21 490681; **www.dhalia.com**. Malta's largest estate agency.

- Formosa Real Estate Agency (Malta), **t** 21 323926; **www.mol.net.mt/formosa**.

- **Frank Salt Real Estate** (Malta), **t** 21 353696; **www.franksalt.com.mt**. Perhaps Malta's most established estate agent, with eight branches and guides to buying on the islands.

- **www.maltarealestateindex.com**: the website of the Malta and Gozo Real Estate Index, which features a list of property for sale and to let direct from owners.

- **Sara Grech** (Malta), **t** 21 331354; **www.saragrech.com.mt**. Specialises in classic rural houses throughout the island.

Mexico

Why buy here?

Pros: Winter on Mexico's Pacific coast is like the Mediterranean in the height of summer and, most attractively for a UK resident, offers year-round sunshine including guaranteed winter sun.

Cons: Apart from the distance, coastal Mexico can be very, very hot and humid during the summer. Mexico City suffers from major pollution problems.

Access: British Airways flies to Mexico City and Air 2000 runs a charter service to Puerto Vallarta. Domestic carriers Mexicana and Aeromexico connect all major cities in the country itself.

Property

Types: New developments of apartments and villas along the coast, as well as rural inland period properties in need of renovation, going for a song.

Where to buy: Among the rainforest-covered mountains of the west coast is Puerto Vallarta, a resort busily being developed and attracting the interest of European buyers especially. There are several good golf courses here.

Property prices: Prices are gradually rising but they are still cheaper than in Europe and the USA. The cheapest properties are in the undeveloped inland towns and villages.

At Puerto Vallarta, a one-bed waterside apartment with a shared pool costs about £50,000 while a three-bedroom house with a pool is around £90,000. The gated Punta Mita resort here has villas costing £1 million-plus.

Legal restrictions: Foreigners buying property in the restricted zone, which is generally coastal and border areas, are required to apply for a permit from the Department of Foreign Relations. This permits them to own property via a trust that gives them full ownership rights. The trust is administered and held by a bank.

Finance

Currency and exchange rate: Mexican pesos; £1 = 20.85 Mexican pesos

Local mortgages: The local lending market is limited and, therefore, obtaining a loan in your home country is likely to be preferable.

The buying process: Most estate agents can sell each others' properties if they are members of the AMPI (the Mexican Board of Estate Agents).

A notary oversees the buying process, executing searches, preparing the deed, carrying out the property transfer and recording the deed with the public property registry.

Costs of buying: This generally works out at around 5 to 7 per cent of the purchase price. Administration of the trust for the property, as required if the buyer is a foreigner, costs about £300 annually.

Is property a good investment? Coastal properties especially have been appreciating well in recent years – by as much as 35 per cent in two years in some areas. Rental returns can be extremely good for the right property, attracting North American and Canadian retirees.

Selling: Capital gains tax is charged at 33 per cent of the rise in value of the property. Foreigners may be exempt from paying CGT in certain cases.

Inheritance tax: This varies depending on the worth of the estate.

Living in Mexico

Mexico generally has a very pleasant climate with warm seas and temperatures in excess of 80°F/26.6°C common even in the height of winter. Britons require an FM3 immigration document to live full time in Mexico. Property taxes of about 0.004 per cent of the value of the property are payable annually.

Further information

- **Mexico: t** (00 52)

Estate agents

- **Century 21** (Mexico), t 322 222 3054; **www.century21vallarta.com**.
- **Coldwell Banker La Costa** (Mexico), t 322 223 0055; **www.cblacosta.com**.
- **La Punta Realty** (Mexico), t 329 291 6420; **www.puntarealty.com**.

Montenegro

Why buy here?

Pros: Although it was once the playground of superstars such as Richard Burton, Elizabeth Taylor, Princess Margaret and Sophia Loren, properties are very affordable in this small country on the Adriatic coast of the Balkan peninsula. It is situated on the southern border of Croatia and neighboured by Bosnia, Serbia and Albania. Formerly part of Yugoslavia, it offers a wealth of stunning scenery, history and culture. Add the unspoilt beauty and increasing speculation that Montenegro may join the EU (a referendum is planned for 2006), and interest is mushrooming. The adventurous will enjoy diving, white-water rafting, climbing and paragliding as well as skiing in winter.

Cons: Montenegro has, in the past, worked towards acting as one country with Serbia. Montenegro is now split into those who want it to separate from Serbia, and those who wish it to remain as part of it. If it moves towards independent status from Serbia, there is no guarantee that if, or when, it happens, it will be straightforward or peaceful.

Also, land registry is not as stringent as in the UK and there is a possibility of issues with title.

Access: British Airways and other airlines have regular flights to Dubrovnik in Croatia, 16km over the border. Montenegro has two airports, Tivat and Podgorica, but currently direct flights from the UK are limited although they are available during the summer.

Various coach companies offer services from neighbouring countries to Montenegro and these offer a very cheap option; trains operate between Bar and Belgrade.

Property

Types: Beautiful old stone houses overlooking freshwater lakes or the dramatic Adriatic coastline, as well as farmsteads in the rolling green hills, are still widely available at comparatively low prices. There is also a good choice of properties suitable for businesses such as restaurants, bars and hotels.

Where to buy: Around the northern coast, prices are higher and the area more popular than the wilder, more unspoilt south.

Property prices: Prices are generally a third cheaper than in Croatia, and pretty properties abound, especially away from the coast. They are bound to rise steadily in the next few years.

Houses start at under £20,000, and a very sizeable house could be obtained for under £60,000. Recent examples (2004) include a five-bed renovated stone house with glorious sea views near Sveti Stefan for £125,000 and a ten-room hotel with restaurant near Tivat for £400,000. Properties on the coast area are available, unlike in many countries.

Legal restrictions: While there is no problem for EU citizens to buy and own a property in Montenegro, land is rather more complicated. While it is possible for foreigners to buy land, it is owned on a leasehold basis of 99 years, as opposed to property which is freehold. Also, it is not possible for foreigners to register land in their own name, which could have a number of implications. This is still a rather unclear point currently, with quite a number of differing opinions, so on the whole at present it is best to steer clear of buying land.

Finance

Currency and exchange rate: Euro (€); £1 = €1.50. The republic of Montenegro severed its economy from Serbia during the Milosevic era and continues to maintain its own central bank, uses the euro instead of the Yugoslav dinar as official currency, collects customs tariffs, and manages its own budget.

Local mortgages: The local lending market is restricted and buyers would be better off raising funds in their home country.

The buying process: This is straightforward and visas, taxes, residency and general bureaucracy issues have been simplified as much as possible by the Montenegran government, eager to encourage foreign investment. But because the land registry system is less stringent than in many countries, it is important to engage a good solicitor listed at the bar to safeguard your interests as much as possible.

The system is rather similar to the notary system in France, where the lawyer initially draws up a legally binding contract for the buyer and seller to sign. A 10 per cent deposit is usually lodged, and is non-returnable should the buyer back out.

Costs of buying: This is around 10 per cent of the purchase price.

Is property a good investment? Property is very keenly priced at present, and possible accession to the European Union and an increasingly likely split from neighbouring Serbia will undoubtedly cause prices rapidly to move upwards. Tourism is likely to increase greatly soon, which would make investment even more sound.

Selling: Capital gains tax is payable at a varying rate.

Inheritance tax: This is dependent on the size of the estate and the relationship of the deceased and the beneficiary.

Living in Montenegro

Although the Balkan conflict of the early 1990s affected Montenegro's economy a great deal, other aspects were largely unaffected by the war.

The coast enjoys a Mediterranean climate, with summer temperatures in the 30s, while winters are mild. There are around 240 days of sunshine and 180 days when water temperatures reach between 21–27°C per year on average.

Skiing, hunting and fishing are all popular pastimes. The cost of living is comparatively low.

Part of Montenegro's charm is its undeveloped nature compared with many of its European neighbours. For example, credit cards are currently generally only accepted in major hotels, shops, restaurants and travel agents.

Access within the country can be difficult. Main roads are acceptable, but smaller ones can be rough and there are many twisting mountain routes. Taxis are often expensive and local buses tend not to be reliable. For quick, easy access from the airport at Tivat to the north of the country, a car ferry service operates from Kamenari to Lepetane across the Strait of Verige.

An unlimited amount of currency can be brought into the country, but there are limits on how many euros may be taken out.

Medical care is generally of a high standard, although foreigners do not have access to the domestic national health system and private health insurance should be taken out.

Further information

- **Montenegro: t** (00 381)
- **Montenegro Living, t** (UK) (020) 8407 0740; **www.montenegro-living.com.**

Morocco

Why buy here?

Pros: Morocco offers a great climate, a truly exotic location, and value for money. Marrakesh is the most sought-after location, where you can buy traditional houses in a beautiful, unspoilt old city. There is a good rental market for winter holidaymakers.

Cons: The Moroccan conveyancing system isn't for the faint-hearted, and finding the original title deeds is often a problem. The bureaucracy can take over two years to get through.

Restoration costs can be very high and dealing with builders problematic. If there is no vehicular access to the property, which is often the case in areas such as the Marrakesh medina, everything will have to be brought in by donkey. Renovated properties may mask a multitude of building flaws and therefore it is actually an advantage to buy a site full of rubble; where the plaster comes away in your hands, you know exactly what you are getting.

Access: Royal Air Maroc, Air France and British Airways all fly to Marrakesh.

Property

Types: The market interesting to foreign buyers generally has two types of property – a *riad* and a *dar*. In the case of Marrakesh both are found in the oldest part of the city, the medina. A *riad*, from the Arabic word meaning garden, here means a traditional home of semi-open rooms built around a courtyard-cum-central garden with a fountain. The most expensive, restored examples have features like chandeliers, marble and ornate tiling. They convey the sort of atmosphere you may find combined in a mosque, Bedouin tent and Roman villa. The size of the courtyard is important: too small and it could be dark and cold. A *dar* is a similar house without the central garden.

Where to buy: The exotic medina located within the city walls of the glamorous, capital, Marrakesh, is where many foreign buyers head, following in the footsteps of such illustrious *riad*-owners as Jean-Paul Gaultier and Yves St-Laurent. Bear in mind that outside high summer the city can get rather cold.

If Marrakesh's medina is too claustrophobic and chaotic, another option is a neighbourhood of Marrakesh's modern section of the city, such as Gueliz or Hivernage, which has a high proportion of French expatriates as well as upmarket restaurants, cafés and shops. The purpose-built resort of La Palmerie outside the city, on the other hand, which covers nearly 50 square miles and has upmarket holiday homes and golf courses, will suit lovers of all mod-cons but has rather less character than the medina.

Property prices: Prices have soared in recent years: in 1990 you could buy a good Marrakesh *riad* for £1,000. Now those in disrepair start at around £50,000 (count on at least the same again for restoration) and those that have been well restored, have a good location and a large courtyard and are accessible by car can easily fetch over £300,000. A five-bedroom villa with swimming pool at La Palmerie would cost over £750,000.

For a *dar* with two or three bedrooms and a living room in need of restoration, the starting price is around £40,000. Once renovated, the price typically rises to over £130,000.

Legal restrictions: There are no legal restrictions for foreigners when buying in towns and cities, but buying in the countryside requires special authorisation, known as the 'vocation non agricole', allowing land to be used for building.

Finance

Currency and exchange rate: Dirham; £1 = 16.61 dirhams

Local mortgages: For simplicity, mortgages should be taken out in the UK.

The buying process: The buying process can be lengthy, over two years in some cases, not helped by the inheritance laws in Morocco, which state that each person with a claim to a property must give the go-ahead for a sale. It is, therefore, very important to engage a reputable, experienced, local legal representative to make all the checks. Some properties do not have title deeds and getting hold of the paperwork can take many months.

It is vital to ensure that any building works have been carried out to an adequate standard. You need to see photographs of the building works and any bills from builders, architects, engineers and suchlike. As well as your own property, it is important to ensure that any surrounding buildings are secure – you don't want your neighbour's wall crashing down on your own.

A *notaire*, a local authority official, oversees the sale on behalf of both the buyer and seller. He establishes that the deeds are in order, that those with a claim to the property agree to the sale, and that all outstanding acounts are settled. You will probably need to employ a translator as all dealings are in Arabic. When the deposit is paid, which is generally 10 per cent but could be as high as 50 per cent, a completion date is agreed. Be prepared for unusual demands, such as a request from the vendor to stay in the property for several months after the sale while he builds his new home...

Payment for the property is more difficult than normal, too. Moroccan currency cannot be taken out of the country and all money taken into the country has to be banked and documented. Without this proof that the money has been legitimately imported into the country, you cannot change the money back again when you wish to sell.

Costs of buying: Estate agents typically charge around 3 per cent commission. There is a 5 per cent property tax payable on completion, and conveyancing costs average around 3 per cent.

Is property a good investment? Yes, as long as there is no question over owner-ship and steps have been taken to ensure that the restoration has been made to an acceptable standard.

Selling: Capital gains tax is payable on profit made from the selling of a prop-erty. It is quite common, although illegal, for sellers to under-declare the value of their property to avoid full payment of this tax.

Inheritance tax: This varies according to the size of estate and relationship of the beneficiary to the deceased.

Living in Morocco

The average temperature in summer is 35°C and in winter is 22°C. The cost of living is low, but you have to allow extra time for most things. Shopping in the tiny shops, for example, can involve a good deal of haggling and couldn't be more unlike a trip to Tesco.

Further information

- **Morocco: t** (00 212)
- **Moroccan Embassy**, 49 Queen's Gate Gardens, London SW7 5NE, UK, **t** (020) 7581 5001; **www.morocco.embassyhomepage.com.**

Estate agents

- **Max Lawrence Properties, t** (UK) (01380) 828 533, **t** (Morocco) 61 13 44 22; **www.morocco-travel.com.**
- **Arcade Immo Services** (Morocco), **t** 63 03 33 37; **www.arcadeimmoservices.com.**
- **Atlas Immobilier** (Morocco), **t** 44 38 62 75; **www.atlasimmobilier.com.**
- **Kantari** (Morocco), **t** 44 44 00 22; **www.kantari.com.**

• **La Palameraie Golf Palace and Resort** (Morocco), **t** 44 30 19 59; **www.pgp.co.ma.**

• **Marrakech Riads** (Morocco), **t** 44 42 64 63; **www.marrakech-riads.net.**

New Zealand

Why buy here?

Pros: Although air fares are hefty from the UK, both UK buyers of holiday homes and immigrants, often young families, are increasingly being lured by the enviable lifestyle and comparatively low property prices here. Currently more than 4,000 Brits are relocating to New Zealand annually.

As well as its great climate, New Zealand has a stunningly unspoilt and diverse geography, with mountains, forests, glaciers, geysers, lakes, rivers and volcanoes. In addition to the lack of a language barrier, the glorious beaches, many ideal for surfing, the southern island especially has an established skiing industry.

Cons: Obviously the sheer distance from the UK is a serious disadvantage if you were thinking of buying a holiday home rather than a permanent place of residence.

Access: Several airlines offer good-value flights with a choice of stopovers to break the journey.

Property

Types: These vary from city apartments, often called 'units', and town houses, to wooden and brick-built detached houses on generous plots out of the cities.

Where to buy: Apart from the largest cities, such as Christchurch, Wellington and Auckland, popular areas for holiday and retirement homes include the Kapati coast to the north of Wellington, the Coromandel Peninsula in the far north of the North Island and the northern Marlborough region in the South Island. Second homes are also abundant in the Southern Alps, Glaciers, Banks Peninsula, south of Christchurch in the South Island.

Property prices: Property prices have been rising steadily for over five years and generally rose by 10 per cent in 2002. But in some areas, such as Wellington, Auckland, Nelson, Wanaka, Christchurch and Queenstown, prices have surged upwards in the last couple of years. The average home in 2003 was £71,000 compared with £59,000 in 1998. For twice that you can get a seriously good property here.

Two- and three-bedroom houses in the suburbs and rural areas generally range from about £35,000 to £85,000, with central city apartments typically starting at the higher end of this scale. A good-sized family home in Auckland starts at over £200,000, while a 100-year-old four-bedroom villa in Wellington near the centre is about £250,000. Away from the cities, you can get amazing properties for the money. For example, one British buyer recently bought a large country house with 10 acres of orchards at Gisborne, a small seaside town in a wine region, for just £90,000.

Legal restrictions: Unless permanent residence has been obtained, foreign buyers are required to obtain permission to buy from the land value tribunal or district land registrar if the land being purchased exceeds one acre. Foreign buyers may be restricted from buying if the property costs more than NZ$10 million (£3.5 million) or is in a sensitive area such as on the beach or on conservation land.

Finance

Currency and exchange rate: New Zealand dollar (NZ$); £1 = NZ$2.90

Local mortgages: A wide range of mortgages are available, usually for up to 80 per cent of value and for 25 years' duration. On the downside, there is a set-up fee charged by banks of 1 per cent of the amount borrowed, and rates are high compared with the UK, currently over 7.5 per cent. Some local banks, such as Westpac, have recently introduced mortgages for foreigners based on what they earned in their native country.

The buying process: This is generally straightforward and quick, and deals are often completed within one month. Gazumping is illegal. On the signing of an initial contract to buy, which is legally binding, a deposit (typically 10 per cent) is payable. It is a good idea to include a clause stating that the deposit is refundable if there is any question of the title to the property or if the land is found to be liable to compulsory purchase by the government.

It is prudent for buyers to commission an engineer or builder's report to check the condition of the property. Before completion the buyer's lawyer checks the title of the property before obtaining a land information memorandum.

Costs of buying: There is a land transfer registration fee of NZ$150 (around £50) and conveyancing costs average £350 to £700.

Is property a good investment? New Zealand is a very stable country, so the property market is generally reliable and safe.

Selling: There is no capital gains tax, even on second homes.

Inheritance tax: There is no inheritance tax.

Living in New Zealand

Made up of two main islands (North and South Islands) and numerous outlying ones, three-quarters of the country is hilly or mountainous and half-forested. Bigger in area than the UK, yet with just a fifteenth of its population, New Zealand is greener, warmer and friendlier.

The temperate oceanic climate (and sub-tropical climate in the extreme north) offers hot summers and cold winters. The west coast can receive very heavy rainfall, while the east coasts escape with very little. The main cities, Wellington especially, are affected by strong winds at times.

About three-quarters of the population is of European descent and most migrants today are still from Europe. Indigenous Maoris account for about 10 per cent of the four million population. Culturally, though, New Zealand increasingly leans towards its Polynesian roots and is less and less like a bygone Britain, as many people assume. English and Maori are the two official languages.

New Zealand enjoys political stability, a comparatively low cost of living, a very high standard of living – higher than neighbouring Australia – as well as a low crime rate and a good national health system. There are also reciprocal health agreements covering visitors of other countries including the UK.

Britons can stay for six months on a visitor's visa, with an option to extend this to nine months. To stay longer there are several options.

You can apply for a family visa if you marry or live with an existing New Zealand citizen or have immediate family members with citizenship or residency. In the case of your partner being a New Zealander, you would be required to prove that your relationship is genuine and has lasted for a minimum of a year. This is demonstrated by such things as having a joint bank account and other examples of shared commitments.

You can also apply for a general skills visa as a skilled professional, with success linked to age (45 is the cut-off age), qualifications, experience and skills offered using a points system. Applications can take over a year to process. Jobs most in demand include teachers, nurses, accountants, engineers, chefs and workers in the building trades. Typically education, jobs and personal records are examined and numerous references and types of documentation are required. Health and police checks can cost around £1,000. The application can be undertaken by a specialised emigration agent on the applicant's behalf, who will charge from £500 to £2,000.

If you have the funds, a long-term business visa can be considered. Here you would be required to invest in an existing business or start your own. Age and work experience are taken into consideration and a business plan is required.

When you have lived in the country for two years on one of these visas you can apply for permanent residency.

Income tax ranges from 15 per cent to 33 per cent, and there are residential rates and extra charges for such things as water and refuse collection that average around £350 to £700 for most homes. There are no restrictions on holiday letting.

Further information

- **New Zealand: t** (00 64)
- **New Zealand High Commission**, New Zealand House, Haymarket, London SW1Y 4TQ, UK, **t** (020) 7930 8422; **www.nzembassy.com.**
- **New Zealand Embassy**, 37 Observatory Circle, NW, Washington, DC 20008, USA, **t** (202) 328 4800; **www.nzemb.org.**
- **New Zealand Tourist Board**, New Zealand House, Haymarket, London SW1Y 4TQ, UK, **t** (020) 7930 0360.
- **Department of Land Information**, PO Box 5501, 160 Lambton Quay, Wellington, New Zealand, **t** 4 473 5022; **www.linz.govt.nz.**
- **Real Estate Agents Licensing Board**, PO Box 1247, Wellington, New Zealand, **t** 4 520 6949.
- **www.immigration.govt.nz**: government website with details concerning immigration.
- **Global Visas, t** (UK) (020) 7009 3800; **www.globalvisas.com**. A specialist emigration agency that can help with emigration.
- **Westpac Bank, www.westpac.co.nz.**

Estate agents

All are based in New Zealand.

- **Bayleys, t** 9 309 6020; **www.bayleys.co.nz.**
- **Harcourts, t** 3 441 0777; **www.harcourts.co.nz**. Estate agency group with branches nationwide.
- **Premium Real Estate, t** 9 486 1727; **www.premium-realestate.co.nz.**

Poland

Why buy here?

Pros: Poland boasts large tracts of beautiful unspoilt countryside and property prices that are exceptionally low due to low owner-occupation and years of a problematic, sluggish economy. Yet EU membership will change this rapidly. Large-scale EU investment will improve the infrastructure and mortgage finance will become increasingly available to locals, which will cause prices to shoot up. Early investors will be able to rent or sell at a good profit.

Cons: Although EU membership has made things more secure for investors, the necessary legal frameworks and lending services are not as stringent as they could be. Furthermore, the World Bank recently rated real estate as one of the most corrupt areas of Poland's economy. On top of that, reliable estate agents are few and far between.

Access: There are regular direct scheduled and budget flights to Krakow and Warsaw from the UK.

Property

Types: These range between anything from city apartments to sprawling rural detached villas.

Where to buy: Although property in the capital, Warsaw, is very good value by western European standards, the city is widely regarded as ugly and overpriced. Buyers should consider Krakow in the south, which is a significantly more attractive city. Property in Krakow is around half to three-quarters of the price of property in Warsaw. As soon as you leave the cities, beautiful properties in need of renovation are available in spellbinding countryside for unbelievably low prices.

Property prices: A large detached mansion in Warsaw would set you back £600,000 or so, while a two-bed apartment in the centre would, typically, be under £100,000, although studio flats in the centre are still available for under £25,000. Annual capital growth in the city is currently running at about 25 per cent. Rural houses are widely available for under £60,000 and on the outskirts of Warsaw for around £100,000.

In Krakow prices are highest in the Old Town centre, averaging around £35,000 for a small flat, rising to over £120,000 for a more spacious, well-preserved historic apartment.

To give an idea of the low level of prices, land in the lakeside northern Suwalki region currently runs at around £12 a square metre compared with over £100 a square metre just across the border in Germany.

Legal restrictions: Foreigners who are not EU citizens are required to obtain a permit from the Ministry for Internal Affairs in order to purchase a property in Poland. EU citizens are required to obtain a permit if the property is to be used as a second home.

Finance

Currency and exchange rate: Zlotych; £1 = 6.94 Zlotych

Local mortgages: Bear in mind that, like most Eastern European countries, there is no mortgage code of conduct or consumer credit act and it is usually preferable to use a lender in your home country.

The buying process: The buying process is overseen by a notary representing both parties. After the buyers' legal representative has checked that the deeds are in order and there are no encumbrances affecting the property, the notary oversees the signing of the contract by buyer and seller.

Costs of buying: Costs include stamp duty at 2 per cent and a nominal permit fee. Notarial fees are determined by the Minister of Justice and vary from 0.25 per cent plus PLN (Zlotych) 5,800 for properties with a value of over PLN 1 million to 3 per cent plus PLN200 for properties up to PLN15,000. The above fees are subject to 22 per cent VAT. The cost of land registration varies, depending on the transaction, and the estate agent's fee is typically 1 to 2 per cent, usually paid by the owner.

Is property a good investment? Poland's accession to the European Union coupled with its exceptionally low property prices mean that early investors are set to make substantial capital gains as prices are likely to rise significantly in the next few years.

Selling: Capital gains are usually added to the regular income of an individual and based on their income tax rate. If property is sold at least five years after it was purchased, the gain is exempt from tax.

Inheritance tax: The rate is progressive and depends on the relationship between donor and recipient.

Further information

- **Poland: t** (00 48)
- **Polish Tourist Office**, 310–12 Regent Street, London W1, UK, **t** (020) 7580 6688; **www.visitpoland.org**.
- **Polish Real Estate Federation** (Poland), **t** 22 825 39 56; **www.pref.org.pl**.

Estate agents

- **Ober Haus, t** 22 829 1212; **www.ober-haus.ee**.
- **www.viviun.com** and **www.immobel.com**: Polish property listings.

Portugal

Why buy here?

Pros: Portugal offers a splendid climate with plenty of sun just like Spain, but without the overdevelopment seen on so much of the Spanish coast. It boasts a relaxed pace of life, lots of championship-standard golf courses and more than

800km/500 miles of Atlantic coastline. As well as sandy beaches, it offers vast forests, mountains, hilly areas and much grassland.

Cons: Property prices are generally notably higher than in Spain, while some areas, such as parts of the Algarve, are overdeveloped. The standard of driving also leaves much to be desired. Non-linguists may baulk at the language.

Access: There is a wide choice of flights to the Algarve; flights between London and Faro take just under three hours. Flights to Lisbon are cheaper and more frequent, and Lisbon to Faro takes about four hours by car and five hours by train.

Property

Types: These are very varied, from well-constructed but pricey new-build property along the coast to crumbling cottages and farmhouses in the rural areas inland.

Where to buy: The **Algarve**, with its great climate and dramatic coastline, is where the majority of foreign buyers head. Stretching from the south Spanish coast to Cape St Vincent, it has one of the best all-round climates in Europe, with mild winters and hot summers cooled by Atlantic breezes, although April often brings lots of rain. The most popular area extends from Faro to Lagos.

For many years, wealthy foreign buyers have flocked to the neatly manicured luxury golfing estates here. Celebrity home-owners include Cliff Richard, Michael Owen, Alan Shearer, David Seaman, Chris Evans, Judith Chalmers and Annie Lennox. With the Atlantic to the south and west, the Guadiana River to the east and Caldeirão and Monchique mountain ranges to the north, the Algarve region has a character distinct from elsewhere in the country. Luxury leisure resorts are booming and the most popular new developments are within a 45-minute drive of Faro Airport west of the Algarve on the new motorway that opened in 2003.

If you are keen on avoiding the developed areas, note that the region east of Faro boasts numerous unspoilt fishing villages. Although the Algarve is the traditional area targeted by holiday home owners in Portugal, its location in the south of the country makes it a long, uncomfortable journey if you wish to visit by car. Parts of it are marred by overdevelopment (for example around Albufeira, Vilamoura and Quarteira), although a 1993 planning law has put a stop to this.

Focus your sights northwards and a host of possibilities opens up. The Portsmouth and Plymouth ferries to the Spanish ports of **Bilbao** and **Santander** make it a manageable drive to northern Portugal.

The Portuguese consider the **Minho**, the province north of Porto, to be one of the country's most attractive regions, and it boasts unspoilt coastline, wooded hills and river valleys, and pretty villages untouched by modernity.

Pressing on a bit further, the **Beira Litoral** in the centre of the country, dominated by the historic city of Coimbra, is little more than half a day's drive from the north Spanish ports. Rich in relatively inexpensive old farmhouses and cottages, again the area is peaceful and unspoilt.

On the **coast west of Lisbon** are Cascais and Estoril, which are popular with foreign buyers, while the **Silver Coast**, the Obidos area, is also sought after.

The Portuguese islands, **Madeira** and **Porto Santo** (also known as the Funchal Islands) off the Moroccan coast, and the **Azores** in the Atlantic northwest of Madeira, are more exotic options for the property buyer.

Rural inland areas are the best place to look for good-value older properties suitable for renovation.

Property prices: Oddly, properties here are generally considerably more expensive than in many other European sun spots. Even so, prices are cheap when compared with the UK. Portugal has a far higher population density than neighbouring Spain and the country's low interest rates may be encouraging many nationals to buy second homes here, in stark contrast with, say, France. A small Algarve apartment will set you back at least £150,000.

At an upmarket resort with a low density building policy, like Quinta do Lago in the Algarve, resale apartments typically start at over £225,000, while a new villa will set you back over £1.3 million.

Property on Madeira is around a third cheaper than in the Algarve.

For the cheapest properties on the mainland, head into the rural areas. Village properties for sale in the Beira Litoral area, for example, typically include large houses for restoration with mountain views for under £35,000, three-bedroom renovated cottages for under £120,000 and 18th-century spacious manor houses for £275,000 or so.

Legal restrictions: For those wishing to own a property through an offshore company to avoid local taxes and inheritance laws, read on. In January 2004 a law came into effect stating that any offshore company owning a property in Portugal will be liable to an annual charge of 5 per cent of the value of the property unless it is registered in Delaware, Malta or New Zealand. This means that anyone owning a Portuguese property of £300,000 through an offshore company would have to pay £15,000 annually, which means that owning property through offshore companies is no longer an attractive option.

Finance

Currency and exchange rate: Euro (€); £1 = €1.50.

Local mortgages: Portuguese mortgages require proof of income and outgoings, and normally a maximum of 80 per cent of the purchase price can be raised. Life cover is required and repayment mortgages are the most common type of loan.

The buying process: The buying process is regulated by a notary, a neutral official chosen by the government, who is responsible for making various checks on the property and for witnessing and registering the transfer of ownership from the vendor to the purchaser.

It is possible to sell a property without the use of a notary, but the contract would not be binding on a third party wishing to make a claim on the property or a lender wishing to grant a mortgage on it.

Buyers need to engage an experienced, independent, English-speaking lawyer (*advogado*) to protect their interests and safeguard against possible problems such as restrictive clauses or debts relating to the property. Buyers should also only approach government-registered estate agents (*mediator autoizado*).

When buyer and seller have agreed the purchase price, a preliminary contract (*contrato de promessa de compra e venda*) is signed, which is legally binding. This contains such details as the purchase price and completion date. The buyer pays a deposit, commonly 10 per cent but often more, which is normally non-refundable should the buyer later pull out of the deal. If the vendor backs out, he is usually required to pay the buyer double the value of the deposit.

If funds are being imported to buy a property, a licence must be obtained from the Bank of Portugal (*Boletim de Autorizacao de Capitals Privados*).

When buyer and seller are ready to complete, by signing the final contract in front of the notary, which represents the sale and conveyance deed (*escritura de compra e venda*), the balance owing is then paid by the purchaser and the sale is registered at the local land registry office. This last action can take several months.

Costs of buying: This usually translates as around 10 and 12 per cent of the purchase price. A transfer tax of between 0.5 and 15 per cent of the purchase price of the property is applicable, and there are legal (1 to 2 per cent) and notary and registration (3 per cent) fees payable.

Is property a good investment? The Portuguese property market is buoyant, the rental season is long and there are no restrictions on holiday letting.

Selling: Capital gains tax is payable at the same rates at income tax but only for 50 per cent of any gain made from property.

Inheritance tax: This is levied at between 3 and 50 per cent.

Living in Portugal

Portugal's mainland climate largely consists of mild winters and warm summers, although the northeast has longer, colder winters and hot summers. The islands are sub-tropical.

While the official language is Portuguese, English is widely spoken in the resort areas. The standard of living is quite high and, since the country joined the EU in 1986, the cost of living has risen steadily. The crime rate is comparatively low while health care is of a good standard.

Income tax ranges from 12 to 40 per cent. Foreign property owners are required to have a tax card and a fiscal number. Tax is payable by non-residents on income received in Portugal, for example from letting.

An annual property tax (contribuicao predial) of between 0.7 and 2 per cent is payable, based on the assessed value of the property. There are exemptions for some principal homes in urban areas. Local rates (contribucion autarquica) are also payable.

Residence permits are no more than a formality for EU nationals, and work permits unnecessary. Non-EU nationals may have difficulty obtaining a work permit. Visitors may remain in the country for 90 days. If you spend less than 183 days per year in Portugal you are generally classed as a non-resident and are required to appoint a fiscal representative (a friend or lawyer, for example) resident in Portugal to receive correspondence relating to your local affairs.

Further information

- **Portugal: t** (00 351)
- **Portuguese Tourist Office**, 22–25a Sackville Street, London W1S 3LY, UK; t 0906 364 0610; **www.portugalinsite.com**.
- **Portuguese Embassy**, 11 Belgrave Square, London SW1X 8PP, UK, t (020) 7235 5331; **www.portembassy.gla.ac.uk**.
- **Portuguese Embassy**, 2125 Kalorama Road, NW, Washington, DC 20008, USA, t 202 328 8610; **www.portugal.org**.
- **Anglo-Portuguese Society**, 2 Belgrave Square, London SW1X 8PJ, UK, t (020) 7245 9738; **www.portembassy.gla.ac.uk**.
- **www.portugal-info.com**: has English website links.
- **Barclays Bank Portugal**, t 2484 8 632.
- **Caixa Geral de Depositos**, t (UK) (020) 7623 4477; t (Portugal) 21 795 3000; **www.lardocelar.pt/uk/**. Portuguese bank with over 800 branches offering a full local banking service for UK owners of property in Portugal.

Estate agents

- **David Headland Associates** (UK), t (01933) 353333; **www.headlands.co.uk**.
- **Jones Homes Portugal** (UK), t (01625) 548405; **www.joneshomesportugal.com**. New-build properties.
- **World Class Homes** (UK), t (01582) 832001; **www.worldclasshomes.co.uk**.
- **Christopher Garveigh** (Portugal), t 28 276 9341; **www.garveigh.com**.

- **Premier Properties International** (UK), t (01935) 881199; **www.premierpropertiesonline.net**. Specialising in rural properties in central and western Portugal.
- **Country Homes Portugal** (Netherlands), t (00 31) 35 691 8418; **www.rusticportugal.com**.

Schools for English-speaking pupils

- **Carlucci American International School of Lisbon**, Rua Antonio dos Reis 95, Linho 2710–301, Sintra, t 21 923 9800; **www.caislisbon.com**. Co-educational, 3–18 years.
- **St Julian's School**, Quinta Nova, Carcavelos, 2777 Parede, Lisbon, t 21 458 5300. Co-educational, 4–18 years.
- **International School of the Algarve**, Apartado 80, 8400-400 Lagoa, Algarve, t 28 234 2547; **www.internationalschoolofthealgarve.com**. Co-educational, 4–18 years.
- **Oporto British School**, Rua da Cerca 326/350, Foa do Douro, Porto 4150–201, t 22 616 6660. Co-educational, 4–8 years.

Republic of Cyprus (southern, Greek part)

Why buy here?

Pros: If you're looking for a holiday retreat location or for a place to retire, Cyprus – the third largest island in the eastern Mediterranean – is hard to beat. Not only does it have one of the most agreeable climates in the world – around 330 days of bright sunshine and the warmest seas in the Med – but also inexpensive property, a low cost of living, low taxation, very little crime, a disarmingly friendly, widely English-speaking population and plenty of cheap flight connections from the UK.

As well as some great beaches and tranquil pine forests, on the Greek section of the island – 62 per cent of it – you can ski on Mount Olympus from December to April. Water sports are very popular and widespread. Cyprus also has a fascinating history that has left a host of prehistoric settlements, temples, Roman and Venetian fortifications, amphitheatres, Crusader castles, Byzantine churches and monasteries to explore.

Although Cyprus gained its independence in 1960, its history since 1925 as a British Crown Colony is still very influential today. Cyprus is now the fifth most popular foreign destination for British property buyers, behind only Spain,

France, Portugal and Florida. About three-fifths of buyers of holiday homes today are British and the British community now totals over 60,000, compared with a total island population of 750,000.

Cons: Although inland areas are generally unspoilt, over-development, coastal tower blocks and a large tourist industry have resulted in many built-up coastal areas, although the town of Paphos has been protected to an extent by strict building regulations.

The bitter history of troubles on the island and division into a Greek side and Turkish side since 1974 has caused Cyprus to be politically unstable at times in recent years. Well over 100,000 Greek refugees fled the now Turkish side in 1974. There have been numerous attempts to unify the island, most recently in April 2004 when the United Nations drew up a unification plan in advance of the Greek side's joining the European Union. The plan was rejected by 75.8 per cent of Greek Cypriots, even though 64.9 per cent of the Turkish Cypriot minority were in favour of the plan.

Access: Cyprus has two international airports handling numerous 4½-hour chartered and scheduled flights from London and other European cities to choose from each day. Flights start at under £100 return but these are rare, at the last minute or at awkward times. Typical returns between London and Larnaca hover at around £200, rising to £300 or so at peak periods. EU membership could mean lower prices, with low-cost carriers launching routes.

Property

Types: A wide choice, from period properties both in need of renovation and fully restored, to newly built apartments in holiday developments and luxury seaside villas.

Where to buy: Buyers of holiday homes and retirement properties tend to focus on established, popular coastal areas such as Paphos, Larnaca, Protaras, Ayia Napa and Limassol, while the Troodos mountains are also popular. If you are seeking peace and quiet, go to the northwest, which is the least developed.

Property prices: A 2004 survey found property prices to be substantially cheaper than Spain, Italy and Portugal. The wide choice of locations and property types mean budgets from around £40,000 to over £500,000 are accommodated. One-bedroom apartments typically start at around £35,000, with villas starting at just over double that. But a four-bed villa in a good location on the beach could easily exceed £300,000. A three-bed villa at Paphos, the most popular resort, now costs around £400,000. Prices will almost certainly rise following EU membership in May 2004.

Legal restrictions: If Cyprus manages to find some kind of unity, which seemed far more likely from 2003 when border controls were more relaxed than they have ever been since 1974, potential problems over property ownership resulting from the partition in 1974 are likely to be far less serious in the south of the island when compared with the north.

Turkish Cypriot properties in the south have been held in trust by the Greek Cypriot Government and rented to people who came from the north. Turkish Cypriots can do what they like with these properties, and can dispose of them whenever they want.

Non-Cypriots are only permitted to own one property here and there are restrictions on the amount of land that can be owned, usually three *donums* (43,200 square feet/4,012 square metres), or around two-thirds of an acre. This will probably be relaxed some time following EU membership.

Currently, incomers are not permitted to earn money in Cyprus and, therefore, they are required to satisfy the authorities that they have adequate funds to buy the property and support themselves.

Finance

Currency and exchange rate: Cyprus pound; £1 = C£0.88

Local mortgages: Repayment loans are available, commonly for 5–10 years and for under 70 per cent of value of the property, but better terms may be available in the UK. Self-certification and non-status mortgages are not available on the island.

The buying process: Foreign currency must be imported to make a purchase, and the land registry office requires a certificate documenting this.

The house-buying process is based on the British model. A local lawyer familiar with the system should be used. After the purchaser and vendor have signed an agreement or contract to go ahead with the sale and the purchaser has paid a deposit, searches are made to ascertain that the title is unencumbered. It is important that the buyer's lawyer verifies that the seller is the owner of the property and that the property has an unbroken chain of legitimate ownership.

Signing the agreement and paying the deposit cause the buyer to be legally committed and, therefore, there is no 'gazumping', but the purchaser remains legally bound even if problems with the contract or title are later found.

As a formality, the purchaser applies for permission to buy from the Council of Ministers. This is simple, requiring such things as a bank reference, a character reference, criminal record checks and affirmation that only one home will be owned in Cyprus, that the maximum land size is not being exceeded and that minimum required funds to live on the island are available. This process can take up to a year, but in the meantime possession of the property can be taken.

Ownership of the property is transferred from the vendor to the buyer through the Cypriot Land Registry, via a solicitor.

Costs of buying: Stamp duty is C£1.50 (about £1.70) per C£1,000 (£1,135) of the property price up to C£75,000 (£85,000) and C£2 (£2.30) per C£1,000 over C£75,000. Transfer fees of 3 per cent are payable on the first C£50,000 (£57,000) of the value of the property, with 5 per cent payable on the value from C£50,000–100,000, and 8 per cent on the value over C£100,000 payable. A property bought by a couple has a generous allowance on this. Lawyers' fees average around 1 per cent of the purchase price and the application to the Council of Ministers costs approximately £230.

Is property a good investment? In recent years property prices have risen steadily (at over 20 per cent per annum in the last couple of years, and one British agent is claiming rises of up to 48 per cent in 2003 alone). EU membership will accelerate this rise.

Selling: Capital gains tax of 20 per cent may be applicable when the property is sold, although there are exemptions.

Inheritance tax: Inheritance tax is from 10–30%, payable on estates of over C£20,000 (about £22,700). It is payable by non-residents on property owned on the island.

Living in Cyprus

Cyprus can seem very familiar to a British visitor or resident. Cars drive on the left-hand side of the road and road signs are in English and Greek. The legal system is based on the English one. The cost of living is generally very cheap (around 30 per cent lower than the UK), and it is possible to live comfortably for under £8,000 per year. This has been just as well in the past, as it is usually not possible for incomers to gain employment on the island, although an increased number of work permits have been issued as Cyprus has got nearer to EU membership. The crime rate is low and medical facilities are generally excellent.

Buying a property allows purchasers to become resident, subject to approval by the Council of Ministers. Pensions and investment income is subject to 5 per cent income tax for tax residents and a double taxation agreement with the UK means that residents do not have to pay tax in both countries.

An annual property ownership tax is payable: 2 per cent on properties valued at C£101,000–250,000 (about £115,000 to £285,000); 3 per cent on properties of C£250,001–500,000, and 3.5 per cent on properties valued more than that. There is also a municipal tax of under £120 per year levied locally, based on the value of the property. Officially, foreigners are not permitted to let their properties, although this rule is generally not strictly observed and, therefore, many owners do so unofficially.

Further information

- **Republic of Cyprus** (Greek): **t** (00 357)

- **Cyprus High Commission**, 93 Park Street, London W1Y 4ET, UK,
t (020) 7499 8272.

- **Cyprus Embassy**, 2210 R Street, NW, Washington, DC 20008, USA,
t (202) 462 5772.

- **Cyprus Tourism Organisation**, PO Box 24535, 1390 Nicosia, **t** 233 7715;
www.cyprustourism.org.

- **Conti Financial Services**, 204 Church Road, Hove, East Sussex BN3 2DJ, UK;
t (01273) 772811; **www.overseasandukfinance.com**. Offers loans in Cyprus
secured on Cypriot property.

Estate agents

- **Cybarco**, **t** (Cyprus) 22 741300; **t** (UK) (020) 8371 9700; **www.cybarco.com**.
For new properties in Larnaca, Limassol and Paphos.

- **Halcyon Properties**, **t** (UK) (01323) 891639; **www.halcyon-properties.
co.uk**. Greek and Cypriot specialist property consultants, and UK associate
company for Antony Loizou and Associates.

- **Antony Loizou and Associates** (Cyprus), **t** 25 871552; **www.aloizou.com.cy**.
Cyprus's largest estate agents and chartered surveyors with branches in
Limassol, Larnaca, Paphos and Paralimni. The company can assist with
government permits for permanent residency and property acquisition
and provide ongoing maintenance assistance and property management.

- **Aristo Developers** (Cyprus), **t** 26 841841; **www.aristodevelopers.com**.
Various new developments on the island.

- **Pafilia Property Developers** (Cyprus), **t** 26 848800; **www.pafilia.com**.

Schools for English-speaking pupils

- **American Academy**, 3A M Parides Street, PO Box 1967, Nicosia, **t** 246 2886.
Co-educational, 5–18 years.

- **English School**, PO Box 23575, CY-1684, Nicosia, **t** 227 9302;
www.englishschool.ac.cy. Co-educational secondary school for
11- to 18-year-olds.

- **Logos School of English Education**, 33–35 Yialousa Street, PO Box 51075,
3501 Limassol, **t** 253 6061; **www.logos.ac.cy**. Co-educational secondary
school.

Romania

Why buy here?

Pros: This exotic little-known land has gorgeous properties with tiny price tags, as well as great beaches and a sunny climate. Parts of the Black Sea coast are very beautiful.

Its troubled Communist history is very much a thing of the past and the country is now developing rapidly. The fact that Romania is set to join the European Union in 2007 means that the country is likely to improve greatly.

Cons: Bitterly cold winters will cause you to look fondly on the climate of northern Britain. Although the country's infrastructure is rapidly improving, there are still many shortcomings, including bad roads and drab concrete buildings. In addition, some of the countryside is quite tatty compared with many European countries.

Access: British Airways and Tarom offer daily direct flights from the UK.

Property

Types: These vary from newly built city apartments to seaside villas and older, large detached rural houses.

Where to buy: Romania has lots to offer, with a very varied and beautiful landscape including the dramatic forested mountains of Dracula country, the Transylvanian Alps, and vast fertile plains. The Alps, ideal for skiing in the winter and walking in the summer, boast alpine meadows, unspoilt medieval towns, gothic castles and untouched monasteries. Transylvania is home to many undeveloped medieval villages including Sibiu, Prejmer, Nasaud, Bistrita, Harman and Sighisoara, which has a UNESCO-protected historical centre. Winter-sports centres in the region include Poiana Brasov, Predeal, Sinaia and Busteni.

The beautiful 'Romanian Riviera' on the Black Sea is hard to beat. The city of Constanta has an easy-going atmosphere and lively cultural life, with numerous restaurants and bars, an opera house and theatre. North of here is the popular Black Sea resort of Mamaia and others include Cosinesti, Mangalia, Eforie Nord, and Olimp and Neptun by the Comorova forest.

For tranquillity and value for money, head for the unspoilt rural villages, and for vibrant, exotic city life choose Bucharest, although during the oppressive Ceauşescu area much of the historical centre was destroyed. The picturesque town of Brasov, founded in the 12th century, has numerous houses available in need of renovation.

Property prices: You could buy a Swiss-style chalet on the Romanian Riviera for under £30,000. Rural farms with land have been sold recently for under £10,000. Houses in rural villages such as Agigea start at around £5,000.

In Eforie Nord a three-bed villa near the beach would typically set you back £30,000. In Constanta, a new-build two-bed apartment with sea views would be around £25,000, while for £35,000 or so you could get a four-bedroom town house with a large garden.

Legal restrictions: Although overseas purchasers may buy anywhere in the country, they are not allowed to own the land except in the following circumstances:

- Buying the property and taking over the exclusive use of the land for the lifetime of the house, paying a small tax for the land annually.

- Forming a limited company established in Romania to own the land.

- The property being purchased by a foreign person and the land that is part of the property being bought by a Romanian subject who then gives exclusive right of use for the land to the owner of the building for the lifetime of the building. In this third case the Romanian subject is not permitted to sell the land to another party without the express agreement of the owner of the building.

Finance

Currency and exchange rate: Lei (ROL); £1 = ROL 62,000

Local mortgages: Local borrowing opportunies are scarce and it is advisable to use a UK lender.

The buying process: It is advisable only to use an estate agent who is a member of the National Union of Estate Agents (UNAI). It is also advisable to appoint a surveyor to establish the local worth of the property as it is common for Romanian vendors to inflate asking prices if they know that a foreign buyer is interested. Although it is possible to buy without engaging a lawyer, this would open you to possible pitfalls in the system.

Once the purchase price has been agreed, a pre-purchase agreement is drawn up by the estate agent and signed by both parties and then the buyer pays a 10 per cent deposit, which will be lost if he or she reneges on the sale. If the vendor backs out of the deal he or she is liable to pay the purchaser double the value of the deposit. The agent is responsible for the local searches and the transfer of title and registration is handled on behalf of both parties by a notary.

Both parties attend to sign the final contract in front of the notary and then the sale is registered with the land registry.

Costs of buying: Estate agency fees vary greatly in different parts of the country; for example, they are typically around 2 per cent in Brasov and 6 per cent in

Bucharest. In some instances buyers and sellers may both pay a commission charge to the estate agent. Other costs may add around 10 per cent to the purchase price. Notary fees and transfer taxes are in accordance with charges set by the government relating the the value of the property concerned.

Is property a good investment? Property prices are still in the bargain-basement category, but once Romania joins the European Union in 2007 prices are likely to shoot up.

Selling: There is currently no capital gains tax to be paid on selling.

Inheritance tax: The rate is progressive and also depends on the relationship between donor and recipient.

Living in Romania

Romania has a Mediterranean climate and, although the standard of living is lower than much of Europe, the cost of living is very low also. A meal in a good restaurant with wine is unlikely to set you back more than £5.

Further information

- **Romania: t** (00 40)
- **Romanian Embassy**, Arundel House, 4 Palace Green, London W8 4QD, t (020) 79379666; **www.roemb.co.uk**.

Estate agents

- **Elion** (Romania), **t** 241 508 217; **www.elion.ro**.
- **www.viviun.com**: a selection of Romanian properties for sale.

Slovenia

Why buy here?

Pros: Little-known Slovenia, once part of the former Yugoslavia, is tipped for a tourist boom following EU accession in May 2004. The small country, with a population of just two million, boasts a pleasant short coastline on the Adriatic Sea, an alpine interior ideal for skiing, as well as a lovely capital, Ljubljana.

Cons: Language is a real barrier here and not being fluent can cause endless frustration to a homeowner.

Access: Access is improving and easyJet launched regular flights to the capital, Ljubljana, in 2004.

Where to buy: Ljubljana offers both old-world flair and modern entertainment. The pretty Old Town sits along the Ljubljanica river. Ljubljana boasts a beautiful blend of architectural styles as well as many pavement cafés, restaurants and cultural events. Bled, 35 kilometres from Ljubljana airport, has a lake with an idyllic island and is surrounded by stunning unspoilt countryside. Portoroz is a bustling seaside resort. As well as the beach, there are thermal pools, water-front bistros, restaurants and discos.

The Goricko National Park has lots of cheap property in a beautiful rural setting. It is currently being developed for tourism and will soon be linked to Ljubljana by a direct motorway.

Property prices: In the best areas of Ljubljana a two-bed apartment is typically over £125,000, but in the countryside you can get a three-bedroom country house still for under £50,000 or a cottage for half that. Some rural houses are priced at under £15,000.

Finance

Currency and exhange rate: Tolar; £1 = 362 Tolars. The Tolar is expected to be replaced by the euro in a few years.

Local mortgages: Mortgages for foreigners are still a real rarity and the base rate is high anyway. It is, therefore, better either to buy with cash or raise the finance in the UK with an equity release scheme.

The buying process: Foreigners cannot buy property in Slovenia without a tax registration number, obtainable from the local authority. Local banks also require this number before they will open an account.

A government-appointed notary acts for both buyer and seller but it is vital for buyers to appoint an independent English-speaking lawyer.

The buying process is quick and straightforward and greatly helped by a computerised land registry that can complete searches within 24 hours as well as an efficient legal system and high-tech banking.

The sales contract is signed in front of the notary and the law in Slovenia requires that an official court translator is present when the contract is signed to ensure that the purchaser fully understands the contract.

Costs of buying: Estate agents generally charge 3 per cent. The vendor pays stamp duty of 2 per cent of the purchase price. If the property is bought and then re-sold within two years, the tax becomes 10 per cent. The translator of the sales contract receives a small sum, around £25, and the notary receives about £200, sometimes paid by the buyer and sometimes by the seller.

Is property a good investment? Until EU accession it was very difficult for foreigners to buy here, and early exploiters of the change in the law are likely to benefit handsomely financially.

Selling: Capital gains tax is 25 per cent.

Inheritance tax: Heirs of first succession do not pay tax. In the second succession of inheritance, the tax varies from 5 to 14 per cent, while in the third succession the tax is from 8 to 11 per cent. All other individuals pay tax of between 11 and 30 per cent.

Living in Slovenia

The Slovenian language is very difficult and few, if any, words are recognisable in more common languages like English, French or German. However, English is widely taught in schools and many people speak German because German tourists visit the country. Although Slovenia is still developing, in many respects it is changing at a rapid pace and in some areas standards are very up-to-date. For example, the banking system is modern and ATMs are common.

Further information

- **Slovenia: t** (00 386)
- **East European Property Secrets, www.easteuropeanpropertysecrets.co.uk.**

Estate agents

- **Euroburo** (Austria), **t** 00 43 6137 20099; **www.euroburolimited.co.uk.**
- **Nepremianine** (Slovenia), **t** 3 567 91 10; **www.nepremicnine.net.**
- **www.viviun.co.uk**: features properties in Slovenia.

South Africa

Why buy here?

Pros: Most people looking for a holiday home abroad want sun, sea, tranquillity and an inexpensive home situated in a beautiful setting as well as a low cost of living. South Africa certainly meets such criteria – its summer is our winter – and has in recent years become an increasingly popular second home and retirement location for British buyers.

Although it has crime hotspots it is essentially a safe and friendly destination. English is widely spoken, and the country is never more than two hours in advance of the time in the UK. The climate is consistently good and generally healthy, averaging 26.5°C in January on the Cape. As well as 2,900km/1,800 miles of coastline, the varied geography encompasses mountains, vast plains, forest, lakes and rivers. There are numerous game reserves to discover.

Cons: Apartheid officially ended in 1991, and South Africa is one of Africa's most stable countries; the current democracy appears to be relatively stable, too. But before buying in South Africa, there are a number of factors to consider. The country has long had a history of political instability, widespread social and economic problems and civil discontent. As with many other African countries, the possibility of a coup resulting in a change of regime and causing the loss of your home can never totally be discounted.

British buyers may also be concerned about crime and violence in the country. In 2000 there were 20,000 murders in South Africa, for example. The majority of crime is in the cities, especially Durban and Johannesburg. Cape Town is considerably more relaxed, with a slight old-English feel. The crime rate in the Western Cape remains lower than New York or Los Angeles, but electrified fences, residents employing armed response units and guards are a common occurence. Police corruption is common.

Even so, many holiday areas are a long way from crime hotspots. There is virtually no crime at Knysna, for example, which is a sleepy market town: if someone's car is broken into it's almost front page news.

Although flights, at around 11 hours, take no longer than a drive from London to northern Scotland, it is important to ascertain whether you would be prepared to pay for and make the journey often enough to justify buying.

Another disadvantage is that the Atlantic Ocean, with currents coming from the Antarctic, is usually too cold to swim in. The stretch of coastline bordering the Indian Ocean is warmer. Flights are long and expensive. The huge gulf between owning a luxury beachside villa and the sprawling poverty-stricken shanty towns you pass to get there can be an issue for many.

Access: Flights from the UK start from over £600 but have become increasingly economical and frequent off-season, and overnight flights are now available directly into Cape Town, Johannesburg and Durban. Transfers for non-direct flights are usually frequent and cheap. Flights are of around 12 hours' duration. As well as international airports at Cape Town, Durban and Johannesburg, there are six other major airports. Because South Africa is in the same longitude as the UK rather than in a different time zone, jet lag isn't a problem.

Property

Types: A wide range of properties is available including new developments of coastal villas and apartments, attractive period Dutch gabled houses, game lodges, thatched cottages and large, older town houses. If your budget stretches to it (£650,000 or so), in the remote countryside are Cape Dutch homesteads with 18th-century thatched whitewashed houses set in landscaped gardens. The building standards overall are generally high.

Where to buy: Foreign buyers tend to focus on the coastal areas of the Western and Eastern Capes, the Garden Route, game farms in the Mpumalanga region, and KwaZulu-Natal. The attractive city of Cape Town is particularly popular and near to the Kruger National Park. Knysna in the Western Cape embraces a large lagoon which is an inlet to the warm Indian Ocean, with a backdrop of hills leading to forests and mountains inland. The old market town of Knysna is unspoilt, unhurried and tranqil. It is particularly popular as a retirement location, as are the Franschhoek and Paarl wine regions.

False Bay, to the southeast of Cape Town, is a popular area for seaside homes. Upmarket Cape Town suburb Constantiaberg is very popular and also Camps Bay, where the Twelve Apostles mountain range runs south from Table Mountain into the sea above huge expanses of sand. Here there are fabulous architect-designed houses perched on cliffs overlooking lovely sandy bays and the Atlantic.

The Atlantic seaboard is most popular for apartments because of its position between the sea and Table Mountain. The mountain protects it from the chilling southerly wind.

Property prices: Prices have been cheap – especially as a result of spectacular falls in the value of the rand at the end of 2001 – but the property market has experienced something of a boom in recent years, especially in Cape Town, following an increase in political stability and the rand's strengthening considerably. In late 2003 the average house price in South Africa was £38,000, and £41,000 in the Cape Town Metropolitan area.

A number of developments have been springing up, fuelled especially by British, German and other foreign buyers. A good apartment is easily available for under £20,000 and a villa with a pool for under £40,000.

In Cape Town a two-bed flat in the centre starts at around £35,000 and a large villa by the sea with a pool could easily cost £500,000. Move out of the fashionable areas and you get plenty of value. False Bay, West Coast and Walker Bay are all within a two-hour drive from the airport and have a good choice of property.

The Eastern Cape Coast, South Coast and Natal North Coast are current hotspots with a good choice of property. Natal's coastline is less than an hour's drive from Durban and has seen prices rise 30 per cent from early 2003 to early 2004; a villa here will currently cost £200,000 or so, and one-bed apartments a quarter of that.

For about £25,000 you could buy a two-bed flat in the Knysna area while a spacious three-bedroom detached house in the hills overlooking the lagoon costs £35,000 plus. £200,000 would net a luxury residence.

In the KwaZulu-Natal region, three-bedroom apartments begin at £65,000 or so, and a three-bed villa with its own pool would set you back at least £125,000.

Legal restrictions: All funds brought into the country must go through the South African Reserve Bank via a registered banker. This can add another 10 days or so to the buying process. EU citizens may stay for up to six months each year, as long as they can demonstrate that they can support themselves and can produce a return ticket. Longer stays require a residency permit and an employment permit if you plan to work there.

Finance

Currency and exchange rate: Rand; £1 = R11.92. The rand has fluctuated greatly in recent years, by as much as 40 per cent against sterling.

Local mortgages: Known as bonds in South Africa, these are usually considerably more expensive than in Europe. They are available to non-residents for up to 50 per cent of the purchase price of the property; purchasers are required to bring at least 50 per cent of the funds to buy into the country. Residents can obtain 100 per cent loans.

The buying process: Most property is owned with a freehold title. Conveyancing and land registration are relatively straightforward, especially as transactions are in English. The process takes around 10 weeks, but can be as quick as 14 days. Agents are required to register with the Estate Agents Board and often handle much of the paperwork on a buyer's behalf.

Offers to purchase are made in writing and once signed by both parties a contract comes into existence, therefore legal advice should be taken before signing an offer to purchase. The same lawyer acts for both parties, with the vendor selecting one and the buyer paying the fees, on a predetermined scale based on the purchase price.

The buyer then pays 10 per cent deposit to the vendor's estate agent. A contract is drawn up, stating the legal obligations of both parties.

Costs of buying: Conveyancing costs an average of 1–2 per cent of the purchase price, and legal and other fees are another 1 per cent or so. Notary fees for preparing and registering the title deed range from £230–660. Stamp duty is 0.5 per cent of the purchase price.

A transfer duty is payable by the buyer on resale properties. This varies from 1 per cent on the first R60,000 (£5,000 or so), to 5 per cent from R60,001 to R250,000 and 8 per cent on the remainder. Where the purchaser is a trust or company, the duty is at a flat rate of 10 per cent of the purchase price.

Transfer duty is not payable on new properties, which attract 14 per cent value added tax. Stamp duty of 0.2 per cent is payable on a mortgage.

Is property a good investment? If you buy when the rand has fallen and prices are amazingly low, and prices then rise, clearly property here is a good investment. Unfortunately, life is seldom so simple. Those who bought in 2001 saw the value of their properties plunge over the following 12 months, as the rand shot up from 11 to 16 to the pound.

You can let your holiday home for most of the year providing an income that will more than cover the cost of maintaining the property. And property values will increase as more South Africans re-locate from the cities like Johannesburg and Pretoria, which provides a solid investment for overseas buyers. Cape Town saw increases of 20 per cent in prices in each of the three years up to 2004.

Non-residents are entitled to hold title to land via a company or trust, which can be beneficial to tax plannning.

Selling: Any money gained from selling can be taken out of the country, although capital gains tax is levied on gains made from the sale of a non-primary residence.

Inheritance tax: This is applicable at 25 per cent on estates valued in excess of R1 million (about £85,000).

Living in South Africa

As well as its great beauty, one major attraction of South Africa is its particularly low day-to-day cost of living. A good bottle of white wine is about £1.20 and petrol is just 30p per litre, for example. Eating out is extremely good value. Two people can eat out very well for under £10.

Around 65 per cent of the population speak English. Africaans is also widely spoken along with nine other official languages.

Europeans will feel at home: there are around six million residents of European origin including over 500,000 Britons. Areas popular with foreigners have plenty of Dutch, German, French and British buyers. State medical facilities are generally relatively good, but private health insurance is necessary.

The climate is excellent: summer peaks in December and January with temperatures ranging between 20°C and 40°C. The east coast is semi-tropical and can be humid in summer, while around Cape Town the climate is more like that of the Mediterranean. Being warm and sunny much of the year (the rainy season/mild winter is from June to September), South Africa is also ideal for those considering retirement. On the coast the sea breezes mean it does not get humid, and the air quality is superb.

Annual community fees average from around £150 to £1,000 and rates are approximately £100 to £500 depending on property size and location.

Income tax of 19 to 45 per cent is payable on any income gained in the country, such as from renting out a property. A fiscal representative to make your annual tax returns costs under £400. Property taxes are payable, varying by region and size of property.

Applying for a residence permit involves a hefty fee, currently over £1,000, which is non-refundable.

Further information

- **South Africa: t** (00 27)
- **South African High Commission**, Trafalgar Square, London WC2N 5DP, UK; **t** (020) 7451 7299; **www.southafricahouse.com**.
- **South African Embassy**, 3051 Massachusetts Avenue, NW, Washington, DC 20008, USA, **t** (202) 232 4400; **www.southafrica.net**.
- **South African Property Overseas Marketing Association**, **t** 31 573 1966; **www.sapoma.co.za**.
- **Institute of Realtors of South Africa**, **t** 21 531 3180.

Estate agents

- **Elan International**, **t** (UK) (01935) 881762, **t** (South Africa) 31 573 1966; **www.elanpark.co.za**.
- **Cluttons**, **t** (UK) (020) 7403 3669, **t** (South Africa) 21 425 8989.
- **Private Property Listings** (South Africa), **t** 083 913 1000; **www.privateproperty.co.za**.
- **FPD Savills** (UK), **t** (020) 7824 9077; **www.fpdsavills.co.uk**.
- **Sotheby's International Realty** (UK), **t** (020) 7598 1600; **www.sothebysrealty.com**.
- **Pam Golding International** (South Africa), **t** 28 284 9384; **www.pamgolding.co.za**. Largest international estate agent working in conjunction with FPD Savills.
- **Bren Gleeson** (South Africa), **t** 21 782 7692; **www.gleesonprop.co.za**.
- **Seeff Residential Properties**, **t** 23 344 3291; **www.seeff.com**.
- **Capsol**, **t** 21 461 1083; **www.capsolsales.com**. Specialising in the Cape Town area.

International schools

- **St Cyprian's Girls' School**, Gorge Road, Oranjezicht 8001, **t** 021 461 1090; **www.stcyprians.co.za**. 6–18 years.
- **International School of Cape Town**, Woodland Heights, Edinburgh Close, Wynberg, 7800, Cape Town, **t** 21 761 6202; **www.isct.co.za**. Co-educational, 4–19 years.
- **Durban High School**, 255 St Thomas Road, Musgrave 4000, Durban, **t** 31 277 1500; **www.durbanhighschool.co.za**. 11–18 years.

- **American International School of Johannesburg**, Private Bag 4, Bryanston 2021, Jo'burg, **t** 11 464 1505; **www.aisj-jhb.com**. Co-educational, 4–20 years.
- **Redhill School**, 20 Summit Road, Morningside, Sandton, **t** 783 4707; **www.redhill.co.za**. Co-educational, 4–19 years.
- **Glen High School**, Atterbury Road, Pretoria, **t** 12 348 8625; **www.theglenhighschool.co.za**. Co-educational, 12–18 years.

Spain

Why buy here?

Pros: After a relaxing few days of Spanish sun, sea and sangria, it's easy to be seduced into buying a gorgeous villa or farmhouse sporting a price tag that is tiny when compared with property in the UK. It offers magnificent beaches, spectacular countryside, culture for art lovers and fine wines and cuisine.

Spain remains the most popular country by far for Brits purchasing a home abroad. *A Place In The Sun* magazine commissioned a survey in April 2004 that questioned 4,000 people and found that purchasing a villa or apartment in Spain with a private pool and a sea view was the most popular option.

Buyers in Spain are swayed by the glorious sun and the low rainfall. Unlike France, sunshine is guaranteed in most parts of the country for much of the year. Indeed, many people claim that Spain has the best climate in Europe. It also boasts good transport links with the UK, with plenty of cheap flights and, when you're there, it has a low cost of living.

Many buyers appreciate English being widely spoken and the strong British presence that has been long established in many of the beach resorts. The health care system is generally good. All this contributes to the fact that an estimated 750,000 Britons have now bought retirement houses in Spain.

The country has great contrasts: parts of the north can resemble Scotland while much of the south has a Moroccan feel.

Cons: The north may be convenient for the ferry ports, but would you want to visit during a freezing winter? The south of the country may enjoy the most sun, but are you likely to visit regularly if it's a long trek each time? Also, many sections of the coast suffer from overdevelopment and so it can take time and persistence to find the right property.

Access: Spain enjoys a large choice of scheduled, chartered and budget flights, facilitating access to the *costas* and beyond. In recent years, having a weekend retreat in a vibrant Spanish city has become an affordable possibility, with bargain flights available to destinations such as Valencia, Bilbao, Madrid, Jerez and Barcelona.

The greater variety of routes and the expansion of regional airports such as Murcia, serving the Costa Calida and the southern part of the Costa Blanca, means the busiest airports, like Alicante, can be avoided.

Smaller UK regional airports like Glasgow, Bristol and Manchester are increasingly taking traffic away from Heathrow and Gatwick and making a retreat in Spain a far more attractive proposition to British buyers in the west and north of England and in Scotland.

Although the daunting distance causes few motorists to contemplate regular drives to the hot, sunny south, buying a property within comfortable distance of the northern Spanish ports of Santander and Bilbao is another increasingly popular option. Brittany Ferries operates regular services from Plymouth to Santander, while P&O Portsmouth runs from Portsmouth to Bilbao. People don't often buy near these ports because of the lack of sun, but the northeastern *costas* – Brava, Dorada and del Azahar on the Mediterranean – are within easy driving distance thanks to the fast-improving roads. They are a four-hour drive from Bilbao. From Calais, it would take two days to reach here.

Greatly improved travel options such as extended Eurostar/TGV train services and fast motorways are opening whole new areas of Spain to those seeking a holiday or retirement home. The Catalonia region of northeastern Spain, away from the madding crowds, is easily accessible using the A7 motorway linking France with Barcelona and giving much easier access to historic towns such as Girona.

Property

Types: Unlike the French market, where British buyers almost all buy period homes, many Brits in Spain opt for new-build villas and apartments, and this is the section of the market in which many of the companies geared to British buyers operate.

Where to buy: Spain is the second-largest country in western Europe after France and has a coastline totalling 2,125 km/1,320 miles. Yet overwhelming UK interest is concentrated in two small areas. The Costa Blanca and the Costa del Sol account for the majority of Spanish property sales to the British as they have the best accessibility by air and a good selection of properties at all budgets (*see* box, p.147). However, in places areas are so overdeveloped, especially on the Costa del Sol, that people have taken to describing some pockets as almost 'slums in the sun'. Other *costas* have been rapidly rising in popularity, including the Costa Brava, Costa Dorada and the Costa de la Luz. The Balearics (Menorca, Mallorca and Ibiza) and the Canary Islands (Tenerife, Gran Canaria and Lanzarote) are eternally popular and city-lovers are increasingly focusing on Barcelona, Madrid, Seville and Granada.

The most popular and built-up areas include the areas that first saw mass tourism several decades ago, such as Marbella, Puerto Banus, Benidorm and Estepona. The infrastructure is generally good in the popular resort areas, being geared to tourism and expat residents alike.

Spain is also one of the countries in Europe targeted by skiers. Bear in mind that if you choose a detached home in a ski resort, heavy snowfall may greatly impede access, winters can be hard and long, and you may require someone to visit your property regularly to clear the snow and check the central heating. Uncleared snow can result, once the temperature has risen and it re-freezes, in a glacier around the property, which can make access difficult. If you are buying a property in a ski resort, view it also when the snow has melted, as this can reveal ugly features like rubbish tips.

Here is a more detailed run-down of the various pros and cons of just a few of the areas of Spain popular with buyers, and the types of property available.

As well as a fabulous climate, the **Balearic Islands** boast excellent access due to the large range of cheap flights. Britain's favourite holiday destination for retirees, the islands of Menorca and Mallorca are the most popular choice. Ibiza, the third island, today attracts families as well as the young hedonistic clubbers, and away from the beaches and the hubbub it is easy to discover unspoilt villages.

Mallorca, which welcomed 2.5 million British holidaymakers in 2003, is now also one of the UK's most popular second-home destinations. Topographically it offers a great deal, with the coastline ranging from sandy beaches to cliffs, and there are mountains, river valleys, and rich farmlands in the central plain. The island has something for everyone, including lively towns, unspoilt tranquil inland villages and family resorts.

The mountain region between Soller and Valldemossa is popular with celebrities, including Richard Branson, Michael Douglas and Andrew Lloyd Webber. Claudia Schiffer and Boris Becker also have homes on the island.

Environmental controls have restricted the availability of building plots. The capital, Palma, is very attractive, and the property market here is dominated by upmarket apartments and villas. To escape the mass tourism, you need to head away from the large resorts in the south, which are most likely to suffer from overdevelopment.

Many people aspire to an old farmhouse or *finca* to restore but these are increasingly less easy to source.

Menorca boasts a good range of unspoilt beaches and its coastal resorts are quieter and dominated by family-friendly rented apartments and villas rather than hotels, as on Majorca. Its two main towns, Ciutadella and Mahon, are pretty, old ports with good cafés, restaurants, shops and architecture.

Andalucía, in the south, is one of Spain's most varied regions, with the beaches on the **Costa del Sol**, skiing in the Sierra Nevada and sherry production in Jerez.

Access is excellent, and you can fly into Malaga on the Costa del Sol from at least half a dozen UK airports.

The temperature nudges 55°F/12°C to 80°F/27°C the whole year round, and rainfall averages no more than three days per month from June to September.

The coastline is fringed by high mountain ranges and there is extensive woodland. The heart of the Costa del Sol, which has a population of 1.3 million, is the province of Malaga, between Estepona and Nerja. This area is considerably built up and includes Marbella, Fuengirola and Torremolinos. The least developed area is the far western side, which still has large stretches of countryside.

The Costa del Sol is ideal for sports enthusiasts, especially golfers. It is often called the 'Costa del Golf', as there are over 50 golf courses. Robert Kilroy-Silk, Kevin Keegan and Terry Venables all have homes here

Far quieter than the Costa del Sol and, in contrast, hardly touched, is the coast in the far southwest of Andalucia, the **Costa de la Luz** (Coast of Light), which stretches from windsurf capital Tarifa to the border with Portugal. Here you'll find beaches fringed with pines and eucalyptus groves, sleepy villages and wildlife parks like the Coto de Donana, protected national parkland from Tarifa to Conil. The coast is famous for its magnificent sand dunes and windswept marshes. Property is significantly cheaper than on the Costa del Sol and, in character, the region is like Marbella was three decades ago, before the lager louts and fish and chip shops appeared. It has a pleasant climate. although there are strong winds much of the year.

An up-and-coming hotspot here is Chiclana, a seaside town busy with tourists in July and August yet quieter at other times. It has good beaches and lots of restaurants and bars. A three- or four-bedroom villa here near the beach and with a pool costs around £140,000 to £200,000.

The **Costa Blanca** has a population of about 750,000 and extends 100km/63 miles along the east coast, principally in Alicante province. More rural northern Costa Blanca, which boasts a dramatic backdrop of high mountains, is renowned for its unspoilt beauty, and prices are substantially higher than in the south generally. Prices in the select areas have doubled between 2001 and 2004. More and more British buyers have in recent years been favouring the Costa Blanca over the more over-developed Costa del Sol. The Costa Blanca boasts 80 blue flag beaches as well as 12 marinas.

The coast features cliffs and sandy coves while inland there are pretty villages including Orbeta, Orba and Tormos. There are numerous golf courses, although not as many as on the Costa del Sol.

While the temperature in the region is very similar to the Costa del Sol throughout the year, the rainfall is notably higher.

People are attracted to the **Costa Brava**, the wild coast between France and Barcelona, for the quality of life and striking beauty of the surroundings rather than the promise of constant hot weather. While summers are hot (with temperatures over the year almost as high as the Costa del Sol), winters can be bracing and rainfall is substantially higher. However, the climate is ideal for many sports, and facilities ranging from sailing to golf are numerous. Mountain walking and winter skiing are options.

The travel revolution is putting this area on the property map at long last, with the A7 motorway linking France with Barcelona and giving much easier access to historic towns like Girona. The Eurostar/TGV extension of services to Barcelona will make the region even more popular. Ryanair, easyJet, BA and Iberia all fly locally while P&O and Brittany Ferries sail from Portsmouth and Plymouth to Bilbao and Santander.

Catalonia enjoys strict building regulations and, therefore, is not as spoilt as many other areas of the country. Still, it has its fair share of places to avoid, such as the package tour resorts of Estartit at the northern and Lloret de Mar at the southern end of the Costa; Sa Tuna near the medieval hilltop village of Begur, on the other hand, is delightful.

Buying a property on the cooler **northern coast**, known as 'Green Spain', within comfortable distance of the northern Spanish ports of Santander and Bilbao is becoming an increasingly popular option. The **Costa Dorada** is favoured by the Spanish and boasts fine sandy beaches with forested mountains and valleys in the interior. The coast has well-developed resorts but also tiny villages and ports. Apartments, semi-detached and terraced properties are plentiful, but detached houses rarer and, therefore, more pricey.

Their geographical position, and proximity to Africa, gives the volcanic **Canary Islands** a fabulous climate, with a dry heat that is ideal for a number of health conditions. For winter sun you can't beat the Canary Islands. Here you can swim in an outdoor pool in winter (although sea bathing in mid-winter can be only for the hardiest) and wear shirt sleeves in the evening without having to endure a long flight. Even so, the Canaries get their fair share of windy, overcast periods. Apart from windsurfing there isn't a great deal to do.

The islands include Gran Canaria, La Gomera, Lanzarote, Fuerteventura, La Palma, Tenerife, Hierro and numerous other smaller isles.

The islands suffer from the effects of mass tourism, namely ugly apartment blocks, rowdy British pub-style bars and concrete shorelines, but also have some excellent beaches and many opportunities to get off the tourist track.

They offer plentiful apartment complexes with communal pools to choose from. Tenerife and Gran Canaria have the most Spanish flavour and the quieter, more upmarket islands include La Gomera and Lanzarote. Fuerteventura has dramatic mountains, moonscapes and pretty inland villages; it is one of the cheaper, quieter islands.

The **Costa de Almeria**, which is sandwiched between the Costa del Sol and Costa Calida, boasts almost as high annual temperatures as the Costa del Sol

The geography of Britspain

According to Spain's 2001 census, UK citizens form the third-largest foreign community, after Moroccans and Ecuadorians, with 80,183 officially registered British residents. The true figure is probably a great deal higher.

The geography of new British settlement in Spain doesn't hold many surprises: the familiar holiday *costas* – above all the Costa del Sol and Costa Blanca – are the most popular, followed by the major cities, Barcelona and Madrid.

The British have a reputation for being more conservative than other nationalities, notably Germans, in seeking out new areas, such as the Atlantic regions, or the Valencia coast north of the Costa Blanca. The autonomous regions with the most UK residents, from the same 2001 census, are as follows:

Andalucía (includes Costa del Sol, Costa Tropical, Costa de la Luz)	30,664
Valencia (includes Costa Blanca)	27,638
Canaries	11,690
Balearics	7,944
Catalonia (includes Barcelona)	6,681
Madrid	4,856

and less rainfall. It is characterised by busy tourist resorts contrasting with beautiful, unspoilt land. Far less densely populated than the most well-known *costas*, the area contains the national park of Cabo de Gata, a very beautiful marine reserve.

Along the southeast coast, slightly to the north of the Costa del Almeria, lies the cheaper, less developed **Costa Calida**, the coast of Murcia, with the Mar Menor and La Manga resort, which is popular with the Spanish but still relatively untouched by Brits. It has an even climate throughout the year and is flat rather than mountainous and, therefore, ideal for families with young children and those thinking of retiring. Prices are steadily rising and the best properties have seen a threefold increase in prices since 1999.

It's not for people wanting English-style pubs but if you are more adventurous it could be for you. The expansion of Murcia airport and upgraded motorway network mean access is fast improving. Alicante and San Javier airports are other options.

The wine regions of southern **inland Catalonia**, south of Barcelona, have largely been overlooked by British buyers (as well as the Barcelonese) searching for a holiday home. As ever, they prefer colonising the coast. Access here is via Barcelona airport or the airport at the small town of Reus on the Costa Dorada. The Eurostar/TGV train services and motorways are also improving access. Dubbed by some as 'the new Provence', it has village and town houses, and farmhouses in need of restoration in many villages and towns, ranging from under £60,000 in a village such as Albarca or market towns like Villafranca de Penedes, to over £200,000 in a rustic mountain village like Siurana, 20 miles inland from Reus airport. The area has had comparatively little real development, even on the coast.

Turn your back on the sea and head for the hills and you find the real, undeveloped **rural Andalucía**, with plunging property prices to boot. Access is good, with regular Ryanair and British Airways flights to Jerez and Monarch flights to neighbouring Gibraltar.

Inland, just over an hour's drive down twisting roads from the overdeveloped Costa del Sol, the region around the town of Ronda can be a very welcome escape to tranquillity and tradition. A Moorish stronghold for seven centuries, Ronda attracts the bohemian set, such as writers and artists. Properties are scarce, and you could expect to pay £70,000 or so for a comfortable cottage in a village around here, maybe £375,000 for a new four-bed home with a swimming pool.

Antequera is one of a series of quaint red-roofed and white-walled villages, and boasts Baroque churches, a bullring, streets shaded by almond and orange trees and wide marble pavements. Nearby are extensive olive groves as well as the impressive lake of Iznajar. Around here you're going to find old houses ripe for renovation and very little new development. In another nearby village, for example, terraced houses with courtyard gardens go for around £50,000 to £60,000. Isolated properties located in the countryside in rural areas like these often lack utilities – electricity and telephone may not be available, and water only obtainable from a well. English is seldom spoken in such areas.

If you prefer a city apartment, **Barcelona** is Spain's most popular city for foreign buyers, due to its exquisite waterside setting. Interest has also boomed in vibrant **Madrid**. **Valencia**, until now almost always overlooked, will increasingly be considered, especially considering its substantially lower property prices. Indeed it is tipped by analysts as being the next Iberian hot spot, helped by its hosting the 2007 America's Cup yacht race and by the airport's being extended. However, see 'Legal restrictions', below.

Property prices: Most property bought by foreigners is newly built, which tends to be considerably higher in price than period options; most properties under £50,000 tend to be apartments. Even so, little stone cottages in unspoilt inland villages can still be picked up for under £35,000 or so all around the country.

The Costa del Sol has a wide price range, with four-bedroom villas with pools averaging £425,000 and two-bed apartments costing on average £200,000. Inland prices are around 20 per cent lower.

Prices on the Costa Blanca to the north are generally 20 per cent cheaper than the Costa del Sol.

Prices on the Costa Calida and Costa de Almeira are on average almost half those of the Costa del Sol. A two-bedroom apartment on the Costa del Almeira currently averages £110,000, while a four-bed villa is commonly around £225,000.

A three-bed apartment with sea view in a touristy area, such as the coastal town of Rosas on the Costa Brava, is around £250,000 and more than double that around a desirable village like Begur or Llafranc.

A large proportion of new-build homes sell off plan (i.e. before they are built), and in a number of areas there is seldom enough resale property to satisfy the demand.

It is not unusual for properties on the islands to be 25 per cent more than on the Costa del Sol. Good property has become expensive in Menorca, and has more than doubled in the last five years. A good house will typically cost between £800,000 and £1m; therefore the days of selling an average house in the UK to fund an above-average home in the Balearics and still have half your capital left are long gone.

Interest in buying property in Spanish cities has soared recently, and in 2003 prices rose by 20 per cent in Madrid and Barcelona, even to the extent of catching up with Paris in some neighbourhoods – an unthinkable notion a few years ago. Expect to pay around £200,000 to £250,000 for a two- or three-bed flat in the Gracia *barrio* (or district) of Barcelona, popular with artists and intellectuals and around half a mile north of the central Plaça de Catalunya. A one-bed apartment on the harbour front would be in the same ballpark. Barcelona is a popular base for conferences, which means that there is a healthy demand from business people to rent out apartments.

In Madrid, prices are similar to Barcelona and a centrally based two-bedroom apartment is in the region of £400,000. For cheaper Spanish city living (around 30 per cent lower than Madrid and Barcelona) opt for Valencia, which is set to rise considerably in popularity imminently.

Legal restrictions: If you spend less than 183 days a year in Spain you are usually classed a non-resident and will be required to nominate a fiscal representative (a person the tax authorities can correspond with in Spain), pay local rates, make a Spanish income tax declaration, pay car tax and insurance if you have a car in Spain, make a declaration of your capital assets in Spain and possibly pay a small percentage of wealth tax on them, as well as paying regular utilities bills.

Rules governing land can sometimes be a minefield and make it all the more vital for buyers to engage the services of an experienced, English-speaking lawyer. In Valencia province, for example, which includes the Costa Blanca, there is a possibility that land attached to some properties could later either be compulsorily purchased for development and/or the owner liable to pay a large contribution towards development costs. Agents and developers are not legally required to mention this.

Spain has a law of subrogation, where debts connected with a property, such as mortgages, rates, community charges and local taxes, remain with the property and are the responsibility of the buyer, whether the buyer incurred the debt or not. Therefore, it is very important that your legal adviser clarifies whether there are any outstanding debts on the property.

Finance

Currency and exchange rate: Euro (€); £1 = €1.50

Local mortgages: Spanish mortgages require full proof of income and outgoings and do not take into account any potential income from lettings. A deposit of 25 per cent of the purchase price is generally the minimum required, and most mortgages are on a repayment basis.

The buying process: Buying property in Spain can have its problems and therefore it is wise to be aware as possible of the buying process.

As well as using an estate agent (*inmobiliaria*), it is worth checking out locations as many Spaniards sell privately to avoid paying commission. Notice for sale (*se vende*) signs; in rural areas properties may be advertised in bars.

Spanish property transactions are overseen by a notary (*notario*) appointed by the government. This public official is paid by the purchaser and/or vendor. He/she is not required to verify clauses or safeguard against fraud and therefore is no substitute for independent legal advice.

When you have found the property you wish to buy, as property laws vary considerably in Spain it is important to engage an English-speaking lawyer specialising in overseas legal services.

Few people take as much professional advice as they should when buying in Spain and it is common for buyers to sign documents casually and hand over money before realising that there is no title to the property, it has not been built yet, or it was built without planning permission. Appropriately experienced legal firms can carry out the property acquisition, which involves vetting the contract, providing translations and carrying out local enquiries and searches. These include checking that the seller has legal title to the property and that there are no unpaid debts accrued against the property, ascertaining whether the local authority has imposed any building restrictions and checking the boundaries of the surrounding land.

Some specialist firms can also advise about related matters such as commissioning a survey, raising finance, timeshare sales, emigration and retirement, setting up in business in Spain, dealing with taxation, and dealing with foreign inheritance laws.

Generally, when you have selected a property, a private sale and purchase contract, completely binding on both parties, is drawn up by the estate agent or your lawyer. If the contract, the *contrato privado de compraventa*, is drawn up by the estate agent your lawyer should vet the contract before signing. This contract typically states details of the purchaser and vendor, amount of deposit (usually 10 per cent of the agreed sale price), completion date, payment method, extras the buyer has agreed to buy and any other conditions. The contract fixes the price, eliminating gazumping, and states the date of the final payment and signing of the public deeds to the property.

The deposit can only be refunded under certain strict conditions and therefore it is important to be aware of what these are.

If you are offered a deal where the property is officially sold at an artificially low price with the balance as 'cash under the table' to avoid costs, avoid it. Apart from being illegal, such deals can create inflated capital gains tax problems if you later sell the property, as the gain appears to be larger on paper than it is in reality.

Before signing you should be aware of added expenses such as the community fees and annual rates payable, as these can be quite high. You need to see a copy of the deeds, to check that the people claiming to be the owners are those named on them. You need to see the *nota simple*, a land registry document stating who owns the property and indicating whether an outstanding mortgage (which would be passed on to you) or other encumbrance affects the property.

If the property is new or was built in the last few years, you require documents from the local town hall proving that a building licence was obtained and, if the property has already been lived in, a licence of first occupation.

If you are buying 'off-plan', that is, before the building has been built, payments are normally made in agreed stages. Ensure that the contract allows you to retain a final payment for six or 12 months after completion of building works so that any faults that crop up can be rectified.

Rural properties such as an old village cottage or a farm may have been handed down from generation to generation, and therefore deeds may not be in existence. This situation will require specialised legal help and you will probably have to draw up a topographical plan noting such things as boundary lines, rights of way and water rights. Obtaining title deeds for such a property can take considerable time.

The Spanish conveyancing process involves numerous other points that a good legal representative should be able to take you through, such as ensuring that transfer of utilities charges, local taxes and other expenses relating to the property are made on the day of the sale, so that you are not liable for any unpaid previous ones.

The balance of the purchase price and any outstanding fees are payable when the purchaser and vendor sign the definitive contract, which is the same as the title deeds of the property (*escritura de compaventa*) drawn up by the notary. This details all ownership history, which is important as, especially in rural areas, people often hand down property from generation to generation without legal proof of ownership.

All parties involved should attend or otherwise arrange to have someone with power of attorney attend in their absence.

Rural properties seldom have a straightforward *escritura* and for this reason it is imperative that your lawyer check every aspect of the title deeds before you commit yourself. It is common for the property size and boundaries to change over the years with no documentation. Your legal representative should indicate whether there are any possible adverse clauses in the deeds.

After signing, the notary lodges the deeds with the land registry to register the change in title, as in Spain a property's title deeds are assigned after the contract has been sealed rather than before, as in the UK. This can result in an extra three- or four-month wait before the sale can be completed. Land registry fees are then due.

The notary should provide a copy of the deeds for your lawyer to complete other legal formalities. The notary's fees are due on completion.

Costs of buying: Total costs of buying average at least 10 per cent of the purchase price of the property. Transfer tax (*impuesto de transmisiones patrimoniales*) varies from region to region and in Andalucia is 7 per cent of the sale price of the property. There are registration fees of 0.5 per cent, the notary's fee and the lawyer's fee. Other costs include a possible surveying fee, and mortgage valuation. The estate agent's fee, typically between 5 and 10 per cent, but sometimes as much as 15 per cent, is often included in the purchase price. The buyer is also usually obliged by Spanish law to pay 5 per cent of the value of the property to the tax office on account of the seller's potential tax liabilities.

Is property a good investment? Prices in Spain have been rising rapidly in recent years overall, at a rate of 15 per cent in 2002 and 2003. Although slowing in 2004, the prices along the coast will continue to grow steadily, helped by the large increase in numbers of northern Europeans retiring to Spain.

In the south especially, the large number of sunny days per year allows a long season for potential holiday lets on the coast, although a swimming pool is almost always needed to secure healthy rentals. Renting out properties inland is significantly more difficult unless you have an exceptional property.

Unlike in France, where holidaymakers generally prefer to rent out older properties with character, in Spain the trend is for new properties with all mod cons such as satellite TV and a video.

For those wishing to own a property in Spain through an offshore company to avoid local taxes and inheritance laws, the Inland Revenue in the UK has, in

2004, given notice that homes owned through a company structure may be taxed as a benefit in kind. The charge would be based on an assumed value for the property and therefore the more it is thought to be worth, the higher the amount you will pay. The Inland Revenue would assume a rateable value for the first £75,000 and charge what it calls the interest on beneficial loans on any excess amount. The rate is currently 5 per cent.

Selling: Capital gains tax (*impuesto sobre incremento de patrimonio*) is at 18 per cent for residents and 35 per cent for non-residents, but there are various exemptions.

Inheritance tax: Spanish succession tax (also called gift tax) is payable if the recipient of the gift or the heir of an estate resides in Spain, or if the asset being passed on the event of death or gifted is a property in Spain.

The tax is governed by the autonomous communities, or regions, and these are moving towards abolishing succession tax or offering tax relief between spouses, direct blood descendants and adopted children. As the tax position is currently changing, check with a qualified Spanish tax adviser.

Living in Spain

Overall Spain enjoys a superb climate (the climate on the Costa Blanca is considered by the World Health Organisation to be among the healthiest in the world), political stability, a high standard of living yet lower cost of living than much of Europe, as well as a low crime rate and good standard of health care.

Once you have financial dealings in Spain, whether as a resident or non-resident, you are required to have a fiscal number known as a *número de identificaión de entranjero*. Without this you cannot register the deeds of a property, pay or claim back tax, open a bank account or take out insurance, among other things. Non-resident property owners are required to appoint a fiscal representative to deal with their tax dealings.

Families moving to Spain and wanting their children to be schooled there can enrol in a free state school by applying to the provincial governor's office to validate the child's schooling to date. Proof of residency in Spain, passport and Spanish bank account details are required. Most private schools teach in Spanish, like the state ones, but some offer English tuition at primary level. For older children consider an international school, which offers qualifications recognised by universities and works towards the International Baccalaureate.

If you remain in Spain for more than 183 days per year you become a tax resident of Spain and liable for Spanish taxation on worldwide income and investments. Non-resident property owners are liable for income tax if the property is rented out. Income tax is on a sliding scale of up to 43 per cent although personal allowances are more generous than in the UK. There are also local taxes, which vary from region to region.

Property tax (*impuesto sobre bienes inmuebles*) generally varies from 0.3 to 1.7 per cent and is based on the value of a property as assessed by the local authority. The tax is linked to other taxes including income and inheritance tax.

The Spanish health service suffers from waiting lists, underfunding, lack of choice and few English-speaking doctors. However, free public health care is available to employees and dependants paying Spanish social security, retired people with residency rights and who have pensions from countries (including Britain, but not the USA or other non-EU countries) which have reciprocal arrangements with Spain, as well as EU citizens visiting the country.

At 65 you receive two sizeable benefits of retired residency: tax breaks and free private medical care. Spain's health care system is 80 per cent private and therefore there is proper funding as long as you have an E111 form, which ensures the British National Health Service pays your medical bills.

To forecast your pension income and state entitlement if you were to retire in Spain, the DSS in the UK can provide a BR19 form so that you will receive an accurate projection.

There are numerous property developments specifically aimed at the retired, which may have medical clinics, nursing care and shopping facilities within the complex.

Residence permits are a formality for EU nationals, although non-working residents are required to have income sufficient to support themselves in the country. To work in the country, non-EU nationals are required to obtain a work permit, which can be difficult to obtain. Visitors may remain in the country for six months each year without a residence permit.

Further information

- **Spain: t** (00 34)
- **Spanish Tourist Office**, 22–3 Manchester Square, London W1U 3PX, UK; t (020) 7486 8077; **www.tourspain.es.**
- **Spanish Embassy**, 39 Chesham Place, London SW1X 8SB, UK, t (020) 7235 5555; **www.cec-spain.org.uk.**
- **Spanish Embassy**, 2375 Pennyslvania Avenue, NW, Washington, DC 20008, USA, t (202) 452 0100; **www.spainemb.org.**
- **Spanish Consulate General**, 20 Draycott Place, London SW3 2RZ, UK, t (020) 7589 8989.
- **24-hour visa information service, t** 0900 160 0123.
- **Foundation Institute of Foreign Property Owners**, Apartado 418, 03590 Altea, Alicante, Spain, t 96 584 2312; **www.fipe.org.**

• **www.aboutspain.net, www.red2000.com, www.escapetospain.co.uk,
www.idealspain.com, www.tuspain.com, www.typicallyspanish.com,
www.spainexpat.com, www.britishexpat.com, www.directmoving.com**:
advice about Spain, Spanish property, living in Spain and associated
matters.

Finance

• **Banco Halifax Hispania** (UK), **t** (01422) 333868; **www.halifax.es.**
• **Norwich and Peterborough Spanish Home Loans** (UK), **t** (01733) 372006;
www.norwichandpeterborough.co.uk.
• **Barclays Bank Spain** (Spain), **t** 913 36 1 610; **www.barclays.es.**
• **Currencies Direct** (Spain), **t** 965 707 971.

Estate agents

General

• **European Villa Solutions** (UK), **t** (01223) 514241; **www.europeanvs.com.**
• **Mercers** (UK), **t** (01491) 574807; **www.spanishproperty.co.uk.**
• **Property Finder** (UK), **t** (01908) 218753; **www.thepropertyfinder.com.**
• **Catalan Country Life, t** 93 467 1523; **www.catalancountrylife.com.**
• **Your House in Spain** (Spain), **t** 933 063 541; **www.yhis.com.**
• **www.themovechannel.com**: lists websites selling property in Spain.

Catalonia

• **World Class Homes** (UK), **t** 0800 731 4713; **www.worldclasshomes.co.uk.**

Costa Blanca

All agents are based in the UK.

• **Atlas International, t** 0800 531 6500; **www.atlasinternational.com.**
• **Ocean Estates, t** 0800 328 0444; **www.oceanestates.com.**
• **QSD, t** 0800 783 1616; **www.qsdgroup.com.**
• **Ultra Villas, t** (01242) 221500; **www.ultravillas.co.uk.**

Coastal Andalucia

• **Properties Abroad** (UK), **t** (020) 8441 2078; **www.propertiesabroad.com.**

Rural Andalucia

• **The Property Finders** (UK), **t** (01908) 218753;
www.thepropertyfinders.com.

- **Travellers Way** (UK), **t** (01527) 559 000.
- **Flamencoshop** (Spain), **t** 627 989 543; **www.flamencoshop.com**.
- **Intereality** (Spain), **t** 952 706 380; **www.intereality.es**.
- **La Serrania** (Spain), **t** 952 877 286.

Balearic Islands

- **Escape2balerics.com** (UK), **t** (0161) 351 2160; **www.escape2balerics.co.uk**.
- **Kuhn and Partner** (Spain), **t** 9712 28 20; **www.kuhn-partner.com**.
- **Prestige Properties** (Spain), **t** 971 190 455; **www.ibizaprestige.com**.

Canary Islands

- **Main's Amis Estates** (UK), **t** (020) 8311 1110; **www.mainsamisestates.co.uk**.
- **www.amazingpropertyservices.com** (Spain), **t** 922 717 166.
- **Engels and Volkers** (UK), **t** (020) 7590 3170; **www.engelvolkers.com**.

Madrid, Barcelona and Valencia

- **Lonbar** (UK), **t** (0118) 951 9811; **www.lonbar.com**.
- **Proincasa** (UK), **t** (020) 7079 1412; **www.proincasaresidential.com**.
- **Ambassador** (Spain), **t** 915 775 642.
- **John Taylor** (Spain), **t** 932 413 082; **www.johntaylorspain.com**.
- **Knight Frank** (Spain), **t** 917 880 700; **www.knightfrank.co.uk**.
- **Promora** (Spain), **t** 916 504 242; **www.promora.com**.

Ronda

- **Hamptons International** (UK), **t** (020) 7589 8844; **www.hamptonsinternational.co.uk**.

Rural Spain

- **Greenbox Properties** (UK), **t** (01670) 528258; **www.greenbox.co.uk**. Cottages in rural Andalucia and Murcia from £20,000.
- **Real Spain** (UK), **t** 0871 871 6755; **www.real-spain.net**. Resale and period property both on the coast and inland.
- **Inmobiliaria Almanzora** (Spain), **t** 950 120 406; **www.inmobiliaria.com**. A selection of rustic farmhouses and fincas in the Almanzora Valley from £20,000.
- **Siroco Estates** (UK), **t** (01253) 294848/402188; **www.sirocoestates.com**. Country properties half an hour's drive from the coast.

Schools for English-speaking pupils

• **National Association of British Schools in Spain**, Avenida Ciudad de Barcelona 110, Escalera 3-5 D, 28007, Madrid; **www.nabss.org**. For general details about schooling.

• **International College Spain**, Vereda Norte 3, La Moraleja, 28109 Alcobendas, Madrid, **t** 94 6 50 2 398; **www.icsmadrid.com**. Co-educational, 4–18 years.

• **American High School of Bilbao**, Soparda Bidea 10, 48640 Berango, Vizcaya, **t** 946 680 861; **www.sarenet.es/asb/**. Co-educational, 3–16 years.

• **American School of Las Palmas**, Apartado 15, Tarifa Alta, Las Palmas, **t** 928 430 023; **www.aslp.org**. Co-educational, 4–18 years.

• **English International College**, Urbanizacion Ricmar, CN 340, Marbella, 29600 Malaga, **t** 952 831 058.

• **English School Los Olivos**, Avenida Pino Panera, 46110 Godella, Valencia; **t** 963 639 938; **www.school-losolivos.com**. Co-educational, 4–12 years.

• **Kensington School**, Carre del Cavallers 31–33, 08034 Barcelona, **t** 932 035 457. Co-educational 4–18 years.

• **Lady Elizabeth School**, Apartado de Correos 233, 03730 Javea, Alicante, **t** 965 731 960; **www.theladyelizabethschool.com**. Co-educational, 4–18 years.

• **Sunny View School**, Apartado 175, Cerro del Toril, Torremolinos, Malaga; **t** 952 383 164; **www.nabss.org/sunny.htm**. Co-educational, 5–18 years.

Switzerland

Why buy here?

Pros: Switzerland, bordered by France, Germany, Italy, Austria and Liechtenstein, is at the crossroads of Europe. It boasts economic stability, almost clinical cleanliness, affluence, neutrality, low taxes and a healthy climate. Not only is Switzerland renowned for its skiing, with the Alps reaching altitudes of over 4,000m/13,000ft, but its breathtaking scenery is also a wonderful backdrop for hot summers. As well as its stunning mountains, it has crystal-clear lakes, vibrant cities and charming little villages.

Many people assume that its property is only for the super-rich, yet there is great opportunity to buy at an affordable price. Switzerland's ultra-efficiency, with such things as trains running on time, is a revelation to many British people used to 'putting up'.

Cons: There are a number of different restrictions concerning property ownership, *see* opposite.

Both the cost of living and of property are high in Switzerland. The super-efficiency and general neatness might be too much for some. Be sure to view properties not only when the snow has fallen, but when the snow has melted too. Snow can cover a multitude of sins, such as ugly roofs and rubbish tips.

Access: There are plenty of flights to Swiss cities from many British airports and carriers include Swissair, British Airways and easyJet.

Property

Types: Chalets and chalet apartments in resort areas are of principal interest to foreign buyers, and, to a lesser extent, apartments in the main cities such as Zurich, Berne and Geneva.

Where to buy: A number of cantons restrict foreign property ownership and this, combined with the comparatively high price of property and a lack of properties for sale, means that there is not a great deal of choice compared with neighbouring countries.

The canton of Bernese Oberland offers rustic wooden chalets among pretty hills, while Switzerland's only Italian-speaking canton, Ticino, offers lakeside villas and a hotter climate. Villas in the western canton of Vaud is near enough for visits to Geneva. Other areas popular with foreign buyers include Montreux and Châteaux d'Oex in the canton of Vaud, Klosters in Canton des Grisons and Gstaad in the Bernese Oberland.

Internationally famous Verbier is popular, boasting more than 600km of pistes. Ever popular with Britons, there are plenty of pubs, clubs, restaurants, excellent shops and a golf course.

Crans-Montana is a chic and elegant resort uniquely situated on a south-facing plateau overlooking the Rhône Valley. It enjoys an unusually sheltered climate and has two good golf courses, four lakes, hotels, restaurants and night-clubs. Nearby, with more family atmosphere, is Anzère, situated just above Sion, which has a relatively high proportion of modern chalet-style apartment complexes.

Property prices: Prices have been rising steadily, at around 12 to 16 per cent in 2003 alone. The pretty, sleepy little town of Châteaux d'Oex has one-bed apartments starting at £115,000. In the swish, cosmopolitan town of Montreux a one-bedroom apartment would typically set you back £150,000 or more, with £200,000 the starting price for two bedrooms. In Villars you would typically pay about 25 per cent more. A five-bed chalet in Chailly, just north of Montreux, would be around £300,000.

At Verbier, studios start at under £50,000, one-bed apartments from about £100,000, two bedrooms from £145,000 and three beds from about £180,000.

Legal restrictions: It is difficult to buy homes outside tourist resorts and in some German-speaking areas. Not all of the country's cantons allow foreigners to buy property, although recent years have seen restrictions relax slightly. Those cantons that do allow sales may have special conditions, such as quota systems, designated regions that foreigners can buy in, restrictions on the type of property that can be bought or on whom a vendor can sell to.

Foreign owners are required to occupy a Swiss property for at least three weeks per year. Letting can be for a maximum of 11 months per year.

Except for certain reasons such as family illness or death, properties cannot be sold for two years after the purchase date, a ruling introduced in an attempt to discourage property speculation.

Finance

Currency and exchange rate: Swiss franc; £1 = Sfr 2.31

Local mortgages: These tend to enjoy lower rates than those in the UK, although there is significantly less choice of mortgage types.

The buying process: Before buying, permission must be obtained from the local canton and the government, which takes anything from two months to three years. Sellers usually do not accept offers below the asking price. An official notary is appointed by the selling agent to act for both buyer and seller, who sign a legally binding contract for the sale, written in French, German or Italian, depending on where the sale is taking place in the country. At the same time the buyer pays a 10 per cent deposit, which is forfeited if the buyer subsequently pulls out. On completion the title deed is registered by both the local land registry and the central land registry situated in Berne.

Costs of buying: The notary and land registry fees and transfer tax usually amount to around 5 per cent of the purchase price of the property.

Is property a good investment? In the long term, property represents a good investment, especially as it is generally in short supply, but various restrictions make it difficult to speculate successfully in the short term.

Selling: Capital gains tax, which is usually only applicable to profits made from property, varies from canton to canton and is dependent on the amount gained and length of ownership.

Inheritance tax: Rates of inheritance tax vary from canton to canton, and it is not levied by Schwyz canton.

Living in Switzerland

Switzerland is split into 26 largely autonomous cantons that have diverse culture, geography and climates. Indeed, its weather conditions are probably Europe's most varied in such a small area. North of the Alps (which extend from west to east) there is a continental climate with hot summers and cold winters, while the south has a Mediterranean climate of hot summers and mild winters.

Politically, Switzerland is very stable. The standard of living is high, yet the cost of living is not as high as people assume and is lower than 20 years ago. German, French and Italian are the official languages, although English is widely spoken.

The crime rate in Switzerland is very low and health care facilities are of a very high standard, although very expensive and, therefore, private health insurance is necessary.

Taxation rates vary in each of the 26 cantons in the country, and non-residents are required to pay Swiss income tax on any income earned in the country. Peculiarly, members of the Catholic, Old Catholic (Protestant) and Reformed churches are required to pay a variable church tax.

Residence permits, except for short-term employment, are difficult to obtain, although it helps if you have a job that is in demand, are over 60 and/or have wealth. Those wishing to retire in Switzerland are required to prove that they have sufficient funds to support themselves and must sign a declaration stating that they will not seek paid employment. Non-residents can spend six months per year in the country for a maximum of three months each time.

Bear in mind that if you choose a detached home in a ski resort, heavy snowfall may greatly impede access, winters can be hard and long, and you may require someone to visit your property regularly to clear the snow and check the central heating. Uncleared snow can result, once the temperature has risen and it re-freezes, in a glacier around the property.

Further information

- **Switzerland: t** (00 41)
- **Swiss Embassy,** 16–18 Montagu Place, London W1H 2BQ, UK, **t** (020) 7723 0701; **www.swissembassy.org.uk.**
- **Swiss Embassy,** 2900 Cathedral Avenue, NW, Washington, DC 20008, USA; **t** (202) 745 7900; **www.swissemb.org.**
- **Switzerland Tourism,** Bellariastr 38, 8027 Zurich, Switzerland, **t** 1 288 1111.
- **British Resident's Association of Switzerland,** Chemin de Chenalettaz 105, 1807 Bloney, Switzerland, **t** 21 943 1788.
- **American Citizens Abroad,** 5 Rue Liotard, 1202 Geneva, Switzerland, **t** 22 340 0233; **www.aca.ch.**

- **www.myswitzerland.com**: tourist information about Switzerland.

Estate agents

All are in the UK.

- **Alpine Apartments Agency, t** (01544) 388234;
www.alpineapartmentsagency.co.uk.
- **Engel and Voelkers, t** (020) 7590 3170; **www.engelvoelkers.ch.**
- **Investors in Property, t** (020) 8905 5511; **www.investorsinproperty.com.**
- **Overseas Homesearch, t** 0870 240 3258;
www.overseashomesearch.co.uk.
- **Sotheby's, t** (020) 7598 1600; **www.sothebysrealty.com.**
- **Villas Abroad, t** (020) 8941 4499.

Schools for English-speaking pupils

- **British School of Berne**, Hintere Dorfgasse 20, 3073 Gumligen, Berne,
t 31 952 7555; **www.geocities.com/britishschool.ch.** Small co-educatioanl
school with pupils aged 3–12.
- **College du Leman**, 74 Route de Sauverny, 1290 Versoux, Geneva.
Co-educational, 8–18 years.
- **Geneva English School**, 36 route de Malagny, 1294 Genthod, Geneva,
t 22 755 1855; **www.geneva-english-school.ch.** Co-educational, 4–12 years.
- **International School of Berne**, Mattenstrasse 3, 3073 Gumlegen bei
Berne, **t** 319 51 2358; **www.isberne.com.** Co-educational, 5–18 years.

Turkey

Why buy here?

Pros: Although Turkey has a long way to go before it could be considered a first
choice as a holiday home location, the surge in popularity in recent years by
tourists for its west coast has caused increasing interest.

Fantastic weather coupled with a very low cost of living, the friendliest of
people and a truly exotic culture as Europe merges with Asia (95 per cent of the
country is in Asia) make Turkey a great choice for buying. Most of the country is
unspoilt and it enjoys a rich, fascinating history and culture.

Cons: Turkey's borders, established only in 1923, are with Iraq, Iran, Syria, Georgia,
Armenia, Greece and Bulgaria – it is hardly the most stable region in the world.

Still, the areas popular with the vast majority of buyers, the Mediterranean and Aegean coasts, are well away from trouble spots in the Middle East.

There are internal problems caused by Islamic militants, and its Kurdish population demanding their own state; it has also had a poor record of democracy and human rights, as well as a long-standing poor relationship with Greece. Yet its stability seems to be improving and in recent years real steps have been taken to resolve the Cyprus problem.

There is also a history of geographical instability (in the form of a tendency for earthquakes), although to put things in perspective, Italy suffers more of these. The Turkish lira has historically also been very unstable and so the exchange rate can vary greatly, which can play havoc with proposed budgets when purchasing.

The property market is unregulated and buyers need to beware of unscrupulous operators who tend to populate the more popular touristic centres.

Access: There is a good choice of scheduled flights to Istanbul. Turkish Airlines has year-round flights from the UK via Istanbul to Bodrum, Izmir and Dalaman, taking around six hours. Cheaper charter flights are generally available from May to September, and there is more choice, such as direct flights from London to Dalaman, taking around four hours.

Property

Types: Properties popular with foreign buyers are generally in new developments with purpose-built holiday facilities such as swimming pools, tennis courts, children's play areas and other sport and leisure features.

Where to buy: Most of the properties popular with foreign buyers are on the Aegean and Mediterranean coasts, not least because there is good infrastructure, many facilities for holidaymakers, a great stretch of coastline and average temperatures of around 28°C/82°F in July and August. The most popular areas are around Fethiye, Bodrum, Izmir, Kalkan, Antalya, Belek and Kas. Some areas, such as Kalkan, enjoy strict conservation laws.

Property prices: These are relatively low, not least because the Turkish lira has been unstable and subject to devaluations. A three-bedroom villa in good condition near the sea at Marmaris would typically be around £90,000, while a one-bed apartment at Kalkan, an unspoilt town east of Marmaris, could be picked up for under £25,000. A spacious four-bedroom villa at Fethiye in southern Turkey on the Mediterranean coast would probably set you back about £120,000.

Legal restrictions: Non-Turkish buyers are required to gain permission from the Turkish government to buy property in Turkey. Nationals of certain countries that do not have reciprocity with Turkey are not permitted to buy property in the country. These countries do not include the UK, USA and most European countries. Property purchase in military areas or security zones and certain villages and towns or outside the boundaries of a municipality are not permitted. However, forming a company to purchase the property may get round this problem.

Finance

Currency and exchange rate: Turkish lira; £1 = 2,700,000 TL

Local mortgages: UK lenders do not, as yet, lend on Turkish property, so you would need to raise cash another way, such as remortgaging or selling a UK home. Turkish banks offer loans, but better terms are usually available abroad and the Turkish lira can be extremely volatile.

The buying process: Strict rules govern foreigners buying property in Turkey and therefore a bilingual lawyer familiar with Turkish conveyancing is essential. It is important that your lawyer explains Turkish inheritance laws as these vary considerably from British ones, which could have significant repercussions.

Accepted market values for properties in Turkey can be non-existent or vague and therefore a good degree of haggling may be necessary before you agree on a price. When vendor and purchaser have agreed the purchase price, they sign a preliminary contract with the vendor's estate agent and the buyer pays a deposit, typically of 10 to 25 per cent. This does not bind the vendor to sell and only incurred expenses can be claimed by the buyer if he pulls out of the deal. The buyer, on the other hand, loses his deposit should he subsequently not go ahead with buying.

The initial contract contains relevant details of the sale such as the completion date, conditional clauses and details about the property and buyer and seller. Conditional clauses should be included to cover you against the possibility of there being debts on the property, no being clear title or your failure to secure a loan on it.

To get around the problem of the vendor's not being bound to sell to you, you can obtain a *sati vaadi sozle mesi*, an undertaking to sell, from the vendor, prepared by a notary public at a cost of an extra 1.2% of the purchase price. This formal contract will include full details of the sale, vendor and purchaser and any conditions.

The purchaser instructs his/her lawyer to make the necessary checks and searches. The transaction is prepared by the land registrar and a contract for the sale is drawn up. This process can all take six months or so. When the sale is ready for completion the deeds are signed in the presence of the land registrar and a copy is given to the purchaser. Buying from another overseas owner is considerably quicker than buying from a Turkish national, as the necessary searches and checks will have already been made.

Costs of buying: Funds for purchasing a property must be imported from abroad, backed up by official proof. There is a property transfer tax of 1.5 per cent of the declared value of the property, which is generally lower than the purchase price. Notary fees are 0.8–1.5 per cent . Both vendor and purchaser pay 4.8 per cent of the declared value of the property in stamp duty.

As well as conveyancing costs, there is a registration fee for the contract of 0.54 per cent of the contract price. Both vendor and purchaser are required to pay estate agency fees of around 3 per cent. The buyer pays 3 per cent of the purchase price to the land registry, although sometimes both buyer and seller agree to split the cost.

Is property a good investment? More and more foreign buyers, a rapidly growing holiday-home market and the increasing possibility of Turkey's joining the EU means that property here could have good investment potential. There are no restrictions on holiday letting, and the letting season generally runs from April to October.

Selling: There is no capital gains tax as long as a property has been owned for at least five years.

Inheritance tax: This varies between 1 and 30 per cent.

Living in Turkey

Turkey is a huge country with a wide variety of climates and ways of life. Although much of eastern Turkey is very undeveloped and in parts winters can be harsh, the areas popular with buyers, around the Aegean, Mediterranean and Marmara coasts, have a Mediterranean climate with more than 300 days of sunshine each year and mild winters.

The majority of the population speak Turkish, with a minority (12%) speaking Kurdish and Arabic, and therefore outside the main cities and tourist areas, English and other major languages are rarely spoken, although many Turks speak German from working in Germany.

The cost of living is a third of that in the UK, although inflation tends to be very high. Income tax varies between 20 and 55 per cent. There is an annual property tax of 0.6 per cent of the estimated market value of land and 0.4 per cent of buildings, although there is a 25 per cent reduction on this on new properties for the first five years. Crime is low and medical facilities are adequate.

Further information

- **Turkey: t** (00 90)
- **Turkish Embassy,** 43 Belgrave Square, London SW1X 8PA, UK, **t** (020) 7393 0202; **www.turkishembassy-london.com.**

• **Turkish Embassy**, 1714 Massachusetts Avenue, NW, Washington, DC 20036, USA, **t** (202) 659 8200; **www.turkey.org/turkey.**

• **Turkish Economic Counsellor's Office**, 43 Belgrave Square, London SW1X 8PA, UK, **t** (020) 7235 2743. This can provide a list of Turkish estate agents.

• **Turkish Tourist Office**, 170–173 Piccadilly, London W1V 9DD, UK, **t** (020) 7629 7711; **www.gototurkey.co.uk.**

• **Turkish Information Office**, 821 United Nations Plaza, New York, NY 10017, USA, **t** (212) 687 2194.

• **Turkish Law Office**, 93 Westway, London W12 0PU, UK, **t** (020) 8740 5581.

• **Turkish Consulate General**, Rutland Lodge, Rutland Gardens, London SW7 1BW, UK, **t** (020) 7589 0949.

• **Turkish visa information** (UK), **t** 0906 834 7348.

Estate agents

• **Kalkan Estates** (UK), **t** 08707 282827; **www.kalkanestates.co.uk.** Specialising in properties around Kalkan and the Kas Peninsula.

• **World Class Homes** (UK), **t** (01582) 832001; **www.worldclasshomes.co.uk.**

• **Kent Property Services** (Turkey), **t** 252 412 2247; **www.kentestateagency. com.** Anglo-Turkish agency operating around Marmaris.

Schools for English-speaking pupils

• **MEF International School**, Ulus Mahallisi Dereboyu Cad, Ortakoy, Istanbul, 34340, **t** 212 287 6900; **www.international.mef.k12.tr.** Small co-educational school for 3–18 years.

• **Robert College of Istanbul**, Arnavutkoy PK1, 34345, Istanbul, **t** 212 359 2222; **www.robocol.k12.tr.** Co-educational, 14–20 years.

Turkish Republic of Northern Cyprus

Why buy here?

Pros: If you're looking to buy a dream holiday home abroad, the Turkish Republic of Northern Cyprus (TRNC) has it all. Possibly the last unspoilt corner of the Mediterranean, this sleepy idyll boasts almost year-round sun, deserted beaches, spectacular mountain ranges, stunning monuments, disarmingly friendly people, no high-rise developments, amazingly low living costs and beautiful historic buildings going for a song. Unsurprisingly, this tiny republic has been enjoying an unprecedented property boom in recent years, mostly fuelled by Brits. There are now more than 30 estate agencies operating in the Kyrenia area alone, where in 1999 there were fewer than five. Official records are scant but it is reckoned that more than 2,000 Britons now own a property on the northern section of the island.

Cons: There's a serious potential catch to owning property here, which could turn a property purchase into a legal and financial nightmare. Cyprus is a volatile island strictly separated into Greek and Turkish sectors after the Turkish military intervention in 1974 led to much bloodshed, disappearance and uprooting of both Turks and Greeks. Turkish Northern Cyprus is officially recognised in the world only by Turkey and is shunned by the UN and most other countries. Because the bitter division between the Greek and Turkish sides of Cyprus is still unresolved, there's a real question mark over the ownership of many of the properties for sale. Many Greek Cypriots whose homes were occupied by or lost to Turkish invading forces in 1974 want their homes back. To counter this, Turkey recently initiated a compensation system in the north in an attempt to prevent court cases over disputed ownership, although the move has elicited little response.

If such homes are not legally owned by their new British buyers, they could in theory be taken away at a moment's notice. Two test cases in the European Court of Human Rights have already found in favour of Greek owners of land in the north and against buyers who bought post-1974.

If you buy a property here, you receive Turkish, foreign or TRNC title deeds. The first two demonstrate Turkish Cypriot or foreign ownership pre-1974 yet properties with TRNC title deeds, which the majority of properties in Northern Cyprus have, were Greek Cypriot-owned prior to 1974. According to the Cyprus High Commission in London, 168,000 Greek Cypriots own property and land in the north and so the scale of the problem is large.

There is a real possibility that if the Cyprus problem is resolved in a way where the Greek who was turfed out of his home in 1974 becomes entitled to reclaim it, the owner with TRNC title deeds to his house will be engulfed in a bitter wrangle over ownership.

A solution to the Cyprus problem has been on the cards for years but faced many setbacks. As recently as 1998, there were serious fears of war because the Greek Cypriots planned to take delivery of anti-aircraft surface-to-air missiles to counter the huge Turkish army presence in the north of the island. Turkey retaliated by sending F-16 fighter jets.

However, at the time of going to press the island has a better chance of reunification than ever. The lead-up to the island's joining the EU in May 2004 saw an even more exhaustive flurry of discussions to solve the problem, including a UN blueprint, which would involve territory handovers by both sides and large population shifts. Yet a majority of Greek Cypriots rejected the reunification plan even though a majority of Turkish Cypriots voted for it. The willingness to solve the problem by the Turkish side impressed EU officials and there will probably now be noticeably more steps taken to end the economic isolation of the TRNC.

Access: There are several flights each week from London to Northern Cyprus's recently upgraded Ercan airport near Nicosia, but these are significantly more expensive than flights to southern Cyprus and are often booked up weeks in advance. Because Northern Cyprus is unrecognised internationally, flights have to land in Turkey first, and the flight from Turkey to the island is treated as a domestic flight. In practice, travel from London to Northern Cyprus takes almost twice as long as to southern Cyprus, around 7–8 hours.

Yet Northern Cyprus's eagerness to unify with the Greek side as proposed by the United Nations-backed plan in April 2004 is likely to be rewarded with an easing of international embargoes, and one of the first of these is likely to be the granting of direct flights, possibly by the end of 2004.

Property

Types: Small-scale modern holiday developments are increasingly cropping up here, and old properties abound, from glorified piles of rubble to sizeable historic houses.

Where to buy: The most popular village the British have been buying in is Karaman, which is rather like a twee, well-manicured English village, with well-manicured English villagers, rather than locals, in residence. With homes in Karaman increasingly difficult to come by, the new boom village that Brits are flocking to is Lapta, about nine miles west of Kyrenia/Girne.

Lapta, which pre-1974 was the Greek village of Lapithos, has cafes full of men lounging over a Turkish coffee and a game of backgammon, shops selling almost nothing and half-built homes begun before the economy crashed. Polly Peck's Asil Nadir has a pad here. Lapta has plenty of gorgeous old buildings. It recently had for sale a magnificent seven-bedroom villa for £40,000: but as this was Greek-owned pre-1974, there is potentially a huge question mark over ownership. In contrast, a couple of years ago a magnificent old house nearby that was of a similar size with a swimming pool and a small block of six modern apartments was for sale for 10 times that amount, principally because it was English-owned before 1974.

Anyone considering buying a property in Northern Cyprus, until the political problems are sorted out, should only buy a property where it can be proved that ownership was Turkish or foreign, i.e. not Greek, before 1974, unless they are prepared to pay possibly hefty compensation or even lose the property should the owner or descendants of the owner return to claim the property.

Property prices: Property prices have been very low for years, but as the island's planned membership of the EU moves nearer (the Greek side of the island joined the EU in 2004) and a boom in British buyers has occurred, they are moving up steadily. Around Kyrenia/Girne a one-bedroom cottage in need of much renovation would set you back less than £20,000 while three- and four-bed houses start at around £60,000. A villa with swimming pool would now go for around £90,000.

Legal restrictions: According to the Cyprus High Commission in London, selling Greek Cypriot properties in Northern Cyprus is illegal. It says that the legitimate owners can take the new buyers to the European Court of Human Rights. There have been cases where Greek Cypriots have taken the new owners to court and won.

Yet the TRNC says that if there is a settlement on the island, there will be compensation for both the Greek and Turkish Cypriots who had to leave their properties in 1974.

Finance

Currency and exchange rate: Turkish lira; £1 = 2,700,000 TL

Local mortgages: With Northern Cyprus at present being only recognised by Turkey, it would be unwise to investigate funding for a property on the island at present.

The buying process: Buying a property with foreign title deeds is simplest, as checks will have already been made by the government concerning ownership of title. Firstly a contract is drawn up by the purchaser's solicitor, setting down the terms of the sale, including the purchase price, timescale and any special conditions. The contract is signed by both vendor and purchaser and the purchaser pays in full unless a delayed completion is agreed. If that happens the vendor usually receives a 10 per cent deposit with the balance paid on completion. The title is then transferred to the purchaser's name.

When buying a property with a Turkish or TRNC title deed (obviously the latter cannot be recommended) the vendor and purchaser sign a contract stating the terms of the sale and the purchaser provides a 10 per cent deposit. The buyer's solicitor applies for a purchase permit from the Ministry of the Interior, which carries out checks on the title; this typically takes three or four months. When the permit is received the purchaser pays the balance to the vendor and the title is transferred to the purchaser.

Costs of buying: Typically there is a cost of around £600 for applying for the purchase permit, where applicable. Stamp duty is 6 per cent of the purchase price.

Is the property a good investment? As long as you buy a property that was foreign- or Turkish-owned before 1974, the way prices have risen in recent years suggest there is a very good chance that you have made a good investment. If direct flights are granted, making it as easy and cheap to visit the undeveloped north of the island as the overdeveloped south, property prices should increase significantly.

Selling: With Cyprus's volatile history, saleability can be adversely affected very rapidly whenever there are tensions. Selling a property with a TRNC deed (i.e. Greek owned pre-1974), could prove very difficult indeed.

Inheritance tax: No tax is paid by foreign residents; otherwise there is a sliding scale according to the size of estate.

Living in Northern Cyprus

If you like an easy-going, extremely cheap, sun-drenched way of life, Northern Cyprus is hard to beat. Roads are quiet and in good condition, there is very little development and no high-rise buildings. Yet this also means that everything from health facilities to choice in the shops lags behind almost everywhere else in Europe. There are no rates or community taxes except a council tax of under £50 per annum.

Further information

• **TRNC: t** (00 90 392)

• **North Cyprus Tourism Centre**, 29 Bedford Square, London WC1B 3ED, UK; t (020) 7631 1930; **www.go-northcyprus.com.**

Estate agents
All are situated in Girne, Northern Cyprus.

• **Boray Emklak Estate Agency, t** 822 2919; **www.borayestates.com.**
• **Ian Smith Estate Agency, t** 815 7118; **www.iansmithestate.com.**
• **Korinia Real Estate Agency, t** 815 2985; **www.korinia.com.**
• **Stringer Estates, t** 815 8844; **www.stringerestates.com.**
• **Unwin Estates, t** 822 3508; **www.unwinestates.com.**

Schools for English-speaking pupils

• **AEC, The American College**, Karmi Campus, Karaoglanoglu-Girne, Mersin 10, t 822 3381. Co-educational, 3–17 years.

USA

Why buy here?

Pros: US-bound second-homers overwhelmingly flock to Florida, both for the wealth of theme parks and other leisure attractions, and for the good weather: it has a sub-tropical climate, and is so sunny it is known as the Sunshine State. But of course there are endless other options available in a land so varied topographically, from superb ski resorts to stunning coastlines, and from vibrant cities to sleepy rural backwaters. America's largely English-speaking population is another attraction to non-linguists.

Cons: The weather in such a huge country isn't always glorious and in places can be extreme. Even Florida has its fair share of hurricanes and torrential rain.

For Europeans, the long-haul flights are certainly a disadvantage, both for their length and their cost, which is often high, especially around school holidays and in the summer. For a family, the upkeep of a home on the other side of the world, coupled with several expensive flights, can mean visiting here can be very costly.

America is very strict about the amount of time you can stay in the country. Permits to live and work or retire permanently, as well as long-stay visas, are scarce. Breaking the rules even slightly – even by not paying a parking permit issued years earlier or inadvertently staying 91 days instead of 90 on the visa-waiver programme used by most British short-term visitors – is often dealt with in an unpleasant, heavy-handed way by the Bureau of Citizenship and Immigration Services, the new agency responsible for administering America's borders. Since 9/11 there has been an unprecedented number of complaints by British citizens over their treatment by security-conscious customs officers.

The crime rate in America is high, although it varies considerably from state to state and neighbourhood to neighbourhood. It is important to check the crime rate in the area you are buying – you may get a surprise. When deciding to move from London to Florida in 2004, journalist John Price found that according to the Home Office and FBI crime reports of reported offences per 1,000 population, Islington in London notched up 31 violent crimes against the person while New York scored 10 and Miami Beach 13.

Access: There are many flight options from the UK. For Florida, flights to Orlando and Fort Lauderdale are usually cheaper than for Miami.

Property

Types: Obviously, such a huge country has a vast and varied property market, including apartment complexes with facilities like swimming pools and golf courses, waterside homes, homes in ski resorts and large, comfortable detached homes. In Florida it is important to select a property with a pool, either for letting out or resale purposes.

Where to buy: Every state has something to offer both holiday homeowners and residents. Florida, California and New York are the most popular destinations for foreigners. For winter sports, buyers opt for mountainous states like New Mexico, Colorado, Arizona and Idaho, while Virginia, Carolina and Georgia are becoming more popular.

Here is a more detailed run-down of the various pros and cons of just a few of the areas of the USA popular with buyers, and the types of property available.

More and more **Florida**-bound Brits are preferring to buy their own holiday accommodation rather than sink their funds in pricey hotels, as they get far more living space and privacy and often their own pool. Florida has numerous natural attractions, including 12,000 miles of coastline and 30,000 lakes, but most buyers head for the town of Orlando, the biggest tourist attraction in the world. Orlando has a wealth of theme parks and other attractions such as Epcot, Universal Studios and Seaworld; it is the home of Disney World and therefore ideal for families, but is not a place to consider if you like heritage or culture. When buying in Orlando it is important to choose the location of the property carefully to benefit from the maximum rental income in the weeks you're not holidaying. A 20-minute drive away from Disney World, rental demand can drop dramatically.

It is crucial to obtain professional advice and only deal with established companies fully licensed with the State of Florida's Department of Business and Professional Regulation, especially as there can be rental restrictions, and the four counties there have differing rules concerning property. To make sure a property can accommodate short-term lets suitable for holidaymakers, check with City Hall.

Also, homes in Florida, while cheap by UK standards, seldom appreciate significantly in value, both because there is so much building going on, and because buyers tend to go for new, more modern properties rather than resales. Developers of such properties usually offer an ongoing management and letting service so that your property can be rented out the weeks you are not there. They typically offer inspections visits from about £200.

The continued planned expansion of the Orlando area over the next two decades is assured by Disney World's huge investment in its 'Celebration' city residential, shopping and cultural centre as well as new theme parks and other major projects that are planned. For many, this is welcomed development, as it ensures an even greater choice of things to do, but for others such expansion will lead them to seek a more tranquil setting for their vacation.

Many British buyers are indeed now looking further afield to discover quieter locations. The easy-going but sophisticated town of Naples on the southwest

Gulf coast is an increasingly popular alternative to Orlando. Known for its abundant fishing, 55 golf courses and variety of shops, Naples has some of the finest beaches on this coastline, and is becoming one of the hottest towns on the Gulf. Property in Naples is typically 20 per cent more expensive than in the Orlando area, a much older town. It has a higher proportion of retirees not least because it lacks the hustle and bustle of Orlando.

With an increasingly high number of tourists to the Naples area, the rental demand for homes is also growing. Purchasers of typical pool homes can realistically expect to let the home out for over half the year to holidaymakers, generating a valuable income to offset running costs. But while property near Orlando is easy to let out throughout the year due to its many attractions, on the coast it is a different story as the rental market is much more seasonal and there is also great competition from hotel special deals.

For buyers wishing to locate north of Naples, near Fort Myers, the west coast at Port Charlotte, near Venice Beach, offers rich wildlife, including dolphins, pelicans, cormorants, egrets and ibis. All the beaches in the area are ideal for swimming, boating, fishing and diving, and there are superb golf courses and lakes and rivers in abundance.

Miami, despite being an attractive city on the ocean with golden beaches and year-round sunshine, is seldom considered by British buyers. It has an enticing mix of the glamorous film-making set as well as Haitian, Jewish and Cuban contingents. It has architectural gems like the narrow red-brick lanes of Coconut Grove and Art Deco properties at South Beach. Where, at the time of writing in March 2004, the average price of a London home is £262,000, in Miami it is £76,643. According to the National Association of Realtors, the Miami and Sarasota areas have been enjoying property price rises of over 20 per cent in 2004, compared with 8.5 per cent in the Orlando area.

Recently, British buyers have also been heading for the Pensacola area, North Florida, where a five-bed home retails at around £110,000.

Although most Britons planning a property purchase in America set their sights on Florida, a country as gigantic as the USA has much more to offer than that. For example, for sheer variety, **California** is hard to beat. California covers a larger area than any other state except Alaska and Texas. The main attraction is its many environments, with every geographical feature, a very varied climate allowing anything from skiing to sunbathing, a huge coastline, and mountains and lakes. It also boasts beautiful valleys, thick forests, barren deserts and fertile plains as well as natural wonders like redwood groves and volcanic cones. Wide, sandy beaches, excellent golf courses, ski resorts and many other recreational facilities are plentiful.

California has four of America's 20 largest cities: San Diego, San Jose, San Francisco and Los Angeles, home of Hollywood and the luxury excesses of glamorous Beverly Hills. Nearby is Santa Barbara, one of the most beautiful areas along the Californian coast, but also one of the most expensive.

While Florida is hot and steamy and flat as a pancake, Santa Barbara has a true Mediterranean climate, with breezes coming off the ocean. It means it's never too hot and never too cold. Many visitors and new residents are attracted by California's outdoor way of life. The warm, dry climate of southern California permits outdoor recreation almost all the year around.

At Lake Tahoe, for example, the deepest of California's 8,000 lakes and about 150 miles inland east of San Francisco, you can enjoy water sports, hiking, fishing and relaxed mountain living in the summer or skiing and snowboarding at the many local resorts during winter. Year-round the nightlife rivals that of larger urban cities. The South Lake Tahoe area boasts six casinos and excellent restaurants, shops and nightspots. This is a great holiday location and a very environmentally sensitive area. Most property is situated near the huge national forest and is relatively inexpensive. A two-bedroom mountain chalet will typically set you back from £125,000. For £90,000 or so you can get a two-bed furnished apartment in a ski resort.

In contrast, **New England**, midway between Boston and New York, offers wide open spaces, warm summers, glorious red autumns, winter skiing and usually a white Christmas, beautiful countryside, pretty villages, lively city life, culture spots and arts festivals as well as affordable properties. You can go mountain-biking, sailing and canoeing in the many lakes and rivers. Unsurprisingly, numbers soar here during the summer as New Yorkers flee the heat and humidity. The Berkshires, at the western end of Massachusetts, is a particularly delightful spot, and has a high proportion of second homeowners from New York and Boston. Cape Cod is another popular area, with a rocky coastline and sandy coves, and its peninsula is dotted with pretty colonial villages and towns.

Prices are rising by around 10 per cent a year. While a large house with private beach at the offshore island, Martha's Vineyard, as favoured by the rich and famous like Bill Clinton and Carly Simon, is out of reach to most at £6m plus, three-bedroom homes away from the sea and harbour cost around £215,000.

The Lake Sunapee region, 90 minutes from Boston, is a 2004 hotspot, with houses averaging £220,000.

With average house prices presently running at £3m, **Aspen, Colorado** has the world's most expensive real estate and houses a host of celebs including Cher, Melanie Griffith, George Hamilton, Kevin Costner, Don Johnson, Jack Nicholson and Martina Navratilova. No doubt they are attracted to the small-town feel, summer arts festivals and fabulous winter skiing. Aspen, a four-hour drive from Denver Airport, has a permanent population of only around 5,000. Four-fifths of properties here are second homes. Foreign buyers who can't afford the multi-million-dollar properties often tend to opt for timeshare apartments. You can get a couple of designated weeks a year at a fully furnished apartment for around £100,000, and prices are appreciating at about 10 per cent per year.

Property prices: Of course in such a huge country (the third largest country in the world after Canada and China) property prices vary greatly. Overall, they are significantly cheaper than in the UK, although in many areas they do not tend to appreciate in value a great deal. In Florida, coastal properties tend to be very expensive. Affordable properties in the intense building programmes here are all inland. In rural areas and smaller towns, a spacious house in its own grounds is easy to obtain for under £120,000. The same-sized home would be four or five times the cost in San Francisco and as much as 10 times the amount in New York City.

In Miami £300,000 will get you a spacious six-bedroom waterfront property with moorings, and in the plush Bal Harbour district the same amount nets a three-bed ocean-view apartment.

Prices in Florida are kept down by intense competition and tend to be cheapest north of Tampa. A standard three-bedroom villa with a swimming pool in the Orlando area would be around £100,000. In the Tampa Bay area, on the Gulf coast, it would be about £110,000, and in Sarasota nearer £150,000.

One of the most expensive areas is the select neighbourhood of Palm Beach. A three-bedroom property with pool, 15 minutes from the beach, would be in the region of £300,000.

In East Naples, Florida, a two-bedroom, two-bathroom apartment in a private gated community costs from about £130,000. Three- and four-bed villas typically cost from about £180,000, inclusive of a swimming pool. Most homes are located a gentle 10-minute drive from the beaches.

A three-bed chalet or clapboard house in the woods of Connecticut is typically currently about £90,000, while a three-bed period house with land would set you back around twice that. A two-bedroom apartment in Manhattan, New York, would (in early 2004) set you back around £570,000, £20,000 more than for a similar property in London. Prices rose by 40 per cent in New York in 2003 alone, with no signs of faltering.

Legal restrictions: Note that, if you are a citizen of a number of western countries, including Britain, you can only spend 90 days at a time on the visa-waiver programme. If you have ever been arrested you do not qualify for the waiver, regardless of how long ago it was or whether it resulted in a criminal conviction.

Longer stays require a visa, which can be hard to obtain unless you have a business in the USA, blood relatives or a company transfer.

Some counties and communities do not allow short-term lets.

Finance

Currency and exchange rate: US dollar ($); £1 = $1.80

Local mortgages: Foreign mortgage applicants are required to be homeowners in their country of residence. Mortgages of 80 per cent of the purchase price and for up to 30 years are widely available from a variety of sources, although it is probably easier and cheaper to obtain a mortgage in the UK. Sterling mortgages for Britons buying properties in America have recently become available. Interest-only as well as repayment mortgages can be obtained. US anti-discrimination laws make it illegal to refuse a mortgage on the grounds of age and therefore a 60-year-old should be able to obtain a 30-year mortgage.

The buying process: The conveyancing process is reasonably straightforward, which is unsurprising considering that American real estate laws are based on English laws.

Typically, a 1 to 5 per cent deposit is paid and a legally binding contract is then signed by both buyer and seller. Some states, such as California, require all funds to be paid to a neutral third party, known as the 'escrow agent', who is responsible for checking the progress of the transaction and paying out all necessary funds. If you decide to back out from the purchase you either lose your deposit or may be forced to continue with the sale, unless specified conditions of the contract, such as acceptance of a mortgage or there being a satisfactory survey, have not been met. These conditions can vary in different states.

Before purchase, check that all local taxes have been paid to date, as these charges are often transferred to the new owner.

Typically, if you are buying new, you choose your plot (known as a 'lot' in the USA) and house type; construction begins (taking around 4–5 months) when you have paid the first down-payment of around 25 per cent. You can move in after the last payment has been made.

If you are buying an apartment, expect to be 'vetted' by the building's residents' committee. It is common for other residents of a building to want to ensure newcomers are 'suitable' and can pay the ongoing charges.

Land, council and property taxes can be very high, so ensure you know the figure before deciding to purchase. Older homes should have a termite inspection, as wood-boring insects are a common problem.

Costs of buying: Known as completion expenses, these total around 5 per cent of the purchase price and can include a survey, a valuation fee by the lender, conveyancing fees, title search and mortgage tax. Realtor (estate agency) fees, which are higher than in Britain, are usually split between buyer and vendor.

Is property a good investment? Property in North America is often significantly cheaper than in the UK, but in many areas it does not tend to appreciate in value a great deal. Popular cities like New York and San Francisco are a notable exception, being pricier but also in constant demand.

Selling: Non-residents usually pay capital gains tax at 15 per cent up to US$23,350 (around £13,000) and at 28 per cent over this amount.

Inheritance tax: There are federal estate and gift tax rates from 18 to 55 per cent and some states also impose estate tax on estates left to a spouse or child.

Living in America

America's climate cannot really be summed up, as it varies greatly, from sub-tropical to arctic. It has one of the highest standards as well as lowest costs of living.

Britons can stay for 90 days at a time. To stay for a maximum of six months a year you need a tourist visa. To obtain visas for a greater length of time can take several months to process and usually requires the help of an experienced immigration lawyer.

Annual property and council taxes vary greatly from state to state. An average new-build home in Florida will attract real-estate taxes of 1 per cent of the value of the property.

Federal income taxes also greatly vary, from around 15 to 40 per cent of earnings, and some states, including Florida, have no state income tax at all. Tax relief on business expenses is more generous than in the UK. Some states and counties also impose further local income taxes as well as other taxes such as sales tax and tourist development tax on letting income.

There are no reciprocal health agreements between the USA and the UK and, as health care in America is prohibitively expensive, good private health insurance is vital.

Unless you are a close relative of a US citizen it can be difficult to obtain a work permit, a green (residence) card allowing you to live and work in the USA, unless you are able to buy or invest into a US business or have a particular work skill that is rare to find locally. Note that US residents are subject to tax on the worldwide income.

As permanent visas can be difficult to obtain, full-time retirement in the USA can be difficult to arrange. Many retirees have to be rich enough to keep up another home in the UK and allocate funds for flights back and forth. Further information is available on the US Embassy websites.

Further information

- **USA: t** (00 1)
- **United States Embassy**, 24 Grosvenor Square, London W1A 1AE, UK, **t** (020) 7499 9000; **www.usembassy.org.uk.**
- **Department of Housing and Urban Development**, 451 7th Street, SW, Washington, DC 20410, USA, **t** (202) 708 1112; **www.hud.gov.**
- **United National Real Estate**, 4700 Belleview, PO Box 11400, Kansas City, Missouri 64112, USA, **t** 800 999 1020; **www.unitedcountry.com.**
- **American Citizens Abroad**, 5 Rue Liotard, 1202, Geneva, Switzerland, **t** (00 41) 22 340 0233; **www.aca.ch.**

- **Immigration and Naturalization Service, www.ins.usdoj.gov.**
- Florida's official tourism website is **www.flausa.com**, while **www.sunnysarasota.com** is a website for Sarasota, Florida.
- **American Association of Retired Persons**, 601 East Street, NW, Washington, DC 20049, USA, **t** 1800 424 3410; **www.aarp.org.**
- **British Home Loans** (UK), **t** 0800 096 5989; **www.britishhomeloans florida.com.** A mortgage brokerage based in Orlando, Florida.
- **www.worldlawdirect.com**: free advice on American property law.
- **Florida Brits Group** (UK), **t** (01904) 471800; **www.floridabritsgroup.com.** A property advisory service and support group for more than 1,200 British homeowners in Florida.

Estate agents (realtors)

Florida

- **Florida Countryside** (UK), **t** (01702) 481600; **www.floridacountryside.com.**
- **Florida Homes International** (UK), **t** (01703) 262888; **www.floridahomesint.com.**
- **Overseas Homes and Investments** (USA), **t** (351) 9185 40151; **www.oshomes.co.uk.**
- **Sotheby's Realty** (USA), **t** (561) 659 3555; **www.sothebysrealty.com.**
- **Waterfront Brevard** (USA), **t** (321) 268 3640; **www.waterfrontbrevard.com.**

Miami, Florida
All are situated in the USA.

- **Joe Warren, t** (305) 531 5803; **www.jwrealtor.com.**
- **Buy Beach, t** (305) 531 6929; **www.buybeach.com.**
- **Exquisite Properties, t** (305) 538 7123; **www.exquisiteproperties.com.**
- **Yolande Citro, t** (305) 535 4162; **www.yolandecitro.com.**

New York
All are situated in the USA.

- **Cobble Heights Realty, t** (718) 596 3333; **www.cobbleheights.com.**
- **Coldwell Banker, Hunter Kennedy, t** (212) 255 4000; **www.cbhk.com.**
- **Sotheby's International Realty, t** (212) 431 2440; **www.sothebysrealty.com.**
- **Stribling, t** (212) 570 2440; **www.striblingny.com.**
- **Timothy Scott, t** (212) 813 3573; **www.tscottre.com.**

San Francisco
All are situated in the USA.

- **Betty Brachman, t** (415) 345 3125; **www.bettybrachman.com.**
- **McGuire, t** (415) 351 4663; **www.mcguire.com.**
- **www.realtor.com, t** (415) 229 1393.

Lake Tahoe
All are situated in the USA.

- **McCall Realty, t** (530) 544 1881; **www.mccallrealty.com.**
- **Village Properties, t** (805) 969 8900; **www.villagesite.com.**

New England
All are situated in the USA.

- **Brockman Real Estate, t** (413) 528 4859; **www.berkshirerealty.com.**
- **Elyse Harney Real Estate, t** (860) 435 2200; **www.harneyre.com.**
- **Harding Realty Corp, t** (508) 563 9777; **www.hardingrealtycorp.com.**
- **Newcastle Square Rentals, t** (207) 563 6500; **www.mainecoastproperties.**
- **Sotheby's International Realty, t** (617) 536 6632; **www.sothebysrealty.com.**

Aspen
All are situated in the USA.

- **BJ Adams, t** (970) 923 2111; **www.bjadamsandcompany.com.**
- **Brian L Hazen, t** (970) 920 0563; **www.realestateaspen.com.**

Selecting a Property

You have decided to buy a property abroad and have considered, in part, at least the financial implications of what you are planning to do. You have also taken a good look at the countries that you might like to consider. Now you have to get down to the nitty gritty and do some detailed and specific research. This is a massive commitment you are hoping to make and you cannot afford to get it wrong. You must be well informed about what to expect so that you can make the best choice possible. The time has come to consider access, the expense of travelling to and fro, infrastructure, what you require in terms of location, communication, property demands and responsibilities, and how you are to set about finding and viewing a property that fulfils your expectations and desires.

Travel

Unless you plan to stay at your home abroad all, or the majority of, the time, the speed, cost and ease of transport to and from the country will be a very important consideration. Will you be able to go effortlessly door to door by train, or does the trip involve a myriad of connections by train, ferry and taxi or aeroplane and bus? Do transport services operate adequately throughout the year, and do prices remain similar from season to season?

Before purchasing a property, research transport options thoroughly. Study timetables: many routes operate only at the most popular times, such as from May to October, rather than all year round.

Study price structures: if the only low-cost flights are available at inconvenient times and for only a few days in the depths of winter, and summer prices are astronomical, think again. Also, often outgoing and incoming flights, trains and ferries can vary enormously in price, causing any bargain to evaporate.

Ideally there should be more than one option offering affordable fares a comfortable distance from the property, to cover the very real possibility of a route being discontinued or carrier or ferry operator going bust.

Fully research the journey to and from airports. If the flight is cheap and quick but travel from home and to the property takes several hours, the property is unlikely to be suitable for regular short breaks.

By air

Where easy access to a ferry port was once crucial in determining where to buy a holiday home abroad, now closeness to an airport is increasingly the deciding factor.

With the recent huge growth in bargain air flights, commonly from under £35 return to an ever-expanding array of destinations and now with more than 50 low-cost airlines across Europe, today's purchasers of holiday homes can cast their nets far further than ever before. Indeed, today it is often easier and cheaper to fly abroad than catch a train in the UK to many other places in Britain. Now a second home for weekends in the South of France or maybe an Italian city is an affordable, practical reality, and the only problem is in selecting which country or region to opt for.

But beware of allowing the existence of a budget flight to an airport near your preferred destination to influence your decision to buy significantly. A number of budget routes have been discontinued in recent years, and in February 2004 a European Commission ruling banned Ryanair from receiving subsidies to fly to Charleroi, in Belgium, which could accelerate the closure of further routes in Europe. Such a development would probably cause a surge in British-owned property coming onto the market in affected areas, at comparatively low prices.

Certainly subsequent developments in 2004 indicate that it certainly is not a good idea to buy a property simply because a low-cost airline has launched a service there. In May, easyJet's share calculation fell 20 per cent and it admitted 'unprofitable and unrealistic pricing' while Ryanair axed three French routes, Reims, Clermont-Ferrand and Brest, after an earlier profit-warning. In addition, Birmingham airline Duo went out of business, the ninth European airline to fail from September 2001 to May 2004. More closures of both airlines and routes seem likely at the time of writing.

How much of a bargain are the bargain air fares?

The amazing fares being offered by the so-called bargain airlines are well known, and an increasing number of travellers have even managed to buy tickets at crazy prices – or even been given tickets for free, with only the airport taxes to pay. But if you cannot be very flexible over flight timings, are the prices offered by no-frills airlines really significantly lower than those of the main-stream airlines?

In 2002 I conducted an an extensive survey of air fares for the *Guardian* news-paper and found that at popular times the bargains offered by the no-frills airlines often disappear, especially when taxes and surcharges are added, or if you don't book weeks in advance. Generally, the low-cost airlines increasingly live up to their name the further you fly. A number of fares were monitored for a duration of four weeks, for a weekend break, i.e. taking Friday and Sunday afternoon/evening flights, with flight timings as similar as possible. If a flight became unavailable, the fare of the next available flight was checked until none was being offered for the departure dates.

• The cost of a **British Airways London Heathrow** to **Glasgow International** flight on 24 May 2002, returning on 26 May 2002, varied in cost from £114 to £268.30 during the month before departure.

- Around the same time on the same dates, return **easyJet** flights from **London Luton** to **Glasgow International** varied from £65 to £225 during the month before departure.

- **Ryanair's London Stansted** to **Glasgow Prestwick** flights varied from £113.16 to £193.16 during the month.

- **British Airways** flights from **London Heathrow** to **Nice** and back on these days varied very little, from £569.30 to £570 during the month.

- **EasyJet's** flights from **London Luton** to **Nice** varied in cost from £244.59 to £364.59 during the month before departure.

- Return flights with **BMIbaby** from **East Midlands** to **Nice** varied from £195.00 to £245.00 during the month before departure.

Opting for a low-cost carrier can leave you using an inconvenient departure airport, enduring significant delays, and spending time and money at the other end getting from an obscure rural airport to the centre of town. You also forego complimentary snacks. Most bargain airlines do not offer child discounts and apply hefty charges for excess luggage.

If you are prepared or able to take the least popular flights offered by no-frills carriers, typically very early or late in the day and outside the summer and school holidays, and are happy to use one carrier one way, another for the return (which could mean returning to a different airport), then your chances of low ticket prices somewhat increase.

Travellers able to be flexible over airports are of course even more likely to land a bargain, although it can be inconvenient when you arrive. Ryanair flies to Glasgow Prestwick, for example, although it really should be called Ayr Airport as it is adjacent to that city, an hour's drive from Glasgow.

Yet if you cannot be flexible and want to fly at a popular time then there can be surprisingly little difference in price, whichever airline you choose. Also, the survey revealed that prices offered by the no-frills airlines can shoot up or plunge down alarmingly from day to day.

Airlines and where they fly

European destinations are shown below for those airlines that offer flights from various airports in the UK. Only European destinations are shown. Many of the airlines included offer further flights from the destinations shown.

Operator	Telephone	Website	Destinations
Aer Aerann	t 0800 587 2324	www.aerarann.ie	Cork, Derry, Donegal, Galway, Kerry, Waterford
Aer Lingus	t 0845 084 4444	www.aerlingus.com	Cork, Dublin
Aeroflot	t (020) 8577 9570	www.aeroflot.co.uk	Moscow, St Petersburg

Operator	Telephone	Website	Destinations
Air Baltic	t (021753) 685020	www.airbaltic.com	Riga
Air Berlin	t 0870 738 8880	www.airberlin.com	Berlin, Dortmund, Hamburg, Hanover, M'Gladbach, Munster, Nuremberg, Paderborn, Vienna
Air Europa	t 0870 240 240 1501	www.aireuropa.com	Madrid, Palma
Air France	t 0845 0845 111	www.airfrance.com	Many destinations
Air Malta	t (020) 8785 3199	www.airmalta.com	Various destinations
Air Polonia	t 48 22 575 0000	www.airpolonia.com	Gdansk, Katowice, Poznan, Slupsk, Warsaw
Air Scotland	t (0141) 848 4990	www.air-scotland.com	Alicante, Barcelona, Fuerteventura, Girona, Gran Canaria, Tenerife
Air Slovakia	t (020) 7436 9009	www.airslovakia.sk	Bratislava
Alitalia	t 0870 544 8259	www.alitalia.co.uk	Various destinations
Austrian Airlines	t (020) 7766 0300	www.aua.com	Bratislava
Basiq Air	t (020) 7365 4997	www.basiqair.com	Amsterdam, Rotterdam
BMIbaby	t 0870 264 2229	www.bmibaby.com	Alicante, Amsterdam, Barcelona, Brussels, Cork, Dublin, Faro, Geneva, Ibiza, Jersey, Malaga, Milan, Munich, Murcia, Nice, Palma, Paris, Pisa, Prague, Toulouse
British Airways	t 0870 850 9850	www.ba.com	Alicante, Almeria, Amsterdam, Athens, Barcelona, Belgrade, Berlin, Bilbao, Bologna, Bordeaux, Brussels, Bucharest, Budapest, Cologne, Copenhagen, Dublin, Dubrovnik, Dusseldorf, Faro, Frankfurt, Fuerteventura, Geneva, Genoa, Gibraltar, Girona, Gothenburg, Gran Canaria, Hamburg,

Operator	Telephone	Website	Destinations
			Hanover, Helsinki, Istanbul, Jerez, Kiev, Knock, Krakow, Lanzarote, Larnaca, Lisbon, Luxembourg, Lyons, Madeira, Madrid, Malaga, Malta, Marseille, Menorca, Milan, Montpellier, Moscow, Munich, Murcia, Naples, Nice, Oporto, Oslo, Palma, Paphos, Paris, Pisa, Prague, Pristina, Riga, Rome, St Petersburg, Seville, Shannon, Sofia, Stockholm, Stuttgart, Tenerife, Toulon, Toulouse, Turin, Valencia, Venice, Verona, Vienna, Warsaw, Zurich
British Midland (BMI)	t 0870 607 0555	www.flybmi.com	Alicante, Amsterdam, Berlin, Brussels, Cologne, Copenhagen, Cork, Dublin, Dusseldorf, Esbjerg, Frankfurt, Gothen-burg, Hanover, Jersey, Madrid, Milan, Nice, Oslo, Palma, Paris, Stockholm,, Stuttgart, Tenerife, Toulouse, Venice
Cirrus Airlines	t 0845 773 7747	www.cirrusairlines.de	Leipzig
Croatia Airlines	t (020) 8563 0022	www.croatiaairlines.hr	Various destinations
Czech Airlines	t 0870 444 3747	www.czechairlines.com	Various destinations
easyJet	t 0870 600 0000	www.easyjet.com	Alicante, Amsterdam, Athens, Barcelona, Bilbao, Bologna, Budapest, Copenhagen, Faro, Geneva, Ibiza, Ljubljana, Lyon, Madrid, Malaga, Marseille, Milan, Munich, Naples, Nice,

Operator	Telephone	Website	Destinations
			Palma, Paris, Prague, Riga, Rome, Tallinn, Venice, Zurich
Finnair	t (020) 7408 1222	www.finnair.com	Helsinki
Flybe	t 0870 567 6676	www.flybe.com	Alicante, Bergerac, Bordeaux, Chambéry, Cork, Dublin, Faro, Geneva, Ibiza, Lyon, Malaga, Milan, Murcia, Nantes, Paris, Perpignan, Prague, Salzburg, Shannon, Toulouse
German Wings	t (020) 8321 7255	www.germanwings.com	Cologne
Germania Express	t 01292 511 060	www.gexx.de	Berlin
Hapag-Lloyd Express	t 0870 606 0519;	www.hlx.com	Cologne
Helios Airways	t (020) 8819 8819	www.helios-airways.com	Larnaca, Paphos
Iberia	t 0845 601 2854	www.iberia.com	Various destinations
Iceland Air	t (020) 7874 1000	www.icelandair.co.uk	Reykjavik
Iceland Express	t 0870 850 0737	www.icelandexpress.com	Reykjavik
JAT	t (020) 7627 2007	www.jatlondon.com	Belgrade, Tivat
Jet2	t 0870 737 8282	www.jet2.com	Alicante, Amsterdam, Barcelona, Faro, Geneva, Malaga, Milan, Nice, Palma, Prague
Jetmagic	t 0870 1780 135	www.jetmagic.com	Cork
KLM	t 0870 5074 074	www.klm.com	Various destinations
LOT Polish Airlines	t 0845 601 0949	www.lot.com	Warsaw
Lufthansa	t 0845 7737 747	www.lufthansa.co.uk	Various destinations
Luxair	t (01293) 596 633	www.luxair.lu	Luxembourg
Maersk Air	t (020) 7333 0066	www.maersk-air.com	Aarhus, Athens, Copenhagen, Oslo, Stockholm
Malev Hungarian Airlines	t (020) 7439 0577	www.malev.hu	Budapest
Monarch	t 0870 040 5040	www.fly-monarch.com	Alicante, Barcelona, Faro, Gibraltar, Malaga, Menorca, Palma, Tenerife

Operator	Telephone	Website	Destinations
MyTravelLite	t 0870 1564 564	www.mytravellite.com	Alicante, Almeria, Amsterdam, Barcelona, Faro, Knock, Malaga, Murcia, Palma, Pisa, Tenerife
Olympic Airways	t 0870 606 0460	www.olympic-airways.gr	Various destinations
Portugalia	t 0161 4895 049	www.pga.pt	Lisbon, Oporto
Ryanair	t 0871 246 0000	www.ryanair.com	Aachen, Aarhus, Alghero, Ancona, Baden-Baden, Bergerac, Berlin, Biarritz, Brescia, Brussels, Carcassonne, Cork, Dinard, Dublin, Dusseldorf, Eindhoven, Esbjerg, Forli, Frankfurt, Friedrichshafen, Genoa, Girona, Gothenburg, Graz, Groningen, Haugesund, Jerez, Kerry, Klagenfurt, Knock, La Rochelle, Leipzig, Limoges, Lubeck, Maastricht, Malaga, Malmo, Milan, Montpelier, Murcia, Nimes, Oslo, Ostend, Palermo, Paris, Pau, Perpignan, Perscara, Pisa, Poitiers, Rodez, Rome, Saltzburg, Shannon, St-Etienne, Stockholm, Tampere, Tours, Treviso, Trieste, Turin, Vasteras
SAS Scandinavian Airlines	t 0870 607 2772	www.scandinavian.net	Various destinations
Scot Airways	t 0870 606 0707	www.scotairways.co.uk	Amsterdam
Sky Europe	t (020) 7365 0365	www.skyeurope.com	Bratislava, Budapest

Operator	Telephone	Website	Destinations
SN Brussels Airlines	t (020) 7559 9787	www.flysn.com	Various destinations
Swiss Airlines	t 0845 601 0956	www.swiss.com	Various destinations
Tap Air Portugal	t 0845 601 0932	www.tap-airportugal.co.uk	Various destinations
Thompson	t 0870 1900 737	www.thomsonfly.com	Ibiza, Malaga, Marseille, Naples, Nice, Palma, Pisa, Rome, Valencia, Venice
Turkish Airlines	t (020) 7766 9300	www.turkishairlines.com	Various destinations
VLM Airlines	t (020) 7476 6677	www.vlm-airlines.com	Antwerp, Brussels, Luxembourg, Rotterdam
Volare	t 0800 032 0992	www.volareweb.com	Cagliari, Rimini, Venice
Wizz Air	t 0048 22 500 9499	www.wizzair.com	Budapest, Katowice

By car

You've found that dream holiday home abroad, a romantic little cottage immersed in a landscape straight from an Impressionist painting – all for the price of a second-hand car. There must be a catch. Unfortunately, there often is. One reason why some holiday homes abroad go for a song is because they are so far from a good port and fast road that getting there can seem only slightly easier than finding Ancient Rome with a London street map.

Fortunately, faster ferries, the Channel Tunnel and ever-improving road networks have in recent years enabled British buyers of second homes to look further and further afield for easily accessible properties that only a few years ago would have entailed a long, strenuous car journey. Some carriers offer discounts to frequent users and European property-owners, further encouraging home ownership abroad.

By ferry

Almost two million Britons took a ferry to the Continent in 2003. This may partly be because the low-cost airlines do not look so attractive after a delay or cancellation or when the bargain fares evaporate just at the time you want to go. Ferries are often the cheapest and most convenient option, once you've compared the cost of taking a ferry with the price of the air fares coupled with extras like airport parking and a hire car or other transport at your destination.

To get an idea of driving times and distances from port to destination check out one of the route-planning websites, such as **www.theaa.com, www.rac.co.uk, www.mappy.com** or **www.viamichelin.com**.

Prices can vary surprisingly throughout the year, so investigate that thoroughly, too. For example, the return price for two adults, two children and a car from Dover to Calais was £38 in May 2004and £394 in August with Hoverspeed, and £40.18 in May and £315.92 in August with P&O.

Hopefully, increased competition will reduce the high prices at peak times. For example, launching in May 2004, SpeedFerries plans to drastically undercut established operators like P&O, SeaFrance, Hoverspeed and Eurotunnel starting with an £80 return crossing in August for a car, two adults and two children, compared with prices ranging from £293 to £394 with the other companies.

Midweek crossings and those at unsocial hours are usually cheapest. Some ferry companies give attractive incentives such as early booking offers and frequent user programmes. Check out sailing times and the facilities on board too – increasingly important the longer the trip. The larger vessels offer cinemas, swimming pools, children's clubs, discos, gyms and casinos.

Note that although the Dover–Calais route is the shortest and quickest and has good road links, it will not necessarily be the most convenient service if you are heading west of Paris. Norfolkline's Dover–Dunkirk service is good for Belgium, Holland and Northern Germany. St-Malo and Dieppe are among the more attractive ports.

The website **www.ferrybooker.com** contains useful information and pricing from all of the ferry operators.

Ferry operators

Note: not all of these services operate throughout the year.

• **Brittany Ferries, t** 0870 366 5333; **www.brittanyferries.com**
Plymouth–Roscoff (France): 6hrs (day); 7hrs (night).
Plymouth–Santander (Spain): 18hrs.
Portsmouth–St-Malo (France): 9hrs (day); 10hrs 45mins (night).
Portsmouth–Cherbourg (France): 4hrs 30mins.
Portsmouth–Caen (France): 5hrs 4mins (day); 7hrs 15mins (night).
Poole–Cherbourg (France): 2hrs 15mins or 4hrs 15mins (day); 6hrs 15mins (night).
Cork (Ireland)–*Roscoff* (France): 11hrs.

• **Condor Ferries, t** 0845 345 2000; **www.condorferries.com**
Weymouth–St Malo (France): 4hrs 30mins.
Poole–St Malo (France): 4hrs 30mins.
Portsmouth–Cherbourg (France): 6hrs 30mins.

• **DFDS Seaways, t** 0870 533 3111; **www.dfdsseaways.co.uk**
Newcastle–Gothenburg (Sweden): 25hrs 30mins.
Newcastle–IJmuiden/Amsterdam (Netherlands): 15hrs.
Harwich–Esbjerg (Denmark): 17hrs.
Harwich–Cuxhaven (West Germany): 18hrs 15mins.

- **Fjord Line, t** 0191 296 1313; **www.fjordline.co.uk**
  Newcastle–Bergen via Stavanger, Haugesund (Norway): 18–25hrs.

- **Hoverspeed, t** 0870 240 8282/0870 460 7171; **www.hoverspeed.com**
  Dover–Calais (France): 1hr.
  Newhaven–Dieppe (France): 2hrs.

- **Irish Ferries, t** 0870 517 1717; **www.irishferries.com**
  Rosslare (Ireland)–*Roscoff* (France): 18hrs.
  Rosslare (Ireland)–*Cherbourg* (France): 18hrs.

- **Norfolkline, t** 0870 870 1020; **www.norfolkline.com**
  Dover–Dunkirk (France): 2hrs.

- **P&O Ferries, t** 0870 520 2020; **www.poferries.com**
  Dover–Calais (France): 75–90mins.
  Portsmouth–Le Havre (France): 5hrs 30mins (day); 7hrs 30mins (night).
  Portsmouth–Caen (France): 3hrs 25mins.
  Portsmouth–Cherbourg (France): 2hrs 45mins or 4hrs 45mins (day); 5hrs 30mins (night).
  Portsmouth–Bilbao (Spain): 35hrs (outbound); 29hrs (return).
  Hull–Rotterdam (Netherlands): 10hrs.
  Hull–Zeebrugge (Netherlands): 12hrs 30mins.

- **SeaFrance, t** 0870 571 1711; **www.seafrance.com**
  Dover–Calais (France): 70mins.

- **SpeedFerries, t** (01304) 203000; **www.speedferries.com**
  Dover–Boulogne (France): 90mins.

- **Stena Line, t** 0870 400 6748; **www.stenaline.com**
  Harwich–Hook of Holland (Netherlands): 3hrs 40mins (day); 6hrs 15mins (night).

- **Superfast Ferries, t** 0870 234 0870; **www.superfast.com**
  Rosyth–Hook of Holland (Netherlands): 17hrs 30mins.

- **Transmanche Ferries, t** 0800 917 1201; **www.transmancheferries.com**
  Newhaven–Dieppe (France): 4hrs.

By train

Journeys to all European destinations start at the Eurostar terminals at London Waterloo or Ashford International in Kent. The main transport hubs are Paris, Lille and Brussels, the latter being 2hrs 20mins from London. Overnight services go to such destinations as Nice, Avignon, Barcelona, Madrid, Florence, Rome and Venice.

Eurotunnel

The **Eurotunnel** service (**t** 0870 535 3535/0870 243 0892; **www.eurotunnel.com**) to Calais is, as long as it is working without hitches, fast and convenient, though you pay extra for it. You enter from the M20 near Folkstone and emerge in France on the A16 after being cocooned in your vehicle in a metal tube for 35mins. There are up to four departures per hour at peak times. Eurotunnel operates a Property Owners' Club where, for an annual fee of £35 and a one-off registration fee of £30, substantial savings are made when you book between five and 50 tickets.

The French Motorail sleeper service can whisk you and your car from Calais to Avignon, Nice, Brive, Toulouse, Narbonne, Bordeaux and Biarritz. Prices start at £185 per car and cabin.

Further details are available from **Rail Europe**, 34 Tower View, King's Hill, West Malling, Kent ME19 4ED; **travel centre** at 178 Piccadilly, London W1, **t** (01732) 526700/08702 415415; **www.raileurope.co.uk**.

Transport within each country

It is no good selecting a property abroad that may be relatively easy to reach but is impossible to travel around once you are there. The roads or drivers may be much worse than you are used to and parking spaces in town almost non-existent. Is it worth insuring, taxing and maintaining a car for sole use at your holiday home, or would it be cheaper to hire one each time you visit?

Before buying a property, the state of local public transport should be investigated. Are trains non-existent and buses almost so? Is there an excellent service during the summer months but just a skeleton one at other times?

Driving abroad

Be fully prepared for driving abroad. If you have a foreign-registered car, your nationality plate or sticker needs to be displayed. You may need to produce an array of car-related documents such as the car registration, insurance and MOT certificates at any time. You may require an international driving licence or translation of your UK one. You will probably need local currency for such things as tolls, petrol and possible fines. Your headlights may need to have beam deflectors fitted, and local laws may require such things as a warning triangle (Spain specifies two), a first aid kit and fire extinguisher. A motoring organisation like the **AA** (**t** 0870 600 0371; **www.theaa.com**) or **RAC** (**t** 08705 722 722; **www.rac.co.uk**) will be able to advise of up-to-date regulations.

Ensure you have adequate breakdown cover and insurance. Driving in some European countries requires an international driving certificate (a green card), which in most cases extends your vehicle insurance, but the time limit is usually around three months; longer stays may require local insurance. Legal protection insurance may also be strongly recommended in some countries.

Be aware that vehicle crime may be far higher in the country you are buying into, compared with your home country.

The legal blood level limit varies greatly from country to country, and can be as low as nil, for instance in Turkey. Of course, the local traffic rules, especially if driving is on the other side of the road from which you are accustomed, should be carefully studied before setting off. There can be some quirky rules; for example some countries, such as Norway and Denmark, require low-beam headlights to be on day or night when driving.

Location

Location is obviously of paramount importance, especially if you are planning to make the property your permanent residence. If you are going to work abroad, ease of access to your place of business is a significant factor. You also need to select an area where you would have a good chance of finding other work in the area if necessary. The local schools, health services, public transport and shops all need to be carefully assessed. If you are retiring, shops, leisure facilities, medical services and transport options are all especially important.

Do you require sunshine all year round? If you wish to ski, what is the local snowfall record? Do you wish to integrate into the local community (and are your language skills up to this?) or would you be happier in an area popular with expatriates from your home country?

Is the area susceptible to such things as hurricanes, tornadoes, floods, fires and earthquakes? Does the area become overrun by tourists in the summer season yet all but close down in winter? This may not be an important factor if you are buying a holiday home, but is something to consider seriously if you are moving full time. What are the neighbours at the prospective property like? Could you happily cope with the upkeep of the garden?

City versus country

Many city-dwellers, especially if they have children, at some point consider leaving the urban big smoke for some rural tranquillity. The natural beauty of the countryside is relaxing, even invigorating, and you are usually able to obtain a significantly larger property for your money.

Yet beware of the disadvantages. In the country public transport diminishes and you are likely to be far more reliant on a car, although driving will probably be less of a problem with fewer traffic jams and parking problems.

There are likely to be very reduced employment opportunities outside the cities, and maintenance and domestic fuel costs usually increase in country homes. A small, terraced town house sheltered in a built-up area is likely to be substantially cheaper to light, heat and maintain than a large detached building on a hill.

There are other factors to consider before taking the plunge into the rural lifestyle. For example, does the property have mains drainage, a telephone or electricity supply? Installing such things, or a septic tank, and a generator or solar panels for the electricity supply, can be very expensive and troublesome.

What are the neighbours like? Even if they are some distance away they could spell trouble. A local farm could cause considerable disruption.

Those used to the high density of population in a hectic big town may feel isolated living down a lonely country lane. Many country areas become inhospitable in winter, because of fog, cold and snow. Doctors, hospitals, chemists and schools may be a significant distance away and local shops non-existent or badly stocked.

Socially there can be a lack of choice in the country and it often takes time to become accepted in a community, especially if you are from abroad and your grasp of the local language and foreign ways leaves something to be desired. Yet the slower pace of living can also encourage contact with neighbours and a generally friendlier atmosphere.

Pollution comes in different guises in the country – from chemical sprays used in farming, from spending more time in the car because the shops are 30 miles away instead of three, or from ozone, a pollutant most prevalent in the countryside. Think twice if the dream cottage you wish to buy is near a coal-fired power station that emits sulphur dioxide and causes respiratory problems. Asthma sufferers should seek medical advice before moving from the city in an attempt to improve their condition: the disease can worsen in many rural areas rather than improve on leaving the city owing to the different triggers there.

And then there's noise pollution. Some confirmed townies, while used to next door's ghetto blaster pounding away on a Saturday afternoon, can't abide an inconsiderate cockerel crowing at some godforsaken hour. Prospective country buyers should also ask whether there is an airport nearby. The grounds of that idyllic pile, peaceful when you viewed it, won't be so attractive if it emerges that it is near a fast-growing airport.

The city generally offers more housing choices, more public transport, recreation, entertainment and shopping facilities, health care and schools, although housing is likely to be more costly, health care overstretched and schools suffering from discipline problems. There may be less privacy, more noise and pressure in the city.

The secret to a successful move out of the city to supposed rural bliss is not to attempt too much too soon. Going from a maze of busy streets to the back of beyond can be a costly, time-consuming mistake. It may be safer to consider moving to the edge of suburbia, where you have both rural peace and urban facilities nearby. Or renting in the country for a year to see whether it really is for you.

Property types

Once you have worked out where to buy, work out exactly the kind of property you are looking for. Many prospective buyers waste untold time and money because their search is too vague. Draw up a checklist of requirements. You could start with a wish list of the things you would be looking for in a perfect home. This list could include things like its having at least four bedrooms; being built before 1900; having a garage and a large garden; being situated in a quiet village but near a train station and shops.

Because few people have the budget to buy their ideal home, you could translate your dream list into a checklist of minimum requirements. This list could change to maybe including any property built before 1930; having two bedrooms and a small garden; a regular bus that gives access to both shops and the railway station.

Whatever you choose, don't allow a property's charm to cause you to disregard its practical disadvantages. A chocolate-box exterior is all very well but if the property is riddled with dry rot and renovation works that will see you through to the next century, and excursions to buy a pint of milk take the best part of a day, maybe you should think again.

Buying an old property

Many old properties boast lots of character and are not necessarily more difficult to maintain than newly built homes. Many older properties – though not in all countries – were built to extremely high standards using superior materials and have thick, solid walls that are in complete contrast to the paper-thin walls that many new properties have today. Although building regulations in many countries today are more strict than ever, many housebuilders are more interested in saving money during the building process than in creating long-lasting, maintenance-free homes.

Restoration and refurbishment

Buying and restoring a dilapidated property can net you great savings when you buy and big profits when you sell – if it goes well and there is a strong local property market. Yet often the cost of restoration is far more than first envisaged and is often not recovered when you come to sell. Many foreign buyers take on too large a project, seduced by a very low asking price, underestimating the cost of both restoration and maintenance. Such a project is not for the faint-hearted – especially abroad – and you need huge reserves of patience and commitment. Many things can go wrong, including language mix-ups, bureaucratic mayhem, expanding budget difficulties, unforeseen extra building works, baffling local building regulations and mammoth planning hold-ups.

Many people get into difficulties with restoring and renovating because they underestimate budget and timescales through not taking the time and effort to prepare detailed costings. Don't forget any local taxes that may be added on to any quotations for work to be done.

Properties ripe for renovation typically need a damp-proof course, new windows and doors, a new roof, replaced or repaired walls, timber treatment, a new kitchen and bathroom, re-plumbing, rewiring, installation of central heating, a garden makeover and complete decoration. The cost of rectifying such things can be immense. Bear in mind that the cost of renovation may be very different abroad compared with the UK. For example, DIY items like plywood and plumbing parts can be three or four times more expensive in France when compared with buying in the UK and often British renovators hop onto a ferry and have a spending spree at a B&Q, Homebase or other DIY super-store in Britain for DIY items they need for their French homes.

Many properties for renovation can harbour lots of unforeseen problems. Ideally you should obtain plenty of professional advice, from experts like a surveyor, an architect and builder with experience of similar projects.

When you find a suitable property, ask yourself whether it is right for you. A charming little dark cottage with low ceilings and small windows can't be transformed into an oasis of light without wrecking it, and a high-ceilinged barn won't be cosy and snug. Restoration may need planning or other local permissions so check with the planners at the local council.

Don't be seduced by a low asking price for a property. Restoration costs regularly exceed the market price for the property had it been restored. Installing services like electricity and water to rural properties can be very costly indeed.

Often it is better to employ local builders – if your grasp of the language is sufficient – rather than foreign imports, not least because they are likely to understand the local building techniques, planning laws and building regulations better than outsiders. Using them will ease you into the local community more readily. They are likely to be cheaper and in some countries, such as France, work by registered builders is guaranteed.

The work is likely to require being overseen to ensure instructions and plans are correctly carried out. An architect would charge about 10 per cent of the cost of the job to do this in most cases.

If you plan to renovate, accept that the incessant arrival of huge lorries and a noisy building site disrupting everything for weeks may incur the wrath of your neighbours.

Keep all receipts. If you do everything by the book – which is strongly advised as you can fall foul of some serious laws, attracting large fines in some countries, if you don't – you can often claim back expenses against capital gains tax (see p.220) when you come to sell. If you pay cash in hand you have no protection or proof of payment should problems arise later. Also, doing things by the book means you receive certificates for works done which act as a guarantee.

Resale properties

Properties that are neither brand new nor charming wrecks, but instead are relatively recently built second-hand properties, can be a good bet because they are often good value, any teething problems have probably been resolved, and they are bought as seen, unlike properties bought off-plan.

Buying new

Buying a newly built home can avoid many of the stresses of homebuying. You may sidestep the uncertainties, costs and considerable time of buying a house in a 'sale chain', although some buyers inevitably experience postponed completion dates and other problems. You may avoid an estate agent's fee; you don't have to worry about problems that can beset older properties like rotting timbers, leaking roofs, widespread damp, subsidence and rising damp; and you may be able to take advantage of special offers offered by the developer.

As well as being brand new and spotless, new homes should conform to the latest building standards and advancements, which could include sophisticated security systems and the latest high-tech computer, heating, lighting and audiovisual systems. There may be carpeting, bathroom fittings, a fitted kitchen, new appliances and energy-efficient features.

You will often be able to pay a smaller deposit than for a resale property and there may be attractive deals on such things as conveyancing costs. In many countries properties are covered by a builder's guarantee against structural problems and/or for plumbing, electrical and other installations. The architect may also be responsible for some defects for a set number of years, and the developer may be backed by financial guarantees.

The down side is that you tend to get considerably less space for your money with a new home, and many new properties lack character. Capital growth – the money you make on the property since the time you bought it – can be more difficult to achieve than for older properties. In some regions – such as Florida – your property may not go up in value at all.

It is important to choose the developer carefully. Many countries lack the protection buyers have in the UK, and many developers are vastly underfunded and have financially precarious businesses.

Before buying, take a close look at the site. Is it tidy and well managed? Small developments often grow into larger estates. If the development is next to open ground, check whether it has been earmarked for a later phase of building.

Ask the sales people lots of questions. What is the total number of properties planned for the development? Who looks after communal areas? How long will the construction work for the whole site take?

When the property is supposedly finished, have a good look around to see that the standard of work is acceptable before paying out. For example, has everything that was in the original specification been included? Has the whole of the interior been painted well? Unless any unacceptable or outstanding items are of a minor nature, where you should get a written undertaking that they will be sorted out, you should not complete until the matter is rectified.

Don't be put off by minor cracks around the property. These usually appear when the plaster dries out, although larger cracks should be investigated.

Buying off-plan

Increasing competition for new homes has meant that buying a property from the developer's plans, rather than waiting until it is built, has become increasingly popular, especially in areas with a large presence of new-build developments popular with foreign buyers, such as on the Spanish *costas* and Florida.

There can be great benefits to buying this way, which is known as buying off-plan. Developers often discount properties to get sales moving at a new development, and, if prices rise steeply as word gets round and as the development takes shape, you can have a real bargain on your hands.

You also often have the choice of the best plots with the most impressive views, with the bonus of gaining extra time to save and sort out a mortgage. Another advantage is that you have far more say about how your property will look if you buy off-plan. Developers often have a sizeable range of tiles, carpeting, colour schemes and kitchen and bathroom fittings you can choose from, and you may even be able to rearrange the layout, for example changing two bedrooms into one large room, or maybe two bathrooms into one study and a bathroom.

For all its advantages, buying off-plan can be a gamble, though, especially abroad, and it is therefore particularly important to find a reputable, independent lawyer experienced in this field in the country you wish to buy in who can advise on possible pitfalls. These could include the developer's going bust, failing to complete in time or not building to the specifications given.

Investigate carefully to see how established and financially secure the developer is before committing to buy. In many countries, there are few controls over developers and there is little guarantee that the property, as well as communal areas and infrastructure, such as electricity, swimming pools and parking areas, will ever be completed.

The salespeople working on off-plan developments often earn a hefty commission and can subject potential buyers to a whole host of high-pressure sales techniques to get them to sign on the dotted line.

Do not sign anything written in a foreign language you do not understand until it has been translated fully into English. Also, do not hand over any funds, even if pressurised to do so to secure a property.

Ask the developer to arrange for you to speak to other people who have bought from the company to find out what their experience has been. A developer who is not prepared to do this should be treated with suspicion.

Also bear in mind that when buying off-plan, if the property market contracts, completed homes could cost less than those previously bought off-plan.

Prepare for delays. Factors like bad weather or bureaucratical hold-ups can cause the development to run seriously behind schedule. Examine the developers' plans carefully and refer to them on completion: are neighbouring houses too close or will you have great views of the dustbins?

Consider having a clause included in the contract that allows you to delay completion if there are faults in the property. And if your home is one of the first to be completed, be prepared to live on a building site for weeks or even months.

Managed developments

More and more buyers are opting for a property at a managed development rather than subjecting themselves to the hassle of converting a rambling ruin, which can be a particularly fraught process if you live abroad. In a managed development the maintenance and security of the development will normally be taken care of.

Although the initial cost is more, you have no security worries or maintenance headaches and replace worry about burglars and burst pipes with peace of mind. Often these developments have other features, such as a gymnasium, beauty salon, swimming pool or golf course.

Shared developments

Properties in shared developments, where common elements like the building, land or amenities are shared, are common abroad. There can be a number of advantages. The outside of the building, communal areas and gardens are usually maintained by the managing agents and you share the costs with the other property owners. There may be added security as other homeowners may keep an eye on your property in your absence.

Yet there are disadvantages. An inefficient managing agent can be a real headache, especially if there is a pressing problem that needs to be attended to and they don't appreciate the urgency of sorting it out. You may have little control and still be lumbered with hefty maintenance charges.

Before you commit to buy, make sure you understand the whole range of charges and fees you may be responsible for. Read any agreements governing the property and go through any points you don't understand with your solicitor, who should highlight any points she or he thinks could cause problems. There may be important legally enforceable restrictions such as banning pets or restricting access to part of the grounds, so make sure you have understood every clause.

Service charges can be high and usually include a contribution towards things like repairs and maintenance, communal electricity and buildings insurance.

Before buying, it's a good idea to ask for copies of the service charge demands for the last few years. Have the charges risen sharply, or have there been a high number of costly repairs?

Many managing agents are not regulated by any statutory body and standards vary greatly. Before buying try to speak to other residents to see whether there have been any problems affecting them.

If you are buying a holiday property you may be paying for such things as water and heat throughout the year regardless of whether you are at the property or not, so check the position. In some countries, repairs and upgrading of the building can result in a hefty increase in fees.

Building a home

Another option is to build a home from scratch after buying a plot of land, either an architecturally designed one-off or to a cheaper standard design offered by a builder.

You can get more for your money building this way but in some countries the process can be fraught with difficulty, from ensuring that the land can be built on, to builders following instructions adequately.

Self-builders typically make savings of 25 to 35 per cent by building their homes themselves, although the term 'self-build' is itself rather misleading. Only about 1 per cent of self-builders undertake any of the building work themselves, with most employing a builder to carry out the work for them.

One of the biggest obstacles a self-builder faces is finding a suitable building plot: one that is the right size, an affordable price and unencumbered by insurmountable planning permission problems.

If you opt for self-build, build at least a 15 per cent contingency fund into your budget for the unexpected, which invariably will come up. Pay your builder in stages, not upfront, otherwise you won't have a hold over him if there's a dispute.

Timber-framed homes, such as those offered in kit form by self-build companies, speed up the building process. Companies supplying such homes include:

- **Potton Homes** (UK), **t** (01767) 263300; **www.potton.co.uk.**
- **Border Oak Design and Construction** (UK) ,**t** (01568) 708752; **www.borderoak.com.**
- **Griffner Coilite** (Eire), **t** (01663) 5201; **www.griffnerhomes.com.**
- **Acorn and Deck House** (UK), **t** (01789) 720270; **www.deckhouse.com.**

- **Huf Haus** (UK), **t** (01932) 828502; **www.huf-haus.de.**
- **Swedish House Company** (UK), **t** (01892) 665007; **www.swedishhouses.com**

Often such self-build homes ready for assembly can be shipped anywhere in the world.

The website **www.psa-publishers.com** lists architects around the world and **www.selfbuild.co.uk** has useful self-build information.

The monthly UK self-build magazines have their own websites: *Homebuilding and Renovating* (**www.homebuilding.co.uk**); *Build It* (**www.self-build.co.uk**); *Self Build and Design* (**www.selfbuildanddesign.com**).

Other purchase options

Timeshare

Often the dream of owning a property abroad doesn't work out as planned. You start with the good intention of making regular visits several times a year, but work, education and other mounting commitments result in your visiting the property far less than you would wish. Maybe you should have dipped your toe in the water to start with, to see whether property ownership abroad was really for you.

In such a situation it can seem that a timeshare (also known as holiday or vacation ownership) may be the answer, where you purchase just a short period each year at a property, commonly a couple of weeks.

Unfortunately, in the 1980s, soon after it became popular, timeshare rapidly got a bad name owing to the high-pressure sales techniques many companies applied and also because many developments did not live up to the promises the initial sales literature and banter claimed. Owners of timeshare weeks found out the hard way that, rather than appreciating in value, their timeshare weeks became less and less valuable and often were impossible to sell.

This led to legislation being brought in during the early 1990s to protect customers, and today timeshare has cleaned up its act. Now about one million Britons take timeshare holidays, three times as many as a decade ago. At a rate of about 16 per cent per year it is one of the fastest growing sectors of the travel industry, rapidly conquering new territories.

The market, worth more than $6bn worldwide, is expanding into more and more countries. To many people, timeshare suggests resorts in Spain or America, but the UK has its own growing market, with over 120 resorts, double the number 10 years ago. There are now over 4,700 resorts worldwide in countries as diverse as Hungary, Senegal and India, though Spain remains the most popular. The swift expansion of timeshare is even more impressive when you consider the antics of early players in the market.

The idea of just buying a single unit in one block and being limited to that block for the rest of your life is now history. There are different schemes now. You can be more flexible on the type of unit or time of year, or you can opt for a points system, a currency to exchange, rather than buy at a specific resort.

The bad stories about timeshare focused on the way the product was sold, but traditionally the properties have generally been of good quality. What you are buying is generally superior to a hotel or package holiday. Timeshares have to be better or no one would buy them. A package holiday to Spain costs a family of four typically £2,000–£2,500. With timeshare you typically pay £10,000 now and, apart from flights and an annual maintenance charge, you don't have to pay anything more for 60 years.

Now the sector has put its house in order credibility has been further enhanced by the involvement of major players like **Marriott**, **Disney**, **Airtours**, **Hilton**, **Hyatt**, **Stakis** and **Four Seasons**. Also, a 1997 EU Timeshares Directive giving added protection to purchasers, including a statutory 'cooling off period', has been taken up by many European states, which increases the confidence of buyers.

Additionally, credit card companies Mastercard and Visa introduced a 10-day cooling-off period for holidaymakers who have put down a deposit to be able to cancel the deal if they have second thoughts.

Although timeshares offer a higher standard of accommodation than most package holidays, can save money on future holidays and save on the hassle of arranging the annual break, the spectacular expansion of timeshare is largely due to the opportunity to exchange weeks for those at other resorts.

One reason timeshare appeals to many British holidaymakers is the flexibility and variety offered by the exchange system, where holiday owners can vary their holiday plans, swap weeks or try a different destination. **Interval International** and **Resort Condominiums International** (RCI), the two leading exchange companies, have over 3.2 million customers on their books.

People are retiring earlier and consequently have more time to holiday, and timeshare is ideal for this. People are taking advantage of special offers like bonus weeks and late-break availability. Prices from resellers of timeshare weeks are at least 50 per cent lower than new timeshare purchase prices, sometimes just 10 per cent of the new price.

Even so, for all the advantages and improvements, you can never escape the fact that a timeshare property is never actually your own. And only a few people get to buy the best weeks of the year. A place in the sun isn't an ideal place to visit in the height of winter.

Do not buy in a hurry, as there are still some sharks out there, and loopholes in the system remain. Also, it is not advisable to buy off-plan, i.e. before the apartment or the development's leisure facilities have been built. There is always the possibility that the building won't be completed. Always buy in a resort that has an owners' club that can represent your interests.

Lastly, the handling, community, marketing, maintenance and service charges never go away – and may go up. Timeshares can be very difficult to resell, and instead of making a profit you may have to resort to giving yours away to someone prepared to take over the maintenance contract. And remember that in essence, all you are buying is a long-term reservation on an annual holiday.

Further information

- The **Department of Trade and Industry, t** (020) 7215 5000; **www.dti.gov.uk**, offers a leaflet, *Timeshare – making the right choice*.
- **Organisation for Timeshare in Europe** (OTE), **t** (020) 7821 8845; **www.ote-info.com**.
- **Association of Timeshare Owners Committees, t** 0845 230 2430; **www.tatoc.co.uk**.
- **Timeshare Consumers' Association, t** (01909) 591100; **www.timeshare.org.uk**.
- **Timeshare Users' Group** (USA), **t** 904 298 3185; **www.tug2.net**.

Timeshare companies include:

- **Timeshare Council, t** (020) 7821 8845; **www.timesharecouncil.net**.
- **www.tradingplaces.com** and **www.timeshareresources.com**: resource centres for buying, selling and renting timeshares around the world.
- **Interval International, t** 0870 7444 222; **www.intervalworld.com**.
- **RCI, t** 0870 6090 141; **www.rci.com**.
- **Primeshare, t** (01386) 47813; **www.primeshare.com**.

Holiday property bond

An alternative to timeshare is the holiday property bond, where you purchase part-ownership in a holiday property for around £2,000 to £3,000, which enables you to use rent-free holiday accommodation at 27 locations around the world. You can either keep the bond for as long as you like and pass it on in your will, or after a couple of years you can sell it, almost certainly for less than you paid for it.

An advantage is that, apart from a share of maintenance charges, you have paid for future holiday accommodation and the price never increases. A disadvantage is the lack of locations.

- The **Holiday Property Bond, t** (01638) 660066; **www.hpb.co.uk**.

Shares in a property

Properties at some developments, especially in Florida, can be part-purchased through property companies. For example, at the Parque de Floresta scheme near Lagos in Portugal, buyers have recently been able to purchase a quarter share of a property at £40,000, around a quarter of the full price of the property, which entitles them to stay there for 13 weeks each year forever.

It is not like timeshare. There, you are buying a right to use someone else's property for a set period. Group ownership, on the other hand, boils down to buying shares in your own property. It is an idea that has long been established by people buying boats and aircraft, without the budget to buy outright.

To get around the problem of sharing the property with complete strangers, as you do with a timeshare property, some buyers have persuaded friends and family to buy the other three shares in the property, so that it is jointly owned by them all.

Some people buy in a group privately, without the expense of an agent, allowing them to have access to a much better property than what they could normally afford. A clear, effective contract should be drawn up to protect everyone's interests. It may be advantageous in some countries, such as France, to form a company for ownership of the property so that it is not subject to inheritance laws.

A good way of ensuring fair distribution of weeks is for owners to be given priority in turn. Whoever gets first choice at dates one season or year has the last choice the next.

Group ownership can be very advantageous if you need to sell as the other owners have first call on buying it. Therefore, it is also possible to increase your share as other parties drop out.

The **OwnerGroups Company, t** (01628) 486350; **www.ownergroups.com**, puts together buying groups, finds properties and advises on property management. It can provide a central website for the group so that each owner can bid for the weeks they need each year.

Leaseback

Here a hotel or development company typically sells a suite or apartment at a significant discount (usually around a third off the price) so that the purchaser is entitled to stay at the property for several weeks per year for a set period, typically 20 years. For the weeks they do not use, the owner receives rental income when the property is used by others. Especially popular in Spain and Portugal, prices are not cheap and usually exceed £100,000. It is important to check that you gain full vacant possession at the end of the agreed term.

Searching for a property

Although buying a home abroad is easier than ever before, with new English-speaking agents setting up shop daily and new markets opening around the globe by the week, the process of buying is seldom as simple as viewing a few photos and descriptions, fixing up a weekend visit and putting a deposit down for the first property that takes your fancy.

Firstly, the laws and customs concerning property in many countries can be unclear, even illogical and baffling, and offer many opportunities for the unwary to hit significant problems, or even in some cases be completely fleeced. The need for expert, independent advice – before you have paid a deposit and signed the contract – cannot be overstressed. Never rely on the advice given by someone with a financial interest in the property, such as an agent or a developer, or a professional registered with a recognised body or organisation.

Be aware that in some countries laws to protect the consumer may be inferior – non-existent even – compared with the protection you are used to in your home country. Developers may not necessarily have adequate funds to complete projects, professionals may lack indemnity insurance, and there may be no legal comeback if a service is provided wrongly and causes problems rather than solves them.

Another complication is that choice varies considerably between countries and the regions within them. France is amply represented by English-speaking, often UK-based, specialist companies with hundreds, sometimes thousands of properties to view, initially on the Internet.

Yet for a British buyer buying, for example, a property in next-door Belgium and the Netherlands, it is far more difficult to begin your search from the UK and it would be far more effective to visit local agents in the area you're interested in.

Even in countries well served with property agents geared to the UK market, like France and Spain, many companies only specialise in one small area, and if you want to buy outside the normal holiday regions favoured by the British – such as Brittany, the Dordogne and the South of France in France and the *costas* in Spain – it can be considerably more difficult, especially if you don't speak the local language.

Local estate agents

In most countries estate agents (or real estate agents or property brokers) are regulated by law and are required to be professionally qualified, licensed and in possession of indemnity insurance. Choose one that is a member of a recognised professional association.

Do not take details contained in the property particulars as gospel, and check any measurements stated. Also check that the property is still for sale before travelling to see it.

If a deposit for a property is paid to an agent, this must go into a special protected **escrow account**. Check beforehand exactly what the agent's fee is and whether you will be required to pay any of it if a sale goes ahead, which is normal practice in some countries.

International estate agents

You could try one of the big estate agency chains with a good spread of branches abroad:

- **FPD Savills, t** (020) 7499 8644; **www.fpdsavills.co.uk.**
- **Hamptons International, t** (020) 7589 8844; **www.hamptons.co.uk.**
- **Chesterton International, t** (020) 7201 2070; **www.chesterton.co.uk.**
- **Knight Frank, t** (020) 7629 8171; **www.knightfrank.com.** Sells homes in more than 30 countries on five continents.

When considering using international agents, bear in mind that they usually concentrate on the luxury market so unless you are looking for an estate in Kenya or a beachfront Carribbean villa – rather than a £19,000 studio flat in Benidorm – they may not be able to help.

The Internet

Searching for UK homes on the Internet is now a well established method, but if you're looking overseas the process can still be fraught with difficulty. Typically, either the website hasn't been updated since the millennium, or the property descriptions are all in a bewildering foreign language.

In some countries, notably in Spain, it can be galling to see the same property on several property websites – with several different asking prices and selling fees.

Relocation agents

Property search, buying or relocation agents can help sift out out unsuitable properties. The **European Relocation Association** (EURA) can provide a directory of members.

Typically such firms charge an upfront fee of several hundred pounds as well as a percentage of the purchase price (typically a £500 to £600 or so registration charge plus around 2 to 2.5 per cent of the purchase price), and if you're buying a wreck to do up in rural Greece or France, you may not think their fees are worth it, and likewise they may feel financially it's not worth their while either. Yet often the fee is soon recouped, as a good agent's understanding of the local market can result in an ability to negotiate asking prices downwards. Buying agents can usually also help to arrange mortgages and legal coverage, and to recommend gardeners, builders and electricians.

European relocation agents for people looking for a European holiday home is still a very under-exploited search option. They're strongest in areas where there's a big holiday home market like the Costa Blanca and the Balearics.

Such agents can guide buyers away from unsuitable areas or those that have recently become too expensive to more up-and-coming areas. They can consider a large area, unlike an estate agent, who is only concerned with his own small catchment area.

- **European Relocation Association, t** 08700 726727; **www.euro-relocation. com.** Details on and links to many relocation agents worldwide.

- **Association of Relocation Agents, t** 08700 737475; **www.relocation agents.com.** Details on and links to many relocation agents worldwide.

International UK-based relocation agents include

- The **Property Finders (t** (01908) 218753; **www.thepropertyfinders.com)**

- **County Homesearch International (t** (01872) 223349; **www.wefindhouses.com.**

Inspection trips

Many property companies serving the popular holiday home haunts in Spain, and to a lesser extent Florida, France, Italy and Portugal, offer inspection trips where you are able to see the area in detail as well as properties currently for sale.

These can at first sight be very tempting; indeed, one of the biggest UK firms geared to Spanish buyers currently offers four-day inspection tours of Spanish properties for £49 including accommodation, flights, food and drink.

Yet there is no such thing as a free lunch, and accepting such trips can often – although not always – open you up to incessant high-pressure sales pitches and warnings that if you leave your designated rep during your time abroad you will be charged the full cost of the trip. Typically on these trips you will tour 10 or 12 building sites, show homes and half-completed developments each day, and be encouraged, often with the alcohol flowing, to put your name down for a property bought off-plan. There is likely to be no time to explore the area alone or view older properties, even if you specify an interest in them.

The current situation is reminiscent of the aggressive sales techniques that accompanied the early days of timeshare, which so quickly gave that sector such a bad name. Now, timeshare is far more regulated than the property market and many former timeshare salespeople are concentrating on hard-selling property.

Inspection trips are usually only worth considering if they take small groups rather than whole coachloads on the trips and if they put the buyer under absolutely no pressure. Unfortunately, such trips are few and far between.

Overseas property shows

If you're not set from the start on buying in a specific country, with so many enticing destinations to choose from, one of the biggest problems for those buying a holiday home overseas is deciding where to buy. Should you opt for the sun-drenched beaches of Spain, a villa close to Disneyland and the endless other theme-park-type attractions of Florida, or a home on a sleepy Greek island with little more than a taverna as a distraction?

It can be very fruitful to visit one of the regular international property shows which exhibit regularly around the country and which are often advertised in the property sections of national newspapers as well as the specialist magazines geared to buying property abroad.

Whether interested in a coastal villa, country home or mountain retreat, prospective buyers are usually able to compare how far their budgets stretch in each destination and find out about travel options.

Not only do these 'trade fairs' feature property developers and agents, but often there are representatives from companies who can help in other ways, such as financial advisers, mortgage lenders geared to foreign property ownership and firms of solicitors who specialise in property sales abroad.

Current examples of property shows include the following.

Homes Overseas exhibitions

• **Where:** More than 30 annual exhibitions at major venues including the NEC, Birmingham and Olympia, London. Other cities include Manchester, Belfast, Dublin, Glasgow, Brighton, Exeter, Leeds and Liverpool.

• **When:** Generally held on a Friday, Saturday and Sunday.

• **Details:** *Homes Overseas* **magazine**, Blendon Communications, 207 Providence Square, Mill Street, London SE1 2EW, UK, **t** (UK) (020) 7939 9888, (Spain) **t** 00 34 952 76 8369; **www.homesoverseas.co.uk**.

• **What's there:** Developers, estate agents, mortgage lenders and international lawyers, with seminars covering the purchase process, pensions, investment, tax planning and inheritance. The exhibitions, organised by *Homes Overseas* magazine, provide information on new and resale property from many places such as mainland Spain, the Balearics and Canary Islands, Florida and other US locations, Goa, the Caribbean, Canada, Portugal, Malta, France, Dubai, Czech Republic, Sardinia, Brazil, Monaco, Montenegro, Egypt, Italy, Cyprus, Greece, South Africa, Bulgaria, Hungary, Turkey, Ireland, Switzerland, Australia, Thailand, Egypt, Croatia and Romania.

Overseas Property Expo

• **Where:** Typically at 45 venues in the UK annually including Edgbaston Cricket Ground, Birmingham and Twickenham Stadium or Lords Cricket Ground, London.

• **When:** Fridays to Sundays throughout the year.

• **Details: Overseas Property Expo, t** 0800 3101218; **www.overseasproperty-expo.com**.

• **What's there:** Focusing on Florida, Costa del Sol, Costa Blanca and southern France, there are seminars, buying advice, inspection trips and subsidised flights and accommodation offers.

The Homebuyer Show

• **Where:** ExCel, Docklands, London.

• **When:** The first Friday, Saturday and Sunday in March.

• **Details: Homebuyer Events**, Mantle House, Broomhill Road, London SW18 4JQ, UK, **t** (020) 7069 5000; **www.homebuyershow.co.uk**.

• **What's there:** This is possibly the UK's largest and most comprehensive residential property event, with more than 200 exhibitors and 22,000 visitors in 2003. Both UK and overseas property is covered, with many exhibitors and seminars, and lots of details on hotspots, investment, legal and tax issues.

French Property exhibition

• **Where:** Typically held at venues like Olympia, London, Edgbaston Cricket Ground, Birmingham plus Harrogate and Taunton.

• **When:** A Friday, Saturday and Sunday in January (London), March (Birmingham), May (Harrogate), September (London) and November (Taunton).

• **Details: French Property News**, 6 Burgess Mews, London SW19 1UF, UK; **t** (020) 8543 3113; **www.french-property-news.com**.

• **What's there:** Probably the best French property exhibition, with around 60 exhibitors focusing on France.

The Best of Southern Spain property exhibition

• **Where:** Exhibitions in venues in cities such as London, Birmingham, Manchester, Edinburgh, Brighton, Bristol, Norwich, Brighton and Harrogate.

• **When:** The last Friday to Sunday in February.

• **Details: Viva Estates**, Reserva de Alvarito, Urb Andasol, CN340, KM189, 29600 Marbella, Malaga, Spain, **t** (UK) 0800 298 9594; **www.vivaestates.com**.

• **What's there:** Up to 25 developers and agents. There is relocation, buying, legal, tax, investment, financial and mortgage advice as well as new developments showcased.

QSD Group

• **Where:** various UK venues.

• **When:** Various dates throughout the year.

• **Details: QSD Group**, Avenida de las Naciones, 1-6-03170 Ciudad Questada, Rojales, Alicante, Spain, **t** (UK) 0800 389 8152, (Spain) **t** 00 34 965 725 410; **www.qsdgroup.com**.

MGB Homes international property exhibitions

• **Where:** Hotels in towns and cities including Ashbourne, Bolton, Basingstoke, Ellesmere Port, Bromsgrove, Truro, Swindon and Stratford-upon-Avon.

• **When:** A weekend in late February.

• **Details: MGB Homes**, Centro Commercial La Campana, Punta Prima, Orihuela Costa 03189, Alicante, Spain, **t** (UK) 0808 1800 500, **t** (Spain) 00 34 965 327 804; **www.mgbhomes.com**.

• **What's there:** Focuses on the Costa Blanca, Costa Almeria and Costa Calida.

The International Property Show

• **Where:** A hotel in London and Manchester.

• **When:** The first Friday, Saturday and Sunday in February or March and October.

• **Details: International Property Show**, 7 The Soke, Alresford, Hampshire SO24 9DB, UK, **t** (01962) 736712.

• **What's there:** Usually more than 35 exhibitors have stands to show their properties from around the world including Spain, the Balearics, the Canaries, Gibraltar, Portugal, Florida, Greece, Cyprus, and the Turks and Caicos islands.

International Property Investor Show

- **Where:** A London hotel.
- **When:** First weekend in May.
- **Details: International Homes, t** (01245) 358877; **www.international-homes.com/exhibitions.**
- **What's there:** Co-organised by the publications *International Homes*, *English Homes* and the *Wall Street Journal Europe*, thousands of homes are on offer costing from £35,000 to £6 million. Countries featured include Spain, Cyprus, France, USA, Portugal, South Africa and Malta.

Viva Espana!

- **Where:** NEC Birmingham.
- **When:** A weekend in early May.
- **Details: Viva Espana, t** 0870 120 0332; **www.vivaespana2004.com.**
- **What's there:** Spanish property show.

The Property Investor Show

- **Where:** ExCel, London.
- **When:** A September weekend.
- **Details: Property Investor, t** (020) 8877 3636; **www.propertyinvestor.co.uk.**
- **What's there:** Features developers from around the world.

Destination Sun Homes

- **Where:** various UK venues.
- **When:** Various dates throughout the year.
- **Details: Destination Sun Homes,** 60a High Street, Ingatestone, Essex CM4 9DW, UK, **t** 0870 9911882; **www.destinationsunhomes.com.**
- **What's there:** Focuses on Spain, Florida, the Caribbean and Cyprus.

Visiting properties abroad

Once you have read up on the area you are interested in, blitzed agents with questions, studied reams of property particulars and scanned Internet sites, before long you will have a good grasp of the local property market and will hopefully be able to make a shortlist of the properties or property types you really want to see. This is the time to plan a trip.

Holiday and travel insurance

Before anything, sort out some travel insurance. Check and compare policies carefully as they vary considerably. Note inclusions and exclusions and levels of cover. Although these cover such eventualities as cancelled flights, lost baggage and delays, the most important factor is the provision of medical expenses, which can add up to many thousands of pounds in some territories, such as America. Household policies, private medical insurance policies and credit card companies all often provide holiday and travel insurance, but this is unlikely to be adequate and should be treated as a bonus. An annual policy may be suitable – and cheaper – if you go abroad frequently or for long periods.

Visit the region at different times of year

When you have narrowed things down, visit the area that interests you at different times of year. Nothing beats visiting the region you wish to buy in as often as possible, and really you should get to know the place well, at different times of year, before committing to a purchase rather than buy on the basis of a two-week summer holiday as so many people do. Does the area lose many of its attractions outside the holiday season? Is the transport network good all year round? Can the climate change dramatically from month to month? This is an increasingly important factor the further north you go.

Ask yourself, the agent and the vendor lots of questions

There are lots of questions to answer before committing to buy. Location is a good start. The north of Spain or France may be convenient for the ferry ports, but would you want to visit during a freezing winter? The south of both these countries may enjoy the most sun, but are you likely to visit regularly if it's a long trek each time? Is there an airport, a good train station, attractive town or village nearby?

Is there local animosity to foreign buyers of holiday homes? Is there a good local hospital nearby? More distant destinations like Florida and South Africa may sound very enticing and offer bargain properties, but will you want to endure airports and long-haul flights and fork out the cash for the fare often enough to justify buying there?

There's also security of the property the months you're away to consider, and the expense of buildings and contents insurance.

Conveyancing costs like taxes and lawyers fees can be substantially higher than in the UK. The **Federation of Overseas Property Developers, Agents and Consultants** (FOPDAC) estimates that on average, a buyer can expect to pay 10 or 12 per cent on top of the original purchase price when buying abroad. There may be a minimum purchase price for a property imposed on foreign buyers, as in Malta, for example (*see* p.107).

If you need to let out the property for most of the year to finance it, what is the local rental demand like? Never assume that it will finance the venture, whatever the claims and assurances of agents and sellers, unless they provide proof. Try to be as objective as possible when choosing a property. There may be restrictions on renting your home out, which is a common restriction in developments in Florida, for example. If you rent out your second home, income must be declared to the Inland Revenue and involves completing a self-assessment form, although expenses may be offset against this. You will also probably have to pay tax if you sell the property, and the position here should also be clarified.

Property laws vary enormously. Not considering in whose name the property should be bought could risk a hefty inheritance tax bill for the owner, for instance. If you haven't commissioned the services of an independent lawyer (not one nominated by the agent) with experience of foreign property transactions, you could find you've bought yourself a home where the local farmer has the right to drive his tractor over your front lawn whenever he pleases, or worse, where there's a question mark over ownership of the land or the property. Most importantly, don't sign any binding documents that you don't understand fully without having them checked by a suitably qualified, preferably UK-based, expert first.

If you are buying in an apartment block, development complex of villas or something similar, you should be made aware of the annual share of the maintenance and other costs you will be required to pay with the other owners as well as terms, such as the frequency of exterior painting of the properties in the complex, for which you will have to contribute an amount.

Renting before buying

If you are not sure what kind of property or location you want, it is a good idea to consider renting a similar property to the type you have in mind, in different seasons if possible.

Renting for an extended period not only gives you the opportunity to search for the most ideal home at your leisure but also gives you the opportunity to check out the climate, the locals and facilities and perhaps to hear the experiences of other foreign buyers who have already taken the plunge.

Home exchange

A cheaper alternative to renting is to exchange your home for a set period, if you have no problem with allowing strangers to move into your home in the UK. Agencies that organise home exchanges include:

- **Green Theme International Home Exchange Holiday Service** (UK), t (01208) 873123; **www.gti-home-exchange.com**.

- **Home Base Holidays** (UK), **t** (020) 8886 8752; **www.homebase-hols.com**.
- **HomeLink International** (UK), **t** (01962) 886882; **www.homelink.org.uk**.
- **Intervac International Home Exchange** (UK), **t** (01249) 461101, (USA) **t** 415 435 3497; **www.intervac-online.com**.
- **The Invented City** (USA), **t** 415 846 7588; **www.invented-city.com**.

Viewing

Don't necessarily disregard a property just because it does not look attractive in a photo. Appearances can be deceptive, and the cosmetics of the house can often be easily changed – whereas the location cannot.

Unless you have an unlimited budget, you need to have a flexible approach. Still, it is easy to be seduced by a property where you're so keen to move in that you overlook the disadvantages that could cause problems later on. To ensure that this doesn't happen, work through a checklist of things to look out for from the very first viewing. Make notes as you go round, especially if you are looking at other properties in the day as you can soon forget what features were in which particular house or apartment.

Do not allow the seller or estate agent to rush you. Ask them lots of questions. How long has the property been on the market? Has anyone else made an offer and why did the sale not proceed? How ready and able is the seller to move? Are there copies of bills showing running costs or guarantees for work done available? Is there an indication of the annual running costs?

Although it's easy to change the wallpaper or the fitted kitchen, you won't be able to change the position of the property, its views and the light it receives, so focus on these closely. Look out for trees nearby that could lock out light. If the approach to the property is steep, will access be a problem in the winter? If industry or a farm is nearby, would noise, pollution or smoke be a problem?

A nearby river or stream could pose a threat of flooding, and if the property is near the coast there could also be the problem of coastal erosion. Such factors could affect insurance cover. Visit the property again at different times of day and look for possible causes of disturbance in the locality. A nearby seemingly quiet bar may spring to life and create disturbance in the evening, a school may cause lots of noise and traffic problems at drop-off and pick-up times and a newsagent may get noisy daily deliveries of papers in the early hours.

If, on first viewing, the property looks as if it at least satisfies your minimum requirements, look again in more detail. Will the layout allow you enough space for your needs? Is there adequate space for large items of furniture? Can they easily be brought into the room you plan them for? Measure large items first and check with a tape measure at the property.

Things to look out for

Heating and electrics

What kind of heating is used? Does it look as if it may need updating? Does the electrical system look modern and are there enough power points or does it look as if you would have to consider rewiring – a costly and messy job. Is noise a problem? Open a window to hear the traffic noise.

Dining room and kitchen

Is the dining area or dining room convenient for the kitchen, and is the layout of the kitchen suitable for your needs or simple to change? Is there space for all required appliances? Is the staircase suitable for very young or elderly visitors?

What condition is it in?

If it is an older property, has it been modernised well? It is not usually a problem if the decoration is not to your liking, as the bulk of what you're usually paying for with property comes down to location, and cosmetic things can usually be easily and cheaply changed.

Before committing yourself to buying and possibly paying for a survey you can get a good idea of the condition of a property by looking out for certain indicators. New wallpaper or paint, for instance, could be concealing cracks or damp patches. Cracks around doors and bay windows and long diagonal cracks across walls which look as if they have been repaired but have again cracked could indicate subsidence where the foundations of the property are not secure and which can be very costly to rectify. Doors sticking or not hanging correctly, a sloping floor, bent chimney stack or uneven roof line can also indicate subsidence, as can bulging outside walls. To see if a wall is bulging, stand close to the end of it and look along it to see whether it is straight.

Cracked or sagging plaster ceilings in older houses can be an often underestimated danger and messy to repair. Springy floors can be a sign that the floors themselves or joists underneath may have rotted. A musty smell and cracking in woodwork can indicate dry rot, caused by a fungus (*Serpula lacrynens*), which is usually very expensive to treat, especially as all the affected wood, down to window frames and joists, must be replaced.

Stains on ceilings and walls can indicate damp, although this may be less serious than it looks, perhaps penetrative damp caused by a leaking roof, window or gutter, which should go away once the culprit is fixed. If there is a smell of damp and you can feel moisture on walls, this may indicate rising damp, when a damp-proof course breaks down and the brick walls suck up water from the ground. Typically in this situation you will have wet walls with damp, discoloured wallpaper on the lower portion of walls, possibly a smell of mouldy paper, flaking paintwork and crumbling plaster.

Roof tiles and slates should also be checked by moving some way from the building to have a look at the condition, ideally with binoculars. While outside, also look at the pointing (the mortar between the bricks) because if it is in a bad condition it can allow damp to seep into the property. Nearby trees may have roots that could undermine the property's foundations.

Financing the Purchase and Financial Implications

Finance options

Broadly speaking, when you have found the home abroad that you want to buy, the main options available to finance the purchase are to buy outright, to remortgage your UK home or to take out an overseas mortgage.

Buying outright

Buying outright, where you have the capital available for the total cost of the purchase is, of course, the most straightforward option, but beware of using all your funds for the purchase, leaving you with little or no spare cash for any unforeseen expenses.

Remortgaging your existing home

If you have sufficient equity in your UK home, you could raise the required amount for the purchase by remortgaging or taking out a second mortgage. This may be cheaper, is often simpler to arrange and avoids much baffling paperwork compared with taking out a foreign mortgage.

Mortgages overseas also tend to be more restrictive and have stricter lending criteria, requiring applicants to supply detailed income and expenditure details.

Yet bear in mind that sterling-based finance to fund a foreign asset is subject to currency fluctuations. Also, having bought the property, should you later need to raise money on your foreign home, this is often not possible, as many foreign mortgage markets are far less flexible than that in the UK, do not permit equity release and only allow money to be lent to buy or improve a property.

Borrowing on your existing home means that you are able to present yourself as a cash buyer, which can be a bargaining tool. A disadvantage is the added risk of tying up extra equity in your main home.

Taking out a foreign mortgage

Some foreign mortgages are more expensive and restrictive than those in the UK, while others, conversely, notably many in Europe at the time of writing, offer better rates than those in the UK.

Yet the process of obtaining a mortgage abroad can be far more difficult than in your home country, especially if you do not speak the language of the foreign bank you are dealing with. An international mortgage broker can help smooth the way, although there will usually be an additional fee, usually of around 1 per cent of the loan.

An increasing number of UK lenders are offering loans specifically for properties abroad, although a number of countries are excluded.

Taking out a mortgage in another currency

As well as the option of taking out a mortgage in the currency of the country where your foreign property is situated or your income is paid in, you can also take out a loan in another foreign currency, whether it be US dollars, Australian dollars or euros. In this situation you are exposed, however, to currency swings and devaluations that may not work in your favour.

A UK or foreign mortgage?

The advantages and disadvantages of borrowing in the UK for your property abroad, or in the destination itself, vary from country to country. The differences can be large.

For example, in May 2004 the Bank of England base rate was historically low at 4 per cent, yet the European Central Bank's main interest rate was 2 per cent and the American Federal Reserve's most important lending rate was just 1 per cent. At this time Japan's central bank rate was effectively zero following economic stagnation, resulting in mortgages of just 2 per cent being widely available. If such differences continue, in countries like Spain, France and Italy mortgage interest rates are likely to be lower than if you borrowed in the UK, although the set up charges and administrative requirements may be more. A further point is that some countries allow tax relief against rental income for the interest on a local mortgage but will not allow this on a UK mortgage.

Fluctuating exchange rates can alter monthly payments drastically. According to international legal firm John Howell and Co, over the last 15 years the £ sterling has varied between 280 Spanish pesetas and 162 pesetas. This means that a mortgage of 100,000 pesetas per month would have varied in cost between £357 and £617.

Whatever option you choose, you should obtain expert advice about how the loan could affect tax allowances and liabilities. In some countries, residents receive tax relief on their mortgages, which can mean it is financially beneficial in some circumstances to take out a mortgage if you are resident abroad, even if you can pay cash.

Lenders and other financial companies

• **Conti Financial Services**, 204 Church Road, Hove, East Sussex BN3 2DJ, UK, **t** (01273) 772811; **www.mortgagesoverseas.com**. Mortgage provider for overseas buyers in more than 20 countries including Australia, Canada, the Caribbean, Cyprus, France, Gibraltar, Greece, Ireland, Israel, Italy, Malta, Portugal, New Zealand, South Africa, Spain and the USA.

• **Blevis Franks, t** (020) 7336 1116; **www.blevinsfranks.com**. Specialises in overseas property finance and foreign exchange.

- **PropertyFinance4Less,** 160 Brompton Road, London SW3 1HW, UK; t (020) 7594 0555; **www.propertyfinance4less.com.** Specialises in overseas mortgages, foreign exchange and associated insurance products.

- **Abbey France, t** (UK) 0800 44 90 90, **t** (France) 00 33 3 20 18 18 18; **www.abbey.com.** Provides bilingual mortgage advisers and has a free guide to buying property abroad.

- **Norwich and Peterborough Spanish Home Loans** (UK), **t** (01733) 372006; **www.norwichandpeterborough.co.uk.**

- **Newcastle Building Society Gibraltar, t** 00 350 42136; **www.newcastle.co.uk.**

- **Barclays Bank Spain, t** 00 34 91 336 1610; **www.barclays.es.**

- **Banco Halifax Hispania, t** (UK) (01422) 333868; **www.halifax.es.**

Buying a property through an offshore company

Non-resident buyers of property in some countries buy through an offshore company to legally avoid paying stamp duty and transfer tax, as well as capital gains, wealth and inheritance taxes. Buying an offshore company requires expert legal advice. The practice has been common in France, Spain and Portugal.

In Spain, many homes are sold through a Gibraltar-based company to lessen the Spanish stamp duty bill. In France, setting up a company gives the buyer more control over who can inherit the property.

However, the loophole has increasingly come under threat. In Portugal, for example, the tax rules have been changed recently so that homeowners using an offshore firm are liable for a hefty tax bill.

In the UK, a House of Lords ruling in 2004 introduced the possibility of homes owned through a company structure being taxed as a benefit in kind, although nothing has as yet been confirmed.

Currency exchange

When you have decided on a country to buy within, it is prudent to read up on its recent financial history. Some currencies devalue and strengthen alarmingly in short periods, and buying at the wrong time can cost you thousands more pounds than just a few months before or after. Although one can't predict the future, an overall picture of the economy of a country can be a great asset.

Major events can have a big impact on exchange rates, as they can greatly affect economic confidence. For example, South Africa's rand slipped from R11 to the pound in March 2001 to R20 in December 2001 after September 11.

Exchange rates can make a very big difference, as the following examples show.

If you bought an average-priced property in North America in January 2002 it would have cost $157,000 (then about £97,000). An identical property bought in January 2003 would cost $164,650 (about £89,000). Even though prices rose by 5 per cent over the year, the actual cost in pounds fell by 9.5 per cent.

Conversely, buyers in Europe during the same period would have paid an average of €169,650 (then around £115,000) in 2002 and €183,380 (about £125,000) in 2003. Therefore, a British buyer would have paid around 8 per cent more in 2003 for the same property.

It is possible to forward-buy as much as 18 months ahead, with a **forward contract**, the currency that you need to purchase a property, at an agreed fixed rate. This can provide peace of mind of knowing exactly what you will have to pay, although you will lose out if the currency subsequently weakens.

You can also opt for a **spot transaction**, which allows you to transfer funds immediately, in line with the current exchange rate.

You can also place a **limit order** in the market for a desired exchange rate. The currency is purchased as soon as the market reaches your specified exchange rate, therefore protecting you from negative exchange movements but allowing you to gain from a positive one.

For further currency-related information and online currency converters, try:

- **Currencies Direct, t** (020) 7813 0332; **www.currenciesdirect.com.**
- **Currencies4less, t** (020) 7594 0594; **www.currencies4less.com.**
- **Moneycorp, t** (020) 7823 7700; **www.moneycorp.com.**

Financial implications of buying a property abroad

Taxes

Before buying a property abroad, find out what taxes you will be liable for. These could include transfer taxes and stamp duty when you buy, annual property taxes, rates, residential taxes, real estate taxes and/or council tax once you have bought, wealth tax, inheritance tax and capital gains tax. More cheeringly, there may also be tax incentives to encourage you to live in certain countries, and these should be investigated also.

Property taxes

Annual property taxes, rates, residential taxes, real estate taxes and/or council taxes may be payable and are generally for such things as rubbish collection, road cleaning, street lighting and community services.

Prospective property-owners should check that there are no outstanding taxes of this sort relating to the property, especially as in many cases the new owner is responsible for unpaid property taxes and debts.

Such taxes are usually based on an assessed value of the property. Although this is usually lower than the real current value, it is important that it is not more, as you would then pay more tax than necessary. The assessed value can affect a number of taxes, which can end up being very expensive indeed. For example, in Spain, several taxes relate to the fiscal value of a property, including transfer tax, letting tax and inheritance tax. In some countries the owner is not necessarily sent an annual bill, and it is the responsibility of the owner to find out what taxes are due and pay them. Many properties abroad also attract other taxes. These vary from region to region within each country, but could include, for example, a surcharge in touristic areas for beach-cleaning.

Capital gains tax

In many countries capital gains tax is payable on the profit from the sale of property and sometimes other assets like antiques, jewellery, stocks and shares. It is a complex subject, especially in international terms, and it is advisable to check your tax position with a suitably qualified expert before committing yourself to buying abroad.

Such an expert would be able to clarify your liabilities, any gains that are exempt and capital losses that can be offset against gains. Bills associated with buying, selling, renovating or restoring the property can all be offset against capital gains tax and may be index-linked.

As far as property goes, generally the tax applies to property that is not your principal home. Therefore, if you buy a holiday home abroad the tax would apply to that property according to the tax laws of that country, but if you retain but move from a home in the UK and make a foreign home your principal residence, your UK home may be liable to the tax when you sell, instead.

Often, the longer you own a property in a country, the less you are liable for until you eventually owe nothing. In Spain this is currently a decade and in France it is 32 years.

Wealth tax

Taxes and their implications can vary greatly around the world and many countries have taxes that don't exist in Britain. For example, in some countries a wealth tax is applied, depending on your domicile, where typically your assets (including such things as property, vehicles, shares, jewellery and business ownership) are totalled, with liabilities (such as mortgages and debts), subtracted and a tax on this paid on assets above a certain sum. In France, the tax is exempted at below €700,000 and in Spain the exemption is currently €108,182 and the tax varies from 0.2 to 2.5 per cent.

Income taxes, pensions and savings

Income tax is an important factor in your financial affairs if you are planning to live or work abroad or let out your foreign home, as it is generally payable if you receive income from a local source in a country. In some countries income tax and social security contributions can be very high, so it is essential to clarify the taxation position early on.

As far as the UK goes, to be treated as non-resident for income-tax purposes you need to spend three tax years out of the country. During that period you should spend no more than 90 days in Britain per year.

It is important to plan comfortably in advance so that your finances are set up as efficiently as possible. Contact a financial adviser who specialises in the country you are moving to.

A number of countries, such as France and Spain, have agreements with the UK that mean you don't have to pay tax in two countries. Yet you need to know how the laws determine your tax position and which country you are living in for tax purposes.

Bear in mind that if you are no longer resident in Britain, you give up British tax advantages. PEPs and TESSAs, for example, which are tax-free in the UK, attract tax elsewhere.

If you move abroad you cannot continue to put money into ISAs. However, as far as the Inland Revenue is concerned (Inland Revenue ISA regulations 11 and 22(2)), ISA accounts can be left open and would continue to pay gross interest as before. Even so, some companies could require you to cash in their accounts.

Income derived from rent, even if there is no overall profit, must be declared and tax paid on any gain. If you have a UK business it remains subject to UK income tax even if you are a non-resident. Interest on bank and building society accounts held in the UK remains subject to UK tax. UK pensions, whether state, occupational or personal, are subject to UK tax even if paid to you abroad.

Inheritance and gift tax

Inheritance tax, estate tax or death duty is payable in most countries on the estate of someone who dies. Whether you are a resident or non-resident, the tax is usually applicable in the country you own property in. You generally pay inheritance tax in the country the tax authorities deem is your domicile.

Inheritance tax can be paid by the estate or, as in the case of Spain and France, by the beneficiaries of the estate. Inheritance tax (and gift tax) varies greatly from country to country and can differ a lot depending on such factors as the relationship of the beneficiary to the deceased or the beneficiary's own wealth. A lawyer or financial adviser specialising in the taxation system of the country concerned can advise on ways to avoid or reduce inheritance tax. It is a good idea to decide how to do this before purchasing the property to avoid complications later.

Points to consider before buying

• **Who will own the property?** The decision of whether you, you and your partner, your children, you and your children, a company or trust own the property should be carefully considered and discussed with a suitably experienced lawyer or financial adviser, as the wrong decision could have very costly tax implications.

• **What are the implications if you die?** Who you leave your property to can also lead to expensive tax implications. Even if you have a situation with the archetypical family of two adults plus two children, the spouses cannot necessarily leave all the property to each other or all to their children, which can cause great problems. Many experts advise drawing up a local will to ensure that your property is passed on to your descendants rather than the state when you die.

Those in second marriages or who live together but are unmarried can experience further complications. There can be restrictions. For example, in France you cannot leave your property to whoever you want as certain relatives have a priority claim to it. Again, a lawyer experienced in the property laws of the country concerned should be consulted before purchase.

It is usually beneficial to make a local will when you buy, as the expenses and tax liability for your heirs if you use a UK one are likely to be significantly higher.

• **What will the property be used for?** Letting out or altering the property is likely to require official permission. Obtaining this can vary greatly from country to country.

Making the Purchase and Moving In

Ideally, as soon as you start looking for properties you should start to plan ahead so that everything is in place once you are ready to buy. You should already have checked out the implications of where you want to buy to avoid any disappointing shocks or mistakes later on.

You will need to appoint a solicitor and the sooner you find one the better. He or she will check the title of the property and potential problems like boundaries, rights of way or major developments that might be planned for the locality that could affect the property. Your solicitor will oversee the transfer of funds to complete the sale and formally register the change of ownership with the authorities.

The legal process

Engaging a lawyer

As property laws vary considerably abroad and have many potential pitfalls, a buyer ideally needs to engage an English-speaking lawyer familiar with both the law of the country where the property is located as well as the law of the country the buyer is resident in.

The legal process can be slow in many parts of the world and hold-ups can lose you the property, so choose your solicitor with care. Ideally, you should look for one who has a good command of both your mother tongue and of the language of the country you are buying in. Their fees, expertise and enthusiasm can vary greatly. Obtain quotes and chat to several before making a final choice. Some charge a percentage of the purchase price while others charge by the hour. It will be more expensive to use an international lawyer based in the UK rather than a local one. Ask whether you will be charged a fixed fee and, if so, ask whether this includes everything, down to the search and electronic bank transfer fees, postage and any local taxes. Ask what the charges will be if the sale falls through. If you only obtain a guide price you could be charged for every fax or letter on top.

Buying a property in your own country can be traumatic enough, but when you are buying abroad you are often using a legal system that is completely different in every aspect from what you are used to, from transferring the property through to inheritance law. There are a lot of potential problems that most buyers are unlikely to consider and which can cause far greater difficulties than they would in the UK. Inheritance is usually one of the most important issues (see p.221). This subject can be very complex abroad, especially if things are complicated by such factors as second marriages and cohabitation.

Therefore, there is a great need for a suitably qualified professional to oversee the legal aspects of a purchase or sale, who can be a lawyer (or solicitor) or in some countries, such as Britain, a licensed conveyancer. Conveyancing is also carried out in some countries by a public notary, who oversees the sale on behalf of the government (see p.227).

Such firms carry out the property acquisition, which involves vetting the contract to see that it is legal, clear and fair, providing translations when needed and carrying out local enquiries and searches. The lawyer should ensure that the property has good title (i.e. it belongs to the vendor or that he has legal authority from the owner to sell it) and is not burdened by encumbrances (outstanding mortgages, loans, local taxes, utilities bills or other debts). The property should have no pre-emption rights or restrictive covenants (such as rights of way), and there should be no plans for development that would adversely affect it, such as airports, shops, retail parks or railway lines.

The lawyer should check that the property has the necessary planning permission and building permits and that the property, if applicable, was built according to such permissions.

The lawyer should be able to advise on the subject of under-declaration, where a deflated purchase price is declared to the authorities to reduce the tax liability, a common occurrence in many countries. Under-declaration can carry the risk of heavy penalties.

There are two principal stages where the lawyer is involved: the signing of the preliminary contract and the completion of the sale where the deed of sale is signed by both parties.

Specialist firms can also advise about related matters such as commissioning a survey, raising finance, converting and sending funds, property insurance, timeshare sales, emigration and retirement, setting up in business abroad, taxation, and dealing with foreign inheritance laws. They should ensure your money is protected if you have bought before the property is finished. In such a case there is always the possibility that the developer could go out of business before completion, and the lawyer should make sure that there are safeguards to protect you against this.

UK solicitors specialising in foreign property conveyancing

Countries that these firms of lawyers specialise in are noted.

- **Baily Gibson**, 5 Station Parade, Beaconsfield, Buckinghamshire HP9 2PG, **t** (01494) 672661; **www.bailygibson.co.uk**. Spain.

- **Bennett and Co.**, 144 Knutsford Road, Wilmslow, Cheshire SK9 6JP, UK, **t** (01625) 586937; **www.bennet-and-co.com**. International lawyers dealing with property transactions, inheritance and taxation in Europe, the United States and the Caribbean. Associated firms are in Lisbon, Albufeira, Madrid, Marbella, Alicante, Torrevieja, Tenerife, Barcelona, Majorca, Ibiza, Lanzarote, Paris, Athens, Marseille, Gibraltar, Cyprus and Istanbul.

- **Brooker Grindrod**, Suite 3, Dudley House, High Street, Bracknell, Berkshire RG12 1LL, **t** (01344) 456565. Spain.

- **Carter Slater and Co.**, 41 Harborough Road, Kingsthorpe, Northampton NN2 7SH, **t** (01604) 717505. Spain, Cyprus, Portugal, France.

- **Champion Miller and Honey**, 153 High Street, Tenterden, Kent TN30 6JT, **t** (01580) 762251.

- **Cornish and Co.**, 1–7 Hainault Street, Ilford, Essex IG1 4EL, **t** (020) 8478 3300; **www.cornishco.com**. Spain, France, Cyprus, Italy, Gibraltar, Malta, Greece and Portugal.

- **Croft Baker & Co.**, 95 Aldwych, London WC2B 4JF, **t** (020) 7242 3370. Spain, France, Portugal.

- **De Pinna Notaries**, 35 Piccadilly, London W1V 0PJ, **t** (020) 7208 2900; **www.depinna.co.uk**. France, Spain, Portugal, Germany, Italy.

- **Glaisyers Glickman**, 559 Barlow Moor Road, Chorlton Cum Hardy, Manchester M21 8AN, **t** (0161) 881 5371. Spain.

- **John Howell and Co.**, 17 Maiden Lane, London WC2E 7NL, **t** (020) 7420 0400; **f** (020) 7836 3626; **www.europelaw.com**. This firm covers property conveyancing and related matters in France, Spain, Portugal and Italy.

- **Leathes Prior**, 74 The Close, Norwich NR1 4DR, **t** (01603) 610911; **www.leathesprior.co.uk**. Europe.

- **Lita Gale**, 43 Gower Street, London WC1E 6HH, **t** (020) 7580 2066; **www.litagale.com**. Spain, Portugal, with branches in Lisbon, Faro, Madeira and throughout Spain.

- **Neville de Rougemont**, Greentree, Ascot Road, Holyport, Maidenhead, SL6 2JB, **t** (01628) 778566; **www.nevillederougemont.com**. Portugal, with an office in Lisbon.

- **Sean O'Connor and Co.**, 2 River Walk, Tonbridge, Kent TN9 1DT, **t** (01732) 365378. France.

- **Pannone and Partners**, 123 Deansgate, Manchester M3 2BU, **t** (0161) 909 3000; www.pannone.com. Spain, France.

- **G. Pazzi-Axworthy**, Llys Eira, Birklands Lane, St Albans, Hertfordshire AL1 1EQ, **t** (01727) 823186. Italy.

- **Penningtons**, 69 Old Broad Street, London EC2M 1PE, **t** (020) 7457 3000; **www.penningtons.co.uk**. Most of the European Union, Norway, Switzerland, South Africa, Hong Kong, Denmark and Russia.

- **Prettys**, 25 Elm Street, Ipswich, Suffolk IP1 2AD, **t** (01473) 232121; **www.prettys.co.uk**. Europe.

- **Pritchard Englefield**, 14 New Street, London EC2M 4TR, **t** (020) 7972 9720; **www.pritchardenglefield.eu.com**. France, Germany.

- **Russell-Cooke Potter and Chapman**, **t** (020) 8789 9111; **www.russell-cooke.co.uk**. France.

- **Michael Soul and Associates,** 16 Old Bailey, London EC4M 7EG, **t** (020) 7597 6292; **www.spanishlawyer.co.uk.** Offices in Madrid, Malaga and Marbella.

- **Taylors,** Red Brick House, 28–32 Trippet Lane, Sheffield S1 4EL, **t** (0114) 276 6767; **www.taylorssolicitors.co.uk.** France.

- **John Venn and Sons,** 95 Aldwych, London WC2B 4JF, **t** (020) 7395 4300; **www.johnvenn.co.uk.** Spain, France, Portugal, Italy, Switzerland.

- **Withers,** 16 Old Bailey, London EC4M 7EG, **t** (020) 7936 1000; **www.withers.co.uk.** France, Spain, offices in Milan and New York.

In addition, embassies and consulates can usually provide a list of lawyers, and the **Law Society** (50 Chancery Lane, London WC2A 1SX, UK, **t** (020) 7242 1222; **www.lawsociety.org.uk**) can provide details of lawyers specialising in property sales abroad.

The notary

This public official, who is a crucial part of the conveyancing process in countries such as France, represents neither buyer nor seller but ensures that all documents are in order on behalf of the government.

There are two principal stages where the notary is involved: the signing of the preliminary contract and the completion of the sale where the deed of sale is signed by both parties.

He registers the property and makes sure that all applicable state taxes are paid upon completion, and makes various other checks relating to things such as the sales contract and any developments that could directly affect the property. It is advisable to engage your own lawyer to protect your interests even when a notary is involved in a sale.

When you are ready to buy

Before committing yourself to buying, ensure that an independent, English-speaking lawyer specialising in the conveyancing process of the country you wish to buy in has checked that all matters relating to the property, such as boundaries, access, connection to utilities and current ownership of the property, are clear and satisfactory.

- **Are there any restrictions on things such as further building on the property, making structural alterations, running a business or letting the property out?**

- **Have you had an independent survey carried out by a suitably qualified surveyor? Do you know about all the tax implications of owning a property in the country in question, and of the local inheritance laws?**

• Is the contract to buy satisfactory, stating the correct requirements, such as guaranteed vacant possession on the agreed completion date? Obtain professional advice about property tax, inheritance tax, capital gains tax and other financial matters relating to your purchase.

• Do ensure that you have sufficient funds to cover all fees and expenses relating to the purchase. Don't pay anything until your lawyer says so.

Surveys

Regardless of whether or not it is common practice locally to commission a survey before buying, in most cases you will want a survey to ascertain the condition of the property. Buildings standards vary greatly around the world and some regions offer considerable threats to the stability of a building, such as an increased risk of earthquakes or hurricanes, or wood-boring insects like termites, or poor building land resulting in an increased risk of subsidence. Obviously, the older and more unusual a property is, and worse the condition, the more useful a survey will be. This can be carried out by a surveyor, engineer or technical architect.

Even if the property has a low asking price, a survey may still be needed as the cost of repairing serious defects can far exceed the cost of purchase.

If a property has been restored, ask to see bills detailing works done. Are there guarantees for such things as damp proofing?

Whether you commission a survey or not, there are many things you can check yourself before buying. *See* pp.213–214 for further details. It is worth testing things such as electrical sockets, light switches, doors and windows, taps and drains. Just because they are there doesn't mean that they are in good repair.

Making an offer on a property

Finding the property you want can be difficult enough, but clinching the deal can be a substantial hurdle in itself. By the time you are ready to make the offer, you should have visited the property several times to ensure that it is the property for you. You should be aware of your legal responsibilities once you have made the offer. Would you later be able to pull out from the deal should the need arise, or would you now be legally committed and would walking away from the deal therefore be a very costly or difficult process?

Find out when the vendor is likely to be in a position to move. Would the property be so attractive if there was a lengthy wait for possession – for example, if you were to miss out visiting the property during the upcoming summer?

Clarify exactly what will remain in and what will be removed from the property. Such things as curtains, curtain rails and tracks, carpets and built-in cookers, lamp shades, wall lights, built-in cupboards, shelving, garden furniture and plants and sheds can be very expensive to replace all at once. Would you be interested in buying the refrigerator, dishwasher, washing machine, tumble drier and any other appliances on offer?

If you want to make an offer, you probably won't be taken seriously if you offer substantially less than the asking price unless you know the vendor is desperate to sell, the property has been on the market for a long time or the property has serious problems that need rectifying.

Is the property being offered at a fair price?

There are so many factors that can affect the value of a home. In the city, a central location will increase the asking price; in the countryside, seclusion, mature gardens, proximity to water, and selling in the summer all help to increase the value of a property, as do easy access to main commuting routes, being well sited in an attractive village or town, such as near a park, on the village green or on the edge of a village.

Factors like noise from a flight path, motorway or railway line, a nearby night-club, restaurant, tower block, industrial estate or electricity pylon are among the many things that can hinder a property's value.

More bedrooms does not necessarily mean a more expensive price. Three double bedrooms is better than five cramped boxrooms purporting to be bedrooms. Restructuring a house to reduce five bedrooms to three, if done well, could enhance profitability as the resulting light, spacious design, perhaps with a gallery and other novel features, can be especially appealing. Added space, such as an extension, should be in keeping with the house.

Making the offer

Unlike in England, Wales and Northern Ireland (not Scotland), where vendors usually realise that their property may sell for under the 'asking price', in some countries it is almost unheard of to offer anything below the asking price, and the asking price may on the contrary be simply a starting point for discussions about the final purchase price, which everyone knows will almost certainly be higher. Find out exactly about the traditions of property-buying in the country you are buying in. A good knowledge of the local property market will put you in a stronger bargaining position.

Establish how long the property has been on the market. The longer it is, the more likely the vendor will be receptive to bargaining. If you make a lower offer, justify it by pointing out problems that could be expensive to put right, such as ancient wiring or structural problems. Sell your advantages as a buyer. If you are a cash buyer, remind the vendor.

You may have to wait for a decision, or your offer may be accepted or rejected straight away. You may instead enter a period of haggling. It is probably not worth jeopardising the deal for the sake of a few hundred pounds, if the vendor ups the price slightly or quibbles over the worth of the decrepit washing machine he is leaving behind. In many areas, especially those popular with British buyers in France, Italy and Spain, it can be important to move fast to ensure that the sale goes through. If it fails because you quibbled over £500 it could cost you far more to start the home searching process all over again.

After you have made the offer on the property you want, and it is accepted, contact your solicitor frequently to make sure your file stays at the top of their invariably large pile of clients.

The stages of buying

The preliminary contract

The first stage of buying is normally the signing of a purchase contract indicating your intent to buy. It is very advisable to have this preliminary contract checked by a lawyer before signing. If the contract requires translating, be aware that the translation may be inaccurate and is not legally binding.

- **Be wary of being tied to conditions you may not be able to keep to, such as completing within a specified time a short period from signing the preliminary contract. Some contracts specify that simply losing your deposit is not an option should you wish to pull out of the sale, but you are instead legally compelled to go ahead with the sale whatever the circumstances.**

- **Ask your lawyer to insert clauses to cover you against circumstances outside your control – the most common being a clause releasing you from the contract should you fail to obtain a mortgage.**

- **You usually pay a deposit of between 5 and 10 per cent of the purchase price on signing the contract. Make sure you know by which terms you could lose or have your deposit returned.**

Payment for your home

Your solicitor will be able to advise of the best form of payment for the balance owing on the property before completion. Transfer of large sums should be at the commercial rate of exchange rather than the higher tourist rate.

Importing and exporting money

Most countries present few or no barriers to the import or export of funds, although it is common for countries to require foreigners to declare the importation or exportation of funds over a set amount. There may be a limit to the amount of cash that can be brought in or taken out of many countries. If required, it is important to declare funds used for buying a home, as otherwise they could later be confiscated.

Payment methods

- **Personal cheque:** These can take considerable time to clear abroad.

- **Bank draft:** These should always be sent by registered or recorded mail and the disadvantage is that if a draft is lost or stolen it cannot be cancelled. Some banks treat them as normal cheques and the recipient has to wait for the draft to clear.

- **International money transfers:** In today's electronic age, making international money transfers (also known as swift transfers) is usually quick; normally they are processed within three days, and are relatively inexpensive. Most banks and building societies can arrange them and usually either charge a percentage of the amount you are moving (for example 0.25 per cent is charged by Lloyds TSB) and others charge a flat fee (Nationwide charges £20). Ask your bank how it calculates exchange rates and whether the rate is fixed for the day of transfer.

Completion

When it comes to signing the deed of sale, of which you receive a copy, you should check that the property is in the same condition as it was when you agreed to buy. You should be clear about the capital gains tax and inheritance tax consequences of signing the deed.

Properties in some countries do not have title deeds, and in this case ownership is shown by registration of the property at the land registry.

Preparing for moving day

There are a variety of things to do before you can move house. You need to consider the logistics of the move – who will do what? You also need to think about a variety of insurances in case anything gets broken along the way or something unlikely happens to your property – storms, fallen trees or fires have been known to happen within hours of moving in. You also need to think about closing off utilities in your former home, informing relevant agencies of your new address and ensuring that everything is available when you need it in your new property. Make lists and take time to think things through logically so that everything dovetails as you hope.

Removals

When the removal company comes to quote for the work, be sure to show everything that is to be moved. It's easy to forget an attic or garden shed stuffed with boxes, and it can be an unwelcome shock if the extra cost for these only emerges on moving day. Homes that have been altered so that furniture that originally went in can't be removed easily, and cumbersome, heavy objects like a piano on the first floor, will bump up the price.

You also need to consider things such as whether you want removers to take down curtains and dismantle self-assembly beds and furniture and fixtures and fittings. These usually need to be quoted for and will cost extra. Do you have unstraightforward items like antiques, pets, plants or a wine collection that need special care?

If you are tempted to do it all yourself, it may be a false economy when you take into account time off work, the cost of materials, van hire and labour costs. There could also be risks of damage and unforeseen hitches.

Charges by professional removal firms can vary considerably, so shop around for an experienced firm that can offer a competitive quote. Use a removal firm accredited to a recognised trade association.

Ask removal firms whether there a charge for loan of boxes and other packaging. How much work are you required to do in preparation? Bear in mind that many removal firms will not accept a booking until contracts have been exchanged in case the sale falls through.

Will the van be able to access your street? Ensure there is adequate parking and inform the removal firm of any parking restrictions, poor access, spiral staircases and other potential difficulties in advance. Removers are not permitted to interfere with mains services, so contact gas, electricity and water companies well in advance of the move.

You will need to have someone available to oversee what is being moved at both addresses. A clear plan showing where you want furniture placed allows the removers to put it exactly where you want it rather than leaving you with another job to do.

Think carefully about exactly what you need to transport. It is cost-effective to buy many items again at your destination rather than transport existing ones. Check that any electrical goods you wish to take will operate at the new destination. You may need adaptors or voltage transformers.

What will you do with the goods you are leaving behind? Will they remain in the home you are leaving and renting out, should you put them in storage or dispose of them?

The more details about the move you can supply to the removal firm, the more accurate their quote and less likelihood of nasty financial extras on completion of the move. Is the property an easily accessed bungalow or a cramped apartment on the sixth floor with no lift? Are you moving to an island with infrequent ferries or is the property sited just off the highway?

Ask at least three companies for a written quotation that includes the company's full terms and conditions and ask them to supply a quote free of charge and without obligation. Ask plenty of questions. Will the items be moved by boat, air or road? Is packing included or will you be required to pack everything, and will boxes be provided free of charge? Does the quote include items in the attic, basement, garage and garden shed? Is insurance included and is this for 'all risks' to the replacement value of all goods?

- **British Association of Removers Overseas**, 3 Churchill Court, 58 Station Road, North Harrow HA2 7SA, UK, **t** (020) 8861 3331; **www.barmovers.com.** Can provide a list of companies specialising in international relocation.

- **International Federation of International Furniture Removers**, 69 rue Picard B5, 1080 Brussels, Belgium, **t** (00 32) 2 426 51 60; **www.fidi.com.** Can also put you in touch with removal firms and shipping companies.

Removal insurance

Insurance for the move will generally cost about 10 per cent above the total moving cost but is recommended. Check the small print in the policy. Is 'new for old' cover offered or only indemnity cover? Items you pack yourself will generally not be covered. It is a good idea to make a photographic record of your belongings in the event of your needing to make a claim.

Check that the removal firm, if you are using one, is insuring your possessions. It is a good idea also to contact your insurance company to try and get temporary cover through your contents insurance policy, or even a temporary policy for the move.

Household insurance

Usually you should insure your property abroad the moment you own it, for buildings, contents and third-party liability cover. In some countries this can be even more necessary than in the UK, where risks like flooding, hurricanes, earthquakes and storms can be significant.

It is often cheaper to arrange insurance for your home abroad with a local company, but if the documentation is not in English, unless you understand it or can easily get it translated it may be better to pay extra for a policy originating in the UK. And a domestic insurer may provide better cover, claiming may be easier and you may have better protection under UK law. Currently UK insurers that cover homes abroad include **Saga**, **Norwich Union**, **Hiscox** and **Andrew Copeland International**.

Insurance policies vary greatly, even when you're getting identical cover, so be sure to get several quotes for each type of insurance. Check the small print of any policies you consider carefully. Definitions and cover can vary greatly.

It is important to ascertain conditions your insurer may attach to periods when the property is not occupied. You may be required to switch off the water, electricity and gas, and not doing so could cause the insurance to be void. Typically, cover for hazards such as theft may lapse after 30, 60 or 90 days of unoccupancy. You may be able to extend this period to six months or more. Check how 'unoccupancy' is defined. It does not necessarily mean that someone has to be living at the property full time. Weekly visits by a local agent may be enough to define it as occupied.

If your property will have paying guests, check that the policy covers this. Many policies only cover friends and family. Check that you have sufficient legal liability cover against being sued should someone be injured in your home, especially if you are taking out a local rather than UK policy.

Your mortgage deal may include a condition that you buy the lender's insurance; otherwise buy directly from an insurance company or an insurance broker. There may be a small insurance tax added to the premium.

There are two main types of household insurance: buildings and contents. Buildings insurance covers the building itself, its fixtures and fittings, garden walls and fences. Contents insurance covers everything else, things that you would normally take with you if you moved.

By increasing the excess (the amount you pay on any claim) slightly, the cost of insurance policies can reduce surprisingly, so ask how much the premium would be if you took the highest excess. Combining buildings and contents insurance may attract a discount. Policies ideally should be linked to inflation.

Many countries also require third-party cover against financial liability for injuries or accidents to third parties on your property.

Buildings insurance

Not only is it extremely unwise to omit to take out buildings insurance – which pays for repairing or rebuilding your home should it be destroyed in a fire or other calamity – but you will be required to have this insurance if you have a mortgage. Your mortgage lender may offer to provide this insurance, and sometimes, though less and less frequently, it may insist you take out its cover.

The cost of the premium relates to the cost of rebuilding your home from scratch. Buildings insurance is for the rebuilding cost rather than for the value of the property, which may be very different. This can be difficult to work out but your lender will state how much to insure for, otherwise there may be a figure in your survey if you had one done, or your insurance company may be able to help. Otherwise, consult a local builder or surveyor.

While the UK has strict building controls and regulations, construction methods can be very different abroad, and this can be reflected in the rebuilding costs. The rebuilding cost for an old property, especially, may be very difficult to assess and could be much more than the market value of the property.

In some countries a proportion of the insurance premium goes to the state insurance fund. In Spain, for example, the *consorcio* provides cover against natural disasters such as floods, and if you were to claim in such a situation you would be claiming against the *consorcio* rather than your insurance company. A similar system operates in France. In other countries, notably Greece and Italy, earthquake cover is important. Local policies may only provide you with half the sum insured for this risk, so check before taking out the cover.

If you underinsure, any claim is likely to be reduced. The insurance should commence before you take ownership of the property.

If you live in a flat or apartment block, there may be a communal insurance policy covering the whole building, for which you pay a share.

Policies generally cover eventualities like flood, fire and water damage and may include malicious acts, like vandalism. You can add on extras like accidental damage, and legal protection covering fees in the event of a legal dispute. For the policy to remain valid, it is important to fulfil all the requirements of the policy, which may be very specific, for example fitting a certain standard of lock. Check the strength of the door or window locks are fitted to – a good lock on rotten wood is useless. Regions prone to risks like flooding or subsidence may incur higher insurance costs.

Contents insurance

Contents insurance can be of two types. The cheaper is indemnity, where your contents are insured for their current worth. Therefore a camera would be valued as being second-hand. Pricier is new-for-old cover, where your contents are insured for what it would cost to replace them.

You can pay extra for accidental cover, which covers anything you break yourself, and you can also pay extra for all-risks cover to insure possessions outside the home.

Make a detailed inventory of everything you own and try to work out the value as accurately as possible, as if you are under-insured your claims will not be met in full and if you over-insure you are wasting money.

Particularly valuable items will usually have to be specified on the policy otherwise only a proportion of their worth will be covered, and you may need to use a professional valuer to obtain a price the insurance company will be happy with if you have items like antiques or collectables, which could be difficult to value.

There are lots of add-ons you can buy covering such things as family legal expenses, garden furniture, freezer contents, plants, cash, and replacement of lost or stolen keys and having locks changed.

The days leading up to the move

If you are relocating abroad rather than buying a second home, the process leading up to the move could go something like this.

• **In good time you should carry out the following:** If you live in rented accommodation you will have to give your landlord notice that you intend to leave. You should arrange for a new school or schools, if applicable, in your new location in good time. Passports should be comfortably within expiry dates and you should check whether there are any special entry requirements such as visas, permits or inoculations. Pets may require inoculations or quarantine. Ascertain the procedure for shipping your belongings and arrange health, travel, buildings, contents and other insurances as necessary. Organise the opening of a bank account in your new country of residence.

If you intend to bring furniture, household goods and other items to furnish your home, check that there are no restrictions on importation. Also, make sure that all electrical items are compatible, either in terms of voltage (which could entail the need for a transformer) or format; for example, videos suitable for a UK video player may not work in an American one.

It may be cheaper and easier to buy things locally for your home abroad, and availability of spares, servicing and repairs may not be good for items that are not commonly available in the country you are going to. UK furniture may not be suitable in the style of your home abroad or for the climate there.

• **With a month to go:** Book the removal firm if applicable, obtaining packing boxes and starting to fill them – with clear labelling on the outside. Put books in small boxes as large ones will be difficult to lift. Chuck out unwanted goods and arrange your final utility bills at your old home. Clear rubbish from the loft or the garage and sell anything of any value at a car boot sale or donate it to charity.

You can start obtaining quotes from removal companies. Being flexible about dates can help get the price down. Will you do the packing yourself or leave it to them? If you do it yourself, label the boxes clearly with the contents and the room they will be going into.

• **With a week to go:** Arrange for professional disconnection of appliances you are removing like a gas cooker; arrange for final readings of gas, water and electricity supplies. Notifying your local authority that you are leaving may result in a refund of rates; you may be due for a rebate on your tax or social security contributions. Cancel direct debits and standing orders connected with your old home (such as gas, electricity and mortgage) and begin new ones at your new home. Cancel milk and newspaper deliveries and pay the final bills; return library books and other borrowed items. Remove fitted items like mirrors, pictures, shelves and so on and pack them carefully.

As well as telling friends and family, inform the following in the UK of your change of address: gas, electricity, water and telephone companies; insurance companies (contents, buildings, car and life insurance); bank and building societies; doctor, dentist and optician; employer; school or schools; pension provider; loan companies; credit and store card companies; Driver and Vehicle

Licensing Authority (DVLA); council tax department; national savings and premium bonds; TV licensing department; electoral register; schools; the Inland Revenue; the Department of Social Security; lawyer; accountant; organisations you have subscriptions with.

• **Just before the move:** Disconnect the cooker and washing machine and defrost the freezer. Check that your solicitor has arranged for the new owner to take over the council tax bill.

Arrange connection of water, gas and electricity at your new address. You may have to pay a deposit and arrange for periodical access to meters for billing. Are there any guarantees or service agreements relating to the property that you will be taking over? Will you be receiving keys for all of the locks in the property, from front door to garden shed?

• **On moving day:** Take electricity and gas meter readings and read the water meter if there is one at your old address. Ask for a final telephone bill. Leave a set of keys with your estate agent at your old property and label the spares. Make sure important documents and emergency numbers are accessible. Leave pre-addressed labels so that new owners can send on any mail that hasn't been redirected. Lock all windows and doors before leaving.

In many countries it is an unwritten rule not to remove things like lightbulbs and light fittings, doorhandles, fireplaces, fitted cupboards or anything cemented down or planted in the garden but in others many such things are routinely removed, so be prepared.

You should leave the property in the condition in which the buyer first saw it, but cleared of all the items that were not included in the purchase price or bought separately by the purchaser.

Be careful not to leave anything as the new owners would be able to claim they are now theirs, making it very difficult to recover them.

• **Soon after arrival:** In some countries foreigners are required to register with the police and it may be a good idea in some destinations to register with your local embassy or consulate after taking up residence abroad. Also register with your local social security office.

Managing finance

Appointing a local financial professional such as an accountant or a tax adviser to deal with your local financial affairs is sensible, and in some cases mandatory, for example in Spain, where a fiscal representative is required by the government to be appointed by non-resident property owners to deal with their taxation matters.

> ### Moving in
>
> Make lists of everything that you need to do and give yourself enough time to research and organise things calmly. Above all, do not leave your finances to chance and remember to do the following – it will make the move safer and far more stress-free:
>
> • Insure the buildings and contents, using a reputable insurer. Your policy should cover long periods of absence or of being let, if this will be the case.
>
> • Make a will in the country you have bought in and revise your British will. Investigate your tax position and liabilities using a specialist lawyer or accountant.
>
> • Open a bank account in the country you have bought in, to pay all utilities services, local taxes and other required payments.

A local bank account

Although many owners of homes abroad get by using a combination of travellers' cheques, credit cards and cash exchanged at a *bureau de change*, in the long term this is less secure, more expensive and more troublesome than opening a local bank account, which may, anyway, be necessary for paying utility and tax bills. Be aware that in many countries overdrawing on a bank account is not treated as lightly as it often is in the UK, but is treated as a criminal offence and can greatly hinder your credit rating and financial dealings abroad in the future.

You may be able to open a foreign account with a bank that has branches in your home country. For example, an increasing number of British high street banks have a presence abroad, notably in France and Spain. Some banks abroad offer a multilingual service.

Financial services

Some financial companies are offering convenient services organising currency transfers for regular payments like overseas mortgage payments, repatriating foreign income, spending money and pension transfers. It takes the hassle out of regularly buying currency to settle monthly financial commitments, which can be time-consuming and also makes efficient budgeting impossible due to currency fluctuations. They generally make their money on the exchange rate and do not charge fees or commissions like the international transfer fees and commissions charged by banks. Rates can usually be fixed for a set period such as six months or two years.

• **HIFX**, 59–60 Thames Street, Windsor, Berkshire SL4 1TX, **t** (01753) 859159; **www.hifx.co.uk/mpa**. Offers a 'monthly payments abroad' service.

Securing your home

Crime prevention has advanced greatly in recent years, with increasingly sophisticated alarms coming as standard. As well as alarms that are monitored 24 hours a day, there are even systems that allow you to monitor your property remotely from another country using a computer link.

If you have valuable furniture or antiques, microchips linked to tracking systems can be injected into upholstery or into a tiny hole drilled into the back of a picture frame.

Although you can never make your home completely secure, you can make it so much trouble to burgle that the casual thief will move on to the next property. Sensored external security lights, prickly bushes, noisy gravel and large, cumbersome window boxes with large plants can all help deter a burglar. Ladders, tools and climbing frames left around the garden can help a thief.

As far as fire prevention and protection goes, at the very least fit a smoke alarm on each floor. These are a legal requirement in some countries. The cheapest, ionization alarms, are sensitive to smoke from flaming fires, while optical alarms are better at detecting smouldering fires.

Conclusion and summary: final tips on buying abroad

- Decide exactly what you need from the start, especially the things you can and cannot live without.
- Research thoroughly and decide upon an area before looking at any properties.
- Never underestimate the cost of restoration, especially as large properties are often more affordable abroad.
- Take into account the full amount of the associated costs of buying (lawyers fees, land registry and notary's fees, taxes, bank charges, etc.), which can add significantly to the purchase price in many countries.
- Visit the area in winter as well as in summer.
- Never assume holiday lets will finance the venture and check rental income claims.
- Bear in mind that as many British second-home hotspots have been funded by a buoyant UK property market, any UK property market slump would hit the second-home market far more strongly than many buyers often appreciate.

- Consult an independent English-speaking lawyer experienced in the conveyancing system of the country you are buying in, not one nominated by the estate agent or local notary.

- Ensure everything relating to a property such as rights of way, boundaries, proposed nearby developments, contract conditions etc are clarified before committing to buy.

- Work with registered tradespeople.

- Always get written quotes for any work to be done, and invoices when it is finished.

- Check the exchange rate: foreign property transactions are at risk of foreign exchange turbulence, which could considerably increase costs between paying a deposit and paying the balance.

- Renovate in the local style: turn your property in a British home and it may be difficult to sell.

- Adequately budget for transportation of household goods and furniture to your home abroad.

- You need to plan for capital gains tax and inheritance tax and possibly other taxes such as property tax, and income tax if you receive rental income.

- Consider carefully in whose name the property should be bought to avoid a future possible heavy inheritance tax bill. Also, changing the owner after purchase can be costly.

- Review your British will and create a separate will abroad.

- Do not pay any money over to anyone until your lawyer says that you can.

- Do not sign any binding documents you don't understand without having them checked by a suitably qualified expert first.

- Study timetables: do the transport options operate all year round?

- Study price structures of airlines: if the only low-cost flights are available at inconvenient times and for only a few days in the depths of winter, and summer prices are astronomical, think again. Ideally there should be more than one airport offering affordable flights a comfortable distance from the property to cover the possibility of a route being discontinued or carrier going bust.

- Fully research the journey to the property from the motorway/port/airport. Difficult journeys will deter you from visiting the property frequently.

- Acknowledge that it may take far longer to sell your home abroad than you took to buy it. In France, for instance, it is common for British purchasers to buy in a weekend, but take around two years to sell.

Letting and Selling your Property

07

Letting

Many buyers of overseas property aim to finance it by letting it out. Yet although letting can offset some of the costs of financing and maintaining the property, it is rare for it to completely cover costs. **Never buy if rental income has to cover all of your costs, as this can never be guaranteed.**

It is important to thoroughly assess the local rental market before buying, noting the sorts of things that attract renters, such as good access to transport links like airports and motorways, and plenty of tourist attractions nearby. It is a good idea to visit agents and pose as a potential renter yourself before buying a property, to see the current situation of the rental market first-hand rather than relying on the word of a local letting agent. You may for example be presented with scores of properties available to rent at far less than you were hoping to receive for your property.

It is imperative to check that you are actually permitted to rent the property out at all. Some countries (there are widespread limits to letting in the USA, the Republic of Cyprus and Malta, for example) and councils within countries have restrictions on letting and special zoned areas, and many apartment blocks and property complexes also have restrictions.

You have to ask yourself whether, once you have moved in and made the place your own, you will be happy renting out to strangers. Many novice letters assume that their friends and family will flock to rent out the property, too, but this often does not happen, and it can also be difficult charging people you know rental, even at a discounted rate.

If you are not organising lets yourself, choose the letting agent carefully as in the past many have ceased trading, in debt to their clients. Typically, agents charge 20 per cent of the rental income for their fee, although this can vary greatly from country to country and depends on whether a full management service is required. Rental income is taxable in most countries and an annual tax return has to be filed. All property-related expenses are usually deductible against income.

Valuables will have to be safeguarded and the possibility of breakages covered. You will need to be able to pay any shortfall in the event of rental incomes falling short of those expected.

Unfortunately, often the times of highest letting potential are the times you are most likely to want to spend time at the property yourself. You will also need to ensure the place remains in immaculate condition and that all appliances are working properly, and would need to factor in the extra time and cost of such maintenance. The property would have to be furnished to a standard that meets the local safety regulations. You will probably have to pay for professional management of the property, as well as an accountant to calculate the tax you would have to pay on rental income.

Selling

If you decide to sell your home abroad, invest some time in investigating the local property market. There are too many factors at work in the sale of a property for there to be a definitive, ideal time to sell your home, but if you are a vendor it is probably best to follow the pack: the best time to sell is likely to be when the majority of other sellers are trying to, when the market is strong and prices are rising.

If, on the other hand, there is a property slump and prices are falling, it may be better to ride out the storm if you are able to, perhaps by letting out your home long-term until the market has picked up.

Estate agents

Despite the negative view so many people have of estate agents, the overwhelming majority of buyers and sellers still use them both in the UK and abroad.

If your home is at the luxury end of the market, you may be able to use the services of one of the big, well-known international agents like **FPD Savills**, **t** (020) 7499 8644; **www.fpdsavills.co.uk**; **Hamptons International, t** (020) 7589 8844; **www.hamptons.co.uk**; **Sotheby's Realty, t** (020) 7598 1600; **www.soth ebysrealty.com**; **Chesterton International, t** (020) 7201 2070; **www.chesterton. co.uk** or **Knight Frank, t** (020) 7629 8171; **www.knightfrank.com**. These can all give access to wealthy buyers around the world.

But most people will have the option of a local agent in the country the property is located in or, in areas popular with foreign buyers, a British-based agent who specialises in selling foreign properties to Brits.

Take care in choosing an agent, especially as in many countries there are few legal constraints and a high proportion of unscrupulous operators who usually congregate in resorts and other areas popular with foreign buyers. You could initially pose as a buyer and then ask the agent lots of questions. Test out their knowledge of the area and see what other types of property they have on their books. Some may specialise in expensive homes, others may consistently deal with the cheapest ones, or properties in need of modernisation.

Experience counts for a lot. You want an agent who can successfully combine assessing what's been selling recently, seeing where the market is now, and reading how the market will be over the next few months when the property will be on the market.

Note that commission rates can vary widely from country to country; indeed, commission rates in the UK are among the lowest in the world. If you think the rate of commission is too high you could try haggling, especially if the agent has few properties on its books, but bear in mind that an agent's expertise can often get the vendor a better price that more than compensates for the commission charged.

Be clear about what is included in the package. Do you have to pay extra for advertisements in property magazines or the local press, or for a glossy brochure? Ask the agency to confirm its fees and what will be included in writing. You will be given an agreement to sign. Carefully look at the clauses.

Check the estate agent's details. The photographs of your property should be in colour and taken during daylight, ideally in the summer. Good quality interior shots can also help a lot. Check that the agents' descriptions of the property are accurate. Ensure that easily overlooked features that could make your property more attractive or saleable are mentioned.

It is important to obtain several valuations from different agents, which can vary considerably. Ask each agent to back up their valuation with an explanation of how they reached that figure.

For a quick sale it is important to have your home priced accurately. Too high, and you could put off potential buyers, and being forced to make a price-drop a few weeks on could discourage them further.

Bear in mind that some agents go to great lengths to get your business. If one substantially undervalues your home he may simply want to stimulate a quick sale for high turnover of commission, and if you are given a high figure, the agent may instead be trying to flatter you to get your business, with the intention of dropping the price to a realistic figure a few weeks on.

Selling your home yourself

If you have a particularly attractive home and the market is strong, you could consider selling it yourself, thereby avoiding paying an invariably large commission to an estate agent.

When a sale goes well an agent can seem invaluable: preparing accurate, effective sales details, looking after all the viewings, weeding out unsuitable buyers and negotiating the best possible price.

Yet many house sales don't go like that, and vendors are instead left personally to conduct most of the viewings by potential buyers, who have been enticed by inaccurate, imaginative property particulars and who are looking for something completely different.

To have a chance of selling the property yourself, you need plenty of time and energy, and good negotiating skills. You can advertise on an Internet site dedicated to selling homes privately, or even construct your own website solely for selling your home. You could advertise in one of the magazines geared to property-buyers abroad, or within property sections of national papers.

Selling privately is likely to involve considerable legwork, including arranging valuations so that you can decide on an asking price, drawing up particulars, answering enquiries, arranging and carrying out viewings and negotiating. When you find a buyer, the process should then be handed over to your solicitor, who should make sure that the buyer's solicitor sends a formal letter with confirmation of the offer.

It is important when selling privately to ensure that all sale particulars are accurate, as incorrect statements could result in your being sued for damages or cancellation of the contract, or both.

Encouraging a quick sale

Your buyer is likely to have made an initial decision to buy within the first few seconds of arriving at your property for the first time. Therefore, making a good first impression is vital when you come to sell. Both home and garden should be as spotless as possible, the doorbell should work and there should be no clutter; redecorate where necessary.

If you live in an apartment block, ensure that the communal areas are looking as good as possible. Brighten your property's hallway, maybe sanding the floorboards or installing a neutral carpet and adding extra lighting. If the place is small, keep the doors open when you show people around as it makes the rooms look bigger.

By all means bake bread, grind some coffee beans, make a real fire, put soothing music on, use soft lighting and place fresh flowers around the place when prospective buyers come to view, but it is more important to ensure your home is clean, tidy, aired and uncluttered. Salivating, growling dogs, grumpy teenagers and demanding children can be a real turn off. Don't have a bath or shower before viewers arrive as the bathroom will be steamy and may suggest there is a condensation problem.

The overall impression should be clean, light and simple, using lots of neutral, natural materials. Highly patterned wallpapers and fabrics should be used to a minimum, but the odd splash of bright colour is welcome. The general effect should be calm and comfortable, not fussy.

Cover dated or worn sofas and chairs with large throws in a neutral colour and cover carpet stains with neutrally coloured rugs. Paint tiles white with tile paint and regrout if the grout is grubby.

Bear in mind that some initiatives could be a complete waste of money. It's seldom worth splashing out on an expensive new kitchen or bathroom, for instance, as there's little guarantee that potential buyers will like your taste or that it will add value to the property. Complete redecoration is seldom necessary and may prompt suspicion of your trying to hide hidden faults like damp patches or cracks.

Any evidence of faults spells neglect, so eradicate leaking gutters, loose door handles and dripping taps. Things that may be very cheap to put right can put off buyers because it can suggest the possibility of more serious problems. A slate missing from the roof could be rectified easily but if left may suggest to the buyer that the whole roof needs replacing. A few suspect cracks in the walls could simply need filling with a dab of plaster, but it may also suggest serious structural problems like subsidence. Many potential buyers don't want to take the risk, or the cost and trouble to find out how serious the problem is. It's well worth looking into the cost of every repair and improvement before putting the property on the market.

Have utility and maintenance bills, invoices for work done such as rewiring as well as damp-proofing, timber treatment guarantees and similar paperwork to show potential buyers. Do not hover behind viewers as they look around, but give them ample chance to inspect the property at their own pace.

If your property has some interesting aspect to it – maybe it is unusual architecturally or someone famous has lived in it, for example, it may be worth approaching the local paper or even a national, which may be interested in featuring your home.

Further Information

08

Organisations

In 1973 FOPDAC (the Federation of Overseas Property Developers) was formed to unite agents, developers and specialist consultants active in the international property markets whose common aim is to protect the interest of those buying and selling overseas. It is the UK's primary overseas trade federation.

- **Federation of Overseas Property Developers,** Agents and Consultants (FOPDAC), 95 Aldwych, London WC2B 4JF, UK, **t** (020) 8941 5588; **www.fopdac.com.**

Magazines

The websites for many of these publications often have lots of useful information such as online features, property listings, travel information and plenty of links.

Homes Overseas

Published monthly by Blendon Communications, 207 Providence Square, Mill Street, London SE1 2EW, UK, **t** (020) 7939 9888; **www.homesoverseas.co.uk.**
Long-established magazine on all aspects of buying abroad; covers many countries and has regular features on such things as finance, removals and legal issues. *Homes Overseas* is the UK's best-selling specialist international real estate magazine with independent advice and ideas on all aspects of the overseas property purchase.

A Place in the Sun magazine

Published 13 times a year by Brooklands Media, Medway House, Lower Road, Forest Row, East Sussex RH18 5HE, UK, **t** (01342) 828 700; **www.aplaceinthe-sunmag.co.uk.** This newcomer to accompany the popular Channel 4 television programme has country profiles, features and celebrity interviews on a wide range of regions, mostly in Europe.

Spain magazine

Published monthly by The Media Company Publications, 21 Royal Circus, Edinburgh EH3 6TL, UK, **t** (0131) 226 7766; **www.spainmagazine.info.** Lots of features on all things Spanish: travel, food and drink and style as well as property.

France magazine

Published bi-monthly by Archant Life, Archant House, Oriel Road, Cheltenham, Glos GL50 1BB, UK, **t** (01858) 438832; **www.francemag.com.** Lots of features on all things French: travel, food and drink as well as property.

French Magazine

Published bi-monthly by Merricks Media, Charlotte House, 12 Charlotte Street, Bath BA1 2NE, UK, **t** (01225) 786845; **www.frenchmagazine.co.uk**. Lots of features on all things French: travel, food and drink as well as property. Again.

Italy magazine

Published bi-monthly by Poundbury Publishing, Agriculture House, Dorchester, Dorset DT1 1EF, UK, **t** (01305) 266360; **www.italymag.co.uk**. Calls itself the magazine for lovers of all things Italian and includes features on people, places, style, culture, food and property.

Residence

Published four times per year by Mosaic Magazines, 129-131 City Road, London EC1V 1JB, UK, **t** (020) 7250 3007; **www.residence-int.com**.

Relying rather too much on photographs rather than text, this magazine features a handful of countries around the globe each issue.

French Property News

Published monthly by French Property News, 6 Burgess Mews, London SW19 1UF, UK, **t** (020) 8543 3113; **www.french-property-news.com**.

French Property News has more than 400 advertisers in each edition giving access to tens of thousands of properties throughout France as well as access to specialist solicitors, surveyors, removal companies, builders and other services. The company also stages five French property exhibitions throughout Britain each year. Also covered are all aspects of travelling to, buying and living in France.

Living France magazine

Published monthly by Archant Life, Archant House, Oriel Road, Cheltenham, Glos GL50 1BB, UK, **t** (01242) 216050; **www.livingfrance.com**. Lots of features on all things French: French life and culture, wine and gastronomy, property, home interiors and celebrity interviews, plus an in-depth feature on a particular region or department of France. See also *Everything France* magazine, **www.efmag.co.uk**.

Private Villas

Published by DaltonsHolidays.com, 8th Floor, CI Tower, St George's Square, New Malden, Surrey KT3 4JA, UK, **t** (020) 8329 0222; **www.privatevillas.co.uk**. Property-owners wishing to rent out their homes can be included.

World of Property

Published six times per year by Outbound Publishing, 1 Commercial Road, Eastbourne, East Sussex BN21 3QX, UK, **t** (01323) 726040.

International Homes

Published bi-monthly by International Homes, 3 St John's Court, Moulsham Street, Chelmsford, Essex CM2 0JD, UK, **t** (01245) 358877; **www.international-homes.com/exhibitions.**
Features about countries around the world.

Holiday Villas magazine

Published by Merrick Publishing, Wessex Buildings, Somerton Business Park, Somerton, Somerset TA11 6SB, UK, **t** (01458) 274447; **www.holidayvillasmag azine.co.uk**. Property owners wishing to rent out their homes can be included in this magazine.

Resident Abroad

Published by Resident Abroad, 149 Tottenham Court Road, London W1P 9LL, UK, **t** (020) 7896 2525; **www.ra.st.com**. Aimed at British expatriates, with features on finance, property, employment opportunities and living conditions in countries with substantial British expatriate populations.

Spanish Homes magazine

Published quarterly by Spanish Homes Magazine, 116 Greenwich South Street, Greenwich, London, SE10 8UN, UK, **t** (020) 8469 4381; **www.spanishhomes-magazine.com**. Magazine devoted to all things Spanish including property, cuisine, fashion and travel.

Unique Homes

Published by Unique Homes, 327 Wall Street, Princeton, NJ 08540, USA, **www.uniquehomes.com**. This American publication focuses on the luxury market, with anything from European castles to modern oceanfront villas.

Health and travel guides

Dawood, Dr Richard, *Travellers' Health* (OUP, 2003). A very comprehensive yet readable book on the subject.

Hatt, John, *The Tropical Traveller* (Penguin 1993). A well-written, absorbing and entertaining book full of advice on most aspects of travelling in the tropics, anything from money to flying, health, culture shock, animal and human hazards.

Schroeder, Dick, *Staying Healthy in Asia, Africa and Latin America* (Moon Publications). A detailed, good all-round guide.

Wilson-Howarth, Dr Jane, *Bugs, Bites & Bowels* (Cadogan Guides). Now in its third edition, this excellent book offers practical health advice. Indispensable.

Other publications

Eurotunnel (t 08705 353535/08457 697397; **www.eurotunnel.com**) offers seven free regional 'Discover' guides: *Pas-de-Calais*; *Lille and the Nord*; *Seine Maritime*; *Champagne-Ardenne*; *Flemish Coast*; *Wartime Memories*; *Cities of Flanders*.

Websites

Websites with a good spread of properties around the world are a good start to searching for a property abroad. These include the sites for the international estate agency chains such as **www.fpdsavills.co.uk**, **www.hamptons.co.uk**, **www.sothebysrealty.com**, **www.chesterton.co.uk** and **www.knightfrank.com**.

Website **www.viviun.com** has around 3,500 properties from every corner of the world including the more unusual markets such as Brazil, Costa Rica, the Dominican Republic, Panama, the Philippines, Slovakia and Thailand. It also has sections on hotels, castles and islands for sale. **www.escapeartist.com** is another website with international property listings.

Government travel advice is available from the British Foreign and Commonwealth Office (**www.fco.gov.uk**); the US Department of State Travel Advisory Department (**www.travel.state.gov**); the Australian Department of Foreign Affairs (**www.dfat.gov.au**) and the Canadian Department of Foreign Affairs (**www.dfait-maeci.gc.ca**). Other useful websites are listed below.

- **www.newskys.co.uk**: an online magazine dedicated to the overseas homes market.
- **www.siphealth.com**: has information on private health care.
- **www.tradepartners.gov.uk**: gives investment and trade information on different countries.
- **www.fnworldwide.com**: information about relocation.
- **www.wtgonline.com**: World Travel Guide's website has worldwide travel information.
- **www.directmoving.com**: expatriate information and advice.
- **www.britishexpat.com**: useful site for UK expatriates.
- **www.expatexchange.com**: useful for expatriates.
- **www.expatboards.com**, **www.expatworld.net**, **www.peoplegoing global.com**, **www.expatfocus.com**, **www.expatexpert.com**: these sites give expatriate advice and guides.
- **www.escapeartist.com**: a comprehensive site for expatriates and includes property listings.
- **www.spainexpat.com**: geared to the Spanish expat.

- **www.livingabroad.com**, **www.liveabroad.com**: information on living in a variety of countries.
- **www.expatspouse.com**: has information about working abroad.
- **www.womanabroad.com**: advises on family and career matters.
- **www.tckworld.com**: geared to the children of expatriates.
- **www.expatshopping.com**: this can be used for ordering goods from your home country.
- **www.outpostexpat.nl**: Shell Petroleum's website has information on different countries – not only of interest to employees.
- **www.wheretoretire.com**, **www.seniors.com**: these have information on retirement internationally.
- **www.cibfarnham.com**: the Centre for International Briefing provides courses for expatriates.
- **www.informer.it**: information on Italy.
- **www.adrian-barrett.co.uk**: advice on building work.
- **www.countrylife.co.uk**: *Country Life* magazine's website features property from the upper end of the market.
- **www.eca-international.com**: Employment Conditions Abroad (**t** (020) 7351 7151), publishes guides for expatriates for more than 60 countrie.
- **www.adventure-france.com**: an account of experiences of finding, buying and restoring a property in Calvados.
- **www.la-puce.co.uk**: copious advice on looking for a home in France can be found on author George East's website (*see* pp.76–7).
- **www.lamanche.com**: for information on La Manche, the department of Lower Normandy covering the Cherbourg peninsula.
- **www.francetourism.com**: for a map of France showing all the regions and departments and lots of tourist and general information.
- **www.idealspain.com**: information on living in Spain.

Appendix:
Further Countries

09

Obviously there isn't the room in this book to examine the property markets of every country in the world. The following entries give you an introduction to 14 more countries that are not property hot spots, as such, but which could have investment appeal.

Belgium

Although France is still in many areas astoundingly cheap when compared with Britain, some areas are drowning in Brits. To escape your countrymen head for Belgium, so often overlooked and which offers far more than simply beer, chocolates, Poirot, Tintin and the European Parliament.

It boasts a great coast, and the resort of Knokke is particularly popular with buyers of holiday homes. The area enjoys easy access to four fabulous Belgian cities, Bruges, Antwerp, Ghent and Brussels, all bristling with wonderful cafés, restaurants, shops and culture. Belgium is also ideally located for visiting the Netherlands, Luxembourg and northern France.

Coastal properties suitable as holiday homes tend to be in the form of apartments. There is a far better choice of houses when you focus further inland.

For the coast many buyers focus on Knokke-Heist, De Haan and Ostend, while Antwerp, Ghent, Bruges and Brussels are ideal for short city breaks.

But beware. Belgian property can be appreciably more expensive than neighbouring France. Currently around Knokke a four-bedroom villa near the sea would cost around £350,000, a three-bedroom apartment by the sea would come in at around £125,000, and a modern studio near the coast starts at £70,000 or so. Prices in the best areas of the bigger cities like Antwerp and Brussels can almost be on a par with Mayfair or Belgravia in London.

The property market is steady and secure in Belgium and in both 2002 and 2003 prices rose by about 7 per cent.

Access is good. As well as ferries from Dover to Ostend, there is easy access to Belgium via Eurotunnel and the Calais ferries, whose continental ports are little more than an hour's drive away. For northern Brits, Stena Line's Harwich to Hook of Holland service and DFDS Seaways' Newcastle to Amsterdam route both in the Netherlands are possible options.

Further information

- **Belgium: t** (00 32)
- **Belgian Tourist Office**, Brussels and Wallonia, 217 Marsh Wall, London E14 9FJ, UK, **t** 0906 3020 245; **www.belgiumtheplaceto.be.**
- **Belgian Tourist Office**, Brussels and Flanders, 1a Cavendish Square, London W1G 0LD, UK, **t** (020) 7867 0311; **www.visitflanders.co.uk.**

Estate agents

- **Agence Agimobel** (Belgium), **t** 5060 3299. Coastal estate agent based at Knokke-Heist selling mainly apartments.
- **FPD Savills** (Belgium), **t** 2646 2550. Both coastal and city properties are on offer from this international agent.
- **Century 21 Group Agimmo** (Belgium), **t** 2425 0803. For properties in Brussels.
- **Adviesbureau Dewaele**, **t** 5044 4999. For properties in and around Bruges.

Chile

The South American country of Chile can offer a superb untouched coastline coupled with the dramatic Andes mountains and the rainforest, while the lakes region has numerous tranquil retreats. Indeed, it has one of the most varied landscapes in Latin America.

Although it has had a troubled past, stability has taken hold, the economy is improving, the government is democratic, and the future is optimistic.

Prices at this Latin American beauty spot aren't necessarily cheap, and houses of interest to a foreign buyer typically start at around £150,000 at least.

Further information

- **Chile: t** (00 56)

Estate agents

- **Invest in Chile, www.investinchile.com.**
- **www.escapeartists.com**: property listings for Chile.

Costa Rica

This Central American delight sandwiched between Nicaragua and Panama has a gorgeous climate and beautiful flora and fauna, imposing volcanoes and two coastlines with palm-fringed beaches. Both tourism and foreign investment are booming due to a buoyant economy, improving infrastructure and a democratic government. The cost of living is low and people friendly. What more could one want?

Apartments start at just under £100,000 and a really splendid home can be had for under £400,000.

Further information

• **Costa Rica**: t (00 506)

Estate agents

• **Dominical Realty** (Costa Rica), **t** 787 0223; **www.dominicalrealty.com.**

India

The former Portuguese colony of Goa on India's west coast is considered a beautiful place to live and prices, along with the rest of the country, are low compared with Europe. With land prices and salaries in India a fraction of their UK counterparts, you can buy a sizeable piece of land and build a luxurious residence for £50,000, or buy a former colonial residence in need of renovation for less.

The Goan resort of Candolim on the Arabian Sea is popular with the British and houses are available for under £10,000, while newly built one-bedroom apartments, typically with a communal swimming pool, are available for £12,000 or so. Calangute and Baga are also popular areas.

The cost of living is, correspondingly, even cheaper; it is possible to have a three-course meal out for an amazing 50p. Flights from the UK typically start at £300. Prices in Goa are expected to rise as foreign investment rises. The Indian government is also considering granting citizenship to non-resident Indians, which would greatly increase the number of people who would consider investing there, further raising prices.

Another popular area is Kerala in southern India, which has increasingly been a popular tourist destination in recent years. A large modern villa at Ernakulam or Thruvanamthapuram would typically set you back from £35,000.

The Indian conveyancing process and attendant bureaucracy is a maze, and includes a requirement for foreign purchasers to obtain a one- to five-year resident visa. To do this. applicants need to spend at least 182 days (not necessarily in one stretch) in the country in the financial year (1 April to 31 March) previous to the purchase. The deeds for the property cannot be registered until after the 1st of April that year. Another requirement is for foreign purchasers to obtain approval to buy from the local authorities and the Reserve Bank of India before a property purchase can commence.

Rental rates are lower than in Europe, and the money earned from rental cannot be taken out of the country.

Further information

• **India**: t (00 91)
• **High Commission for India**, India House, Aldwych, London WC2B 4NA.

Estate agents

- **Prazeres Resorts** (India), **t** 832 277 064.
- **Homes and Estates** (India), **t** 832 250 115.
- **Kerala Property** (India), **t** 484 235 8947; **www.keralaproperty.com**.

Japan

Japanese property is seldom viewed as an investment as homes are not built to last and prices have fallen for 13 consecutive years. Therefore, the value of properties falls rapidly over the course of several decades and a building that is 50 years old is generally considered to be almost worthless and ready for demolishing.

More positively, the lengthy recession the country has suffered means that the Bank of Japan currently is adhering to a zero interest policy, resulting in mortgages as low as 2 per cent.

Latvia

The Baltic State of Latvia joined the EU on 1 May 2004. This will ensure that its economy will flourish even more than it has done since gaining its independence from Russia in 1991.

Latvia has a less transparent economy and administration than its neighbours, Estonia and Lithuania. It is one of the least costly and least spoilt countries in Europe. It boasts large tracts of beautiful unspoilt countryside and property prices are exceptionally low due to low owner-occupation and years of a problematic, sluggish economy. Yet EU membership in 2004 will change this rapidly with large-scale EU investment improving infrastructure, and mortgage finance will become increasingly available to locals and cause prices to shoot up. Early investors will be able to rent or sell at a good profit.

Although average earnings are a quarter of an average EU salary, Latvia currently has the highest annual growth in GDP in Europe. In early 2004 city apartments were already rising by 20 per cent per year and rental yields were very strong.

But, as with the other Baltic States, Lithuania and Estonia, investment here is seen to be more of a risk than in more familiar eastern European countries like Poland, Hungary and Croatia. It is also not for sun-worshippers: from October to March the country is generally very cold and dark.

For a small country such as this, there is a wide variety of property types, from city apartment blocks to tall merchant's houses, country manor houses and wooden homes in the forests and chalets by the sea. The attractive capital, Riga, is as cheap to live in as it is to buy in. Elsewhere, property prices plummet.

Further information

- **Latvia: t** (00 371)

Estate agents

- **Ober Haus** (Latvia), **t** 371 728 4544; **www.ober-haus.ee.**

The Netherlands (Holland)

Curiously, extremely few Brits buy holiday homes in the Netherlands, popularly known as Holland. Its uncrowded road network is excellent for visiting many attractive towns and cities including the beautiful, fairytale city of Amsterdam, and Haarlem, Delft, Rotterdam and Den Haag.

The country is generally thinly populated and has plenty of pretty, relatively unspoilt towns and villages to choose from. Many areas are suitable, especially along the coast, such as around the coastal resort of Zandvoort. The coastal region has numerous wild stretches of dune and beach. The unspoilt region around the delightful, quiet town of Oudewater, near Gouda, is well located for the most popular towns and cities like Amsterdam, Haarlem, Delft, Rotterdam and Den Haag as well as many of the country's other attractions.

The Netherlands has experienced property boom and bust in recent years. Prices fell in the early 1990s to be followed by a property boom on a par with the UK culminating in a 20 per cent rise in prices in 1999. Since then the property market has been stable and is likely to be a reasonably good investment over the long term. In both 2002 and 2003 prices rose by about 2 per cent per year.

Prices are relatively high compared with, say France or Italy, but substantially cheaper than the UK. Prices for a pretty canal-side property, such as a gabled three-bedroom house in the centre of Oudewater near Gouda, would start at under £200,000, and apartments typically start at under £120,000. A bijou pad in the centre of Amsterdam would typically start at around £180,000.

Stena Line's Harwich to Hook of Holland routing, and DFDS Seaways' Newcastle to Amsterdam service, are the ferries of choice for the Netherlands.

Further information

- **The Netherlands: t** (00 31)
- **Netherlands Tourist Office**, PO Box 30783, London WC2B 6DH (UK), **t** 0906 871 7777; **www.holland.com.**

Estate agents

All are situated in the Netherlands.

- **Groene Hart Huizen, t** 348 564711. Estate agents specialising in the Oudewater region near Gouda.
- **Prismaat, t** 20 662 6364; **www.prismaat.nl.**
- **Ter Haar, t** 20 573 6000; **www.terhaarmakelaars.com.**

Nicaragua

Nicaragua offers beautiful, untouched beaches, elegant, inexpensive colonial houses, cattle ranches at London apartment prices, and islands that are also for sale at very low prices.

Nicaragua has shaken off its troubled past and now, peaceful and democratic, it shows encouraging signs; increased tourism and investment from large hotel chains such as Holiday Inn and Radisson are causing buyers of holiday homes, retirement homes and tourist-related businesses to snowball.

Prices remain very low, even by the ocean. Many buyers are buying colonial homes at Granada on Lake Nicaragua, which start at around £25,000, and a very good example with four bedrooms could be bought for £200,000. One-bed flats are available in Granada for under £10,000. Flights from Miami take just over two hours.

Further information

- **Nicaragua: t** (00 505)

Estate agents

- **Nicaragua Properties** (Nicaragua), **t** 552 3199; **www.nicaraguaproperty.com.**

Russia

Russia's property market, especially in the big cities, has been experiencing a boom owing to Russia's improving economy and growing confidence. But potential buyers should be aware that the legal system is unreliable, conveyancing a minefield and clear land-ownership laws are still evolving, although property is far more secure than even just five years ago.

New moneyed Russians (*novy Russky*) flush with Siberian oil money have been buying up swanky city apartments and grand old dachas with gay abandon, pushing up prices significantly as they do so. The demand for decent properties and a lack of good housing stock has pushed prices up further. Prices have soared in Moscow, by 100 per cent in 2002–2004, and are expected to continue to rise. A two-bedroom flat in the 'Golden Triangle' would now be over £450,000. A one-bedroom flat in a neighbourhood like Park Kultury in central Moscow would set you back about £150,000. But on the outskirts of the city prices plunge to a starting price of about £50,000, although you could easily pay £1 million for a large, traditional home just outside Moscow. A steady stream of affluent foreign tenants are keeping the Moscow lettings market very buoyant.

Move away from Moscow and prices can be amazingly low. In the south of Ukraine and around the Black Sea Port of Odessa a small dacha could be yours for under £15,000. But avoid looking north of Kiev as it is closer to Chernobyl.

As far as borrowing is concerned, local mortgages are very rare – less than 5 per cent of property purchases in the country are made using mortgages and most people deal in cash – but have become increasingly available. Currently only a handful of banks offer mortgages and interest rates are high, but it is predicted that soon the mortgage market will greatly enlarge, with most Russian banks offering loans, competition bringing down rates, and the availability of mortgages driving up prices further.

Further information

- **Russian Federation: t** (00 7)
- **Russian Tourist Office**, 70 Piccadilly, London W1J 8HP, UK, **t** (020) 7495 7555.

Estate agents

- **Knight Frank** (UK), **t** (020) 7629 8171; **www.knightfrank.com**.
- **Beatrix** (Russia), **t** 095 792 5922; **www.beatrix.ru**.
- **Penny Lane Realty** (Russia), **t** 095 232 0099; **www.pennylane.ru**.
- **Sotheby's Realty** (Russia), **t** 00 49 892 280 2894; **www.sothebysrealty.com**.
- **Jones East 8, www.joneseast8.com.ua**.

Slovakia

Attention has increasingly focused on Slovakia since the country obtained European Union membership in May 2004. Access is good now the country has cheap flights. Slovakia is not as 'westernised' as some European countries, which would put off some buyers, although attract others.

Property in the capital, Bratislava, is about 50 per cent cheaper than in Prague, although prices are set to rise now Slovakia has joined the EU, which will increasingly see Bratislava residents commuting to Vienna, just 40 miles away in Austria. Prices start at about £30,000 for older flats, and £65,000 for a new-build two-bed apartment. Houses in the countryside start at about £15,000.

You need to set up a local company to buy property here, and this can usually be arranged by the estate agent or property consultant. The company is subject to tax in the Slovakia but also corporation tax has to be paid in the UK on any company profits, ie when you sell or from rental income. Currently UK corporation tax is 23.75 per cent on profits of between £10,001 and £50,000. However, tax paid on the property overseas can usually be offset against your British tax bill.

Further Information

- **Slovakia: t** (00 421)
- **Slovak Embassy,** 25 Kensington Park Gardens, London W8 4QY, UK, t (020) 7313 6470; **www.slovak-embassy.co.uk.**

Estate agents

- **www.en.redo.sk** and **www.sak.sk**: properties for sale in Slovakia.

Sri Lanka

More than two years after the ceasefire by the Tamil Tigers, the seldom-considered beautiful island of Sri Lanka is a good source of property bargains, although prices have been rising of late in response to increasing foreign interest. Yet prices are still appreciably lower than popular Asian spots like Bali and Thailand. Direct flights are available from the UK to the capital, Colombo. Rich in unspoilt countryside and coastline, former British and Dutch colonial properties abound. One area foreign buyers are focusing on is Galle, on the southern tip of the island. It boasts an imposing fort by the sea, which is a Unesco World Heritage Site. With houses starting at £120,000 here, it has Sri Lanka's most expensive real estate. Just a few miles away prices drop to a fraction of that. Unspoilt beaches with land available to build on abound at Matara and Tangalla further up the coast. As well as the unstable political situation, disputes over land ownership are quite common, and it is important to employ an experienced local lawyer to unearth any possible problems.

Further Information

- **Sri Lanka: t** (00 94)

Estate agents

- **Eden Villas, www.villasinsrilanka.com.**
- **Lanka Real Estate, www.lankarealestate.com.**

Sweden

Sweden is stunningly beautiful and one of the best wilderness areas in Europe with endless opportunities for fishing, hunting, boating, hiking and skiing.

You get a lot for your money in a country widely perceived as astronomical to live in. A restored large rural farmhouse with lake frontage set in several acres would typically cost around £150,000.

Stockholm has a lot to offer: both slick city apartments and easy-going island retreats. Small apartments in the centre, such as the Kungsholmen district, are available for under £75,000, with country properties a few kilometres from the centre commonly costing around £135,000.

Further information

- **Sweden: t** (00 46)
- **Swedish Tourist Office**, Swiss Centre, 10 Wardour Street, London W1D 6QF, UK, **t** 0800 100 200 30; **www.mysweden.com.**

Estate agents

- **Homes in Sweden** (UK), **t** (0131) 663 7605/0777 424 1177; **www.homesinsweden.com.**
- **Notar** (Sweden), **t** 8 545 815 13; **www.notar.se.**

Thailand

Properties in Thailand vary from simple village homes going for a song up to luxury beachfront villas. For example, Knight Frank was recently selling brand new £1.5 million spacious five-bedroom, five-bathroom properties with swimming pools in landscaped gardens overlooking the Andaman Sea at Kamala Bay, Phuket. Expect to pay from around £650,000 to over £2 million for the most luxurious villas, from about £350,000 to £650,000 for mid-range villas, and under £350,000 for smaller villas and apartments. Despite the market crash in the 1997 Asian financial crisis, it has recovered and generally prices have risen by more than 50 per cent in the past three years. Popular areas for foreign buyers include the Thai capital, Bangkok, as well as around the northern city of Chiang Mai and the resort of Phuket in southern Thailand.

Buyers need to engage a reputable English-speaking lawyer experienced in the Thai conveyancing system and able to organise reliable translations of all documents. Your lawyer will need to check the title deed, definition of boundaries and whether there are any outstanding encumbrances against the property. When a purchase price is agreed, both parties sign a preliminary contract binding them to the sale at the agreed price.

Foreigners are only permitted to hold 30-year leases for villas and houses, although they may hold full title in perpetuity in the case of apartments and condominiums.

Thai banks do not organise mortgages for foreigners and therefore finance needs to be sorted out elsewhere. Foreign currency to pay for the transaction is transferred to the receiving bank, which then issues a certificate confirming importation of the funds. This document is known as a *thor tor 3* and is required by the land registry before the final contract can be signed.

In 2001 the Thai government relaxed immigration procedures for people wishing to retire to Thailand. Potential retirees must be at least 50 years of age, and provide legally authenticated proof that they do not have a criminal record in their home country, are not seeking a work permit and have no contagious diseases. Proof of an income of about £11,500 per year is also required.

The Thai bhat is a volatile currency and the market less stable than many regions, and Thai property is unlikely to perform as well as in western Europe.

Further information

- **Thailand: t (00 66)**

Estate agents

- **Andaman Island Group Partnership** (Thailand), **t** 76 355 330; **www.andamanproperty.com.**
- **Andrew Park** (Thailand), **t** 76 354 016; **www.andrewpark.com.**
- **Katamanda** (Thailand), **t** 22 538 528; **www.katamanda.com.**
- **Phuket Land** (Thailand), **t** 76 340 207; **www.phuketland.com.**
- **Knight Frank, www.knightfrankthailand.com.**

Vanuatu

If your wish is for tropical paradise, then Vanuatu, formerly the New Hebrides, in the South Pacific may be the answer. The easygoing way of life here is assisted by a low crime rate and cost of living. However, property is not cheap. Although you could buy a small lagoon-side bungalow for £30,000, a three-bed home is likely to start at £150,000, with the price rising rapidly for a waterside property. Prices are not cheap, for a multitude of reasons, including investors focusing on Vanuatu due to the hand over of Hong Kong to China as well as political and social problems in Papua New Guinea, the Solomon Islands, Fiji and New Caledonia.

The government of Vanuatu encourages foreign investment and has passed legislation to make it easier to invest. Foreigners lease rather than buy the land, usually for 50 years, and leases are registered in the central government Land Records Department, greatly lessening any possibility of land disputes. You do not have to be a resident of Vanuatu or have employment in Vanuatu to purchase residential property.

Income tax is not payable in Vanuatu on any income that the investment earns, and there is also no inheritance tax or capital gains tax to pay. If property is let out, 12.5 per cent sales tax is charged to the tenant and payable to the government.

Further information

- **Vanuatu: t** (00 678)

Estate agents

- **www.transpacificproperty.com**: property listings.

Index